MARY BERENSON
A Self-Portrait from her Letters & Diaries

MARY BERENSON

A Self-Portrait from her Letters & Diaries

Edited by Barbara Strachey
& Jayne Samuels

LONDON
VICTOR GOLLANCZ LTD
1983

British Library Cataloguing in Publication Data
Berenson, Mary
   Mary Berenson.
   1. Berenson, Mary
   I. Title   II. Strachey, Barbara
   III. Samuels, Jayne
   941.082   DA566.9.B/

   ISBN 0-575-03227-8

Phototypeset by Tradespools Limited, Frome, Somerset
Printed in Great Britain by
St Edmundsbury Press, Bury St Edmunds, Suffolk

Contents

Illustrations

Preface

Mary Berenson, like her mother, Hannah Whitall Smith, was not only a compulsive letter writer, but also a naturally gifted and entertaining exponent of what is now, alas, an almost vanished art. For most of her life Mary lived in Italy and her mother in England, and while they were apart they wrote to each other virtually daily. During the summers, which Mary normally spent with her family, unaccompanied by her husband, she wrote as regularly to him, so that the continuity was almost unbroken. She also wrote weekly to Bernard's mother for nearly forty years, very frequently to her sister Alys and to Bernard's sisters, and, as they grew up, to her children and grandchildren as well as to her many friends.

The picture thus presented of her life and character, and that of her husband and their friends, is unusually frank, witty and revealing.

There are a few unfortunate gaps—notably her letters to her first husband and her early letters to Berenson—but the mass of material still in existence amounts to nearly 5 million words. It has therefore been necessary to choose extracts, and it will be appreciated that a great many topics and people have had—reluctantly—to be omitted.

To complete the picture provided by the letters, some extracts from Mary Berenson's diaries have also been included. The diaries cover only some years; the missing years, if they ever existed, have now been lost.

Very occasionally Mary made slips in spelling or punctuation; in these cases the editors have made silent corrections. In this connection it may be noted that until she married Frank Costelloe, Mary spelt words like 'colour' and 'favourite' in the American way (color and favorite) but from then on, throughout her life she spelt them in the English way. The editors have followed her practice.

The material has been collected from many scattered sources, but the largest amount comes from the collection of Mary's family papers in the Smith Archives in the possession of her grand-daughter, Barbara Strachey Halpern. These consist of letters to the following recipients:

Hannah Whitall Smith, Robert Pearsall Smith, Alys Russell, Logan Pearsall Smith, 'Aunt Lill' (Elizabeth Smith), Ray Costelloe Strachey, Karin Costelloe Stephen, Barbara Strachey, Christopher Strachey, Grace Worthington and all joint family letters. Also in the Smith Archives are Letters to a Friend in England and Hermann Obrist (13 April 1895, 30 April 1895, 24 June 1895) and the diaries of 1876 and 1889–90.

The next source of material is the Berenson Archives at the Villa I Tatti. Our thanks are due to Dr Cecil Anrep for permission to consult and use these, and to Professor Craig Smyth and the staff of the Berenson Library at the Harvard Institute for the Study of Italian Renaissance Art, for making this possible. This correspondence consists of letters to:

Bernard Berenson, Nicky Mariano, Geoffrey Scott, Gertrude Hitz Burton, Robert Trevelyan, Hermann Obrist (1 October 1894), and diaries from 1891 to 1937.

One or two draft copies (presumably as sent) have also been included, some personal: to Frank Costelloe (in the Smith Archives), to Eugénie Sellers Strong and Roger Fry (in the Berenson Archives) and some business letters (in the Berenson Archives). These have been so marked in the text.

Letters to the Berenson family are located as follows:

Mrs Judith Berenson, 1 July 1900, 11 October 1914 and 16 July 1919 in the collection of Bernard Berenson Perry; all the others are in the collection of Richard A. Berenson. Letters to Senda Berenson Abbott, 26 November 1906, 18 August 1914 and 18 November 1914 are in the collection of Bernard Berenson Perry. All the others are in the collection of Ralph Barton Perry Jr. All the letters to Bessie Berenson are in the collection of Richard A. Berenson. Joint letters to Senda and Bessie are in the collection of Ralph Barton Perry Jr, and to Senda and Mrs Berenson jointly in the collection of Richard A. Berenson.

Other letters are from the following sources:

Isabella Gardner ... The Isabella Stewart Gardner Museum, Boston.
Carey Thomas ... The Bryn Mawr College Library, Archives.
Carl Hamilton ... The Bryn Mawr College Library, Manuscripts Collection.
Maynard Keynes ... The Keynes Papers, King's College Library, Cambridge.
Edith Wharton and Gertrude Stein ... The Collection of American Literature, Beinecke Rare Books and Manuscripts Library, Yale University.
Walter Lippmann ... The Walter Lippmann Papers, Yale University Library.
Bertrand Russell ... The Russell Archives, McMaster University.
Sir William Rothenstein ... The Rothenstein Papers, Houghton Library, Harvard.
Walt Whitman ... The Charles Feinberg Collection, The Library of Congress, Washington DC.
Lina Waterfield ... Collection of Gordon Waterfield.
John Walker ... Collection of John Walker.

The editors are most grateful to all the above sources for permission to include material in their possession, and to the following people for their kind assistance: Dr Charles Avery, the late David Carritt, Mrs Pamela Diamand, Charles Feinberg, C. Douglas Lewis, Dr John Scott, Meryle Secrest, Julian Trevelyan and Betty and Durrett Wagner.
We are particularly grateful for much kind co-operation to: the Berenson Family, Ruth Berenson Muhlen, Bernard B. Perry, Ralph B. Perry Jr and Richard A. Berenson, to Nancy Clemente and Maud Wilcox of the Harvard Press, Margot Levy, Luisa Vertova Nicolson, John Walker and Gordon Waterfield. Above all we are grateful to Professor Ernest Samuels for his generous willingness to share with us his research for the second volume of his life of Bernard Berenson.

Prologue

In 1891, when she was twenty-seven, Mary Costelloe—born Mary Smith in Philadelphia and married to a London barrister—left her husband and her two small daughters for love of Bernard Berenson and the Italian art of which he was the passionate apostle.

Bernard was a handsome young man, born in Lithuania of Jewish parents, educated in Boston and at Harvard, and destined to become the foremost expert on Italian painting. Mary loved him, quarrelled with him, learned from him and persuaded him to start writing, and when her husband died, nine years later, she married him.

She and 'B.B.', as everyone called him, lived together for over fifty years: working, travelling, making love and money, and pursuing the enjoyment of art and intellectual endeavour. The Villa I Tatti, which they acquired in the hills north-east of Florence, became famous for its cultivated luxury, and from all over the world scholars, artists and art collectors, royalty, statesmen, and the wealthy and fashionable of Europe and America came pouring in to visit them there.

The world to which Mary had been born was a very different one. It was the narrow, pious world of Philadelphia Quaker Orthodoxy. Mary, however, was a natural rebel, and soon rejected her parental standards and beliefs, though she never lost her love for the family. Indeed she was quite unusually devoted to them, as they were to her.

Her mother, Hannah Whitall, was a rebel too, but of another kind. Born a 'birthright' Quaker in 1832, she grew up to find that world under pressure from the Evangelical Revivalism which was then sweeping America. Like Mary, she was a much-loved daughter, and she held from childhood the conviction that women were as much entitled as men to freedom of action and to all the advantages education could offer. Quakers were more inclined to favour such a view than most people at that time, but Hannah's claims and desires outstripped theirs by far. She always remained, however, deeply religious, and confessed in old age that religion had been the romance of her life.

When Hannah was nineteen she fell in love with and married a charming but weak and emotional young man—also a Quaker—called Robert Smith, and they started at once to devote all their energies to Good Works and the search for Salvation. The two of them broke away from the Quaker fold, to the horror of their friends and families, and explored in turn the Plymouth Brethren, the Presbyterians and the Methodists, before arriving at their own version of what was called 'The Higher Life'.

Hannah had a low opinion of the physical side of marriage, but she was an impassioned mother. Seven children were born to her, only three of whom survived to grow up, and these losses added a sharper edge to her love for the remaining three. Her innate feminism meant that she prized daughters more than sons, and when her first daughter, Nelly, died at the age of five, she was inconsolable until Mary was born in 1864. She lavished on this daughter all the adoring, indulgent ambition usually reserved by mothers for promising sons, and continued to do so despite the birth of a boy, Logan, eighteen months later, and of another daughter, Alys, two years later still.

Her husband, Robert, proved to be a brilliant and moving preacher, and in the 1870s he enjoyed a heady success not only at Camp Meetings in America, but also in England—an England that was ripe for Revivalism. On the continent of Europe, too, he won a huge following, even though he preached through an interpreter. Hannah was also a gifted preacher, though in a less emotional style, and the two of them became the spearheads of the 'Higher Life' movement in England. Unfortunately Robert's emotionalism led him to fall into one of the recurrent aberrations to which overheated and undisciplined piety has always been prone: the belief that physical love is the route to divine love.

After he had led immensely successful Conferences at Oxford and at Brighton, rumours began to circulate that he had not only been preaching this heresy, but putting it into practice with one of his female disciples. The more inhibited English Evangelicals, who had sponsored the Smiths, were scandalized, and though Robert claimed to be innocent, he was forced to stop preaching and return forthwith to America. He was a broken man, and within a year or two he had lost his faith entirely.

Hannah regarded this backsliding with scorn, and herself continued undeterred to pursue Salvation in a number of curious places.

14

Oddly enough she yearned to share the mystical raptures of the many fanatics she sought out and later wrote about, although her rational nature and irrepressible sense of humour prevented her from adopting their enthusiasms. Settled once more in Philadelphia, she continued to preach and to attend and conduct Bible Readings. She also wrote a number of down-to-earth but inspiring devotional books, one of which, *The Christian's Secret of a Happy Life*, is still in print, has sold millions of copies, and is regarded as one of the great classics of Evangelical Christianity.

Although she pursued strange beliefs and strange believers with unabated interest, Hannah remained convinced that common sense was a better guide than emotionalism, and that a good rational education—and more particularly a college education—was essential, above all for women. She herself had been forced to abandon her hopes in this direction owing to the early arrival of her children, and the consequent claims of domesticity, and she was determined that her daughters should be given the advantages she had failed to achieve.

After his loss of faith, Robert turned to business, and the family grew more and more prosperous. When he was taken into his father-in-law's glass manufacturing firm, Robert proved to be a first-class salesman, as eloquent in praise of glass as he had once been in preaching Salvation. He suffered, however, like a number of his relatives, from a manic-depressive temperament, his moods swinging between disabling depressions and reckless, extravagant euphoria. Hannah, unyielding in her own strength, had less and less sympathy for such excesses, and her increasing disillusion with Robert led her, eventually, to develop a total scorn for men, particularly in their capacity as husbands.

It was in this matriarchal setting that Mary grew up, and despite her rebellion and the very different life she was to build for herself, she never entirely threw off its influence or its ideas.

CHAPTER ONE

Salad Days

February 1864–July 1885

Hannah Whitall Smith adored her eldest daughter from the start, and though she spoiled all her children, there was no doubt that Mary was the favourite. Soon after her son Logan's birth in 1865, she wrote to her sister-in-law: 'He [Logan] is growing right pretty, and if it were not for his sister's super-abounding sweetness, I expect I should quite fall into raptures over him. But she is *so* splendid that she uses up all my capacity for enthusiasm.'

Mary certainly provided good material for enthusiasm. When she was not yet two years old she was learning her letters, and Hannah told her mother: 'She has a most wonderful memory, and learns every little piece I say to her after hearing it two or three times. And she is beginning to draw on her memory for appropriate quotations, which it seems to me is remarkable for a baby only 21 months old.'

Although Hannah believed in discipline, Mary from a very early age was able to outwit her. As Hannah wrote to her father in 1866: 'She gets a great amount of discipline, but she seems irrepressible, and I am at my wits' end. For she manages *just* to keep within the forbidden limit so exactly that I can't punish her, and yet she has all the fun of disobedience.' Two years later she wrote to her mother: '[She is] neither proper, prudent nor discreet; not at all amenable to reason, with no reverence for authority—no fear of man or woman— ... she is a character to be admired and loved and wondered at, and completely fooled by.... One thing I am very sure of—that she is born to be a leader, and that hers is a royal nature which man can never tame.'

In fact Hannah's efforts at discipline soon melted into a belief that children should be ruled only by love and indulgence—a belief that she was to write and preach about throughout her life and to practise once again when Mary ran away with Bernard Berenson and left her two little daughters to her mother to bring up.

16

Mary was indeed a strong, vital character, possessed of considerable intelligence, and the result of maternal indulgence in her case was to convince her that the only standard by which to judge a course of action was that of her own pleasure and satisfaction. She seriously propounded this philosophy for a time as she grew older, and was never, perhaps, wholly able to shake it off.

Despite her affection for her daughter, Hannah could not entirely approve of her behaviour. The child could wheedle anything she liked out of Robert, who adored her too; she was extravagant and headstrong; and by the time she was twelve she was already an accomplished flirt, and a dominant figure among the twenty or so cousins, many of them up to ten years older than she, who kept each other friendly company in Philadelphia and the nearby suburb of Germantown.

Mary kept intermittent diaries throughout her life, and the earliest of these to survive is dated 1876, when she was twelve.

Diary   24 October 1876   Philadelphia
I went out on Cicero behind the carriage. .... Can you guess *who* I saw *and* what I did? I was going along I don't know exactly how, but pretty joggly, I guess, because Cicero was very frisky, and I saw a carriage with two young men in it. I thought I knew one of them so I stared hard at him till he came nearly opposite and then saw it was Morris Stroud! I had never been introduced to him so I didn't intend to speak to him, but when he was *just* opposite, the horse gave a joggle and I gave a kind of nod with my head and looked straight at him AND smiled!!!!!

Diary   26 December 1876   Philadelphia
It really is disgusting how silly the girls are. Even Sadie and Sophe do talk *ever so much* about boys, but I *do* try not to. In fact I don't think boys are *half* as nice as girls, or as interesting to talk about. Except some!

Diary   2 January 1877   Philadelphia
Whitall, Madge, Bonny, Sadie, John Whitall* and I sat at a little table by ourselves. On that table, the others remarked, all the dishes seemed by degrees to assemble. I will not dispute the truth of this statement, but I will say that we ate a whole turkey between us, and

* All cousins.

an oyster pie, two dishes of green peas, one dish of corn, two dishes of pickled plums, stewed apples and strawberries innumerable, for our first course!!! . . . Oh the ice cream! Oh the cakes! Oh the blancmangers! Oh the grapes! Oh the oranges! Oh the water ices! . . .

First we played Truth. John W[hitall] was asked what he liked best in a girl but he wouldn't tell. However he told me privately afterward that it was flirting. I knew it before.

Despite all these frolics Mary was genuinely eager to learn, and when Hannah came to the conclusion that she needed stricter discipline and more education, she went happily off to boarding school.

Hannah was a brilliant natural letter writer, and showered Mary daily with affection and good advice—to wear more warm clothes; to get at least nine hours' sleep a night; and to enjoy schoolgirl 'smashes' as she herself had done. Mary responded freely and frankly and virtually daily, as she did throughout her life, whenever she was away from her family. In their correspondence, as in their speech, they all preserved, towards each other and to those nearest them, the Quaker usage of 'Thee' and 'Thine'.

To Hannah Whitall Smith   13 October 1877   Howland School
My dearest, sweetest, darlingest mother, Oh! how I love thee. I wish thee could know how much I love thee. And papa too! Really and truly I think I could be about the worst girl in the school if it weren't for you two! The thought of you takes all the wanting to be bad out of me. Last night I could have just been furious at Miss Wythe when she was scolding our table for some fuss, and I could just have walked out of the room *very* haughtily only Mother, I thought of *thee* and of how sorrowful thee would be if I did anything wrong and of how I loved thee and so I let Miss W know I felt sorry. Words *can't* express how much I love thee and papa, I don't think I ever loved you so much when I was at home, but oh! I *do* love you too much for anything. If I study my lessons it is for *thee* I do it, for I know how much thee wants me to be a fine scholar. Please don't think this is the beginning of homesickness, for I do not think it is.

To Hannah Whitall Smith   28 October 1877   Howland School
My own darling mother, I think I will tell thee in the beginning of this that I don't want anybody to see it except 'the family'. Especially not Aunty [deleted] as I don't care to have her go around Germantown saying she don't like my letters at all, and they're nothing but fun and

18

nonsense and wondering if we ever study up here. I know she has been doing that, for Mrs Brown said so in one of her letters to [deleted] and was *rather* doubtful if I was the right kind of companion for Mamie. I'm sure I've a right to write just the kind of letters that I want, and if Aunty don't like them she needn't say so. I don't think it shows I'm not improving here if any letters *aren't* full of lessons and bible classes and I shan't write if people make a fuss about my letters....

Is there such a thing as loving faulty people so that you are *perfectly* blind to their faults? Of course I love thee and papa that way, for I do think you are faultless really and truly. Anyway outside.

I think I shall go crazy sometime, I feel as if I could *now*. Last night I think I must have been a little crazy, for when I got into bed my mind was all in a perfect rush and whirl and I couldn't lie still and I felt just burning up and ready to kill anybody and myself too! I can't describe it. But then I thought of the text 'He shall cover thee with his feathers and under his wings shalt thou trust' and everything seemed suddenly to get quiet and I felt *so* happy....

Does thee know I *think* more than ever since I came up here and I am *so* tired of thinking. Why can't I have a rest? My brain is *so* tired of going on and on all the time. This is one of the 'stages' of a person's existence, I guess. Don't laugh. I expect it's very tiresome.

There is no doubt that Mary had inherited a trace of the troublesome Smith temperament. Later on, not only Robert's brother, Horace, but Mary's brother Logan and her younger daughter Karin were to suffer severely from similar alternations of 'Ups' and 'Downs'—Karin to such a point of misery that she finally took a fatal overdose of morphine when she was sixty-four. Mary's alternations were less frequent and less serious, but she too suffered from a seesaw of moods over the years.

To Robert Pearsall Smith   5 October 1878   Philadelphia
I am sure I do hope your plan of bringing children up with plenty of fun 'tucked under their jackets' will be a success in my case. I am afraid, though, that I am spoiled, for I don't know how I would behave if thee and mother wanted me to do something I didn't want to do. I am *afraid* I should behave horridly and be cross and nasty as I so well know how to be. But I almost always can do what I want to do. I think it must be the right way to let children do what they want, if they don't want anything wrong.... It is so nice to have people approve of you. I don't know how I could stand it, if I thought thee and mother were all the time finding fault with me.

To Robert Pearsall Smith   4 March 1879   Philadelphia
This morning we all went to hear mother preach at a Mr Peper's church, *way* down town. As usual it was very interesting. An old woman who sat by me was sound asleep all the time. Every now and then she would heave deep sighs of content, as if she heard and understood all that mother was saying, and yet I am morally sure that she was asleep, because her head would give great bobs at intervals and then she would snort and open her eyes all of a sudden. *I* shouldn't like to preach to people who were sound asleep but mother don't mind. She says she enjoys seeing them getting so much comfort.

While the children were growing up, Hannah began to work for all sorts of philanthropical causes. She became the National Superintendent of Bible Study and president of her local branch of the Women's Christian Temperance Union, which was headed by her great friend, Frances Willard. She was also caught up in the early stages of the women's movement.

When Mary was seventeen, she was sent to college, and the one chosen was the highly regarded Smith College for girls in Northampton, Massachusetts, where she studied for two years. She was a good deal better off than most of the other girls, and enjoyed herself in a rather lavish manner, among other things bringing her horse 'Anticellere' up to Northampton with her.

To Robert Pearsall Smith   16 September 1881   Smith College
I am too happy to be here, thee can't think how nice it all seems, and nothing to do but study and take exercise.... The only thing that weighs on my mind is my greenness and freshness, which is really immense. I am quite taken down from my conceit by seeing so many girls *so much* cleverer and more intellectual than I am. At home I am a sort of *prodigy* among the girls and it is such a step down to come here and find myself one of the most ignorant and least talented of two or three hundred girls.

To Hannah Whitall Smith   17 September 1881   Smith College
Last night at nine I seemed to hear thee so distinctly saying 'Now! Daughter!' that I had to shut up my books and go to bed. That reminds me—do send me a pillow. I will begin now on what I want. Toothbrush and nailbrush—*Professor at the Breakfast Table* and MY WINTER HATS. I *must* have them.

20

To Hannah Whitall Smith   20 September 1881   Smith College
I cannot thank thee enough for pushing me on to get a college education. You cannot get it the same at home, but here it is perfect for study. Only the girls are not quite so nice as I thought they would be. But maybe when I come to know them better they will prove nicer.

To Hannah Whitall Smith   2 October 1881   Smith College
I cannot understand Fénelon—I will not believe that we, whom God created in His Own Image, are such *utterly* worthless and miserable creatures, unable even to love Him unless He puts it into our hearts. What then is the use of free will, if we cannot even love or obey Him without *He* does it for us? I think it is an awful slander on human nature to talk so about hating and despising your own selves when He made us so, and nothing can convince me that we are all so awfully wicked.

To Robert Pearsall Smith   19 December 1881   Smith College
I do not suppose it will do either of the children the least harm to go now and then to see such funny and bright pieces as Patience ... By all means take them to these jolly little operettas and plays, enjoy the fun of it with them.... For the present I limit myself to Shakespeare.

To Hannah Whitall Smith   8 January 1882   Smith College
I was thinking in church today when the minister was reading 'Do not your alms before men' etc, why you can't have the praise of men along with the giving of alms. I should think you might combine both with a great deal of pleasure. Why ought you to hide the good things you do? I need a few of thy penetrating remarks upon the subject.

To Robert Pearsall Smith   26 February 1882   Smith College
Papa, I *can't* bring 15 girls home with me. There are that many I suppose I could get, Western girls who can't go home in their vacation. But I don't think it would be a pleasure either to them or to us to take them so entirely out of their circle. *I* don't want them, and thee wouldn't if thee knew them.

To Robert Pearsall Smith   8 March 1882   Smith College
For the last two or three days my back has hurt me, and yesterday I gave up and went to bed. With my usual Gummidge*-like cheerful-
* Because she complained so much about her health, Mary had been given the family nickname of 'Mrs Gummidge' after the character in Dickens's *David Copperfield* who 'felt things more than other people'.

ness I thought of course I had some dreadful injury, and I made a plan to come home immediately and settle down into an incurable invalid! But by evening I was able to 'sit up and take a *little* nourishment'.

As the children grew older, Logan revealed a sensitive and reserved character, while Alys, though much prettier than Mary, was less intelligent and striking, and almost *too* good and pliant. It became clearer and clearer, however, that Mary was not going to follow in her parents' footsteps. The Quakers not only ignored, but at that time actively distrusted Art and Music, and even disapproved of much non-religious literature. Mary, on the other hand, took to all these with eager enthusiasm, and encouraged Logan and Alys to do so too.

To Alys Pearsall Smith   18 April 1882   Smith College
It has really given me more than 'Culture' to come here! For the first time I have gone to paintings and statues as a *real* lover. Of course I have often enjoyed them very much when I have been among them, but generally I fear I felt, like Horace Walpole, an 'unruffled regard' for such things. But today I felt tired and sick and ... presently with great pleasure the idea came to me that I might go into the Art Gallery and look at the pictures and statues. So I went and enjoyed myself thoroughly. First they rested and comforted me, and then presently their freshness and spirit crept into my soul, and I was all stirred up and awake. They never had such a strong influence on me before, and I have sometimes wondered if it was worth while for me to cultivate a *real* love for them.

To Robert Pearsall Smith   25 April 1882   Smith College
They think of opening Columbia college to women. If they do, I think I shall study there rather than in Boston, for New York is so much nearer home. O but I should like to be in with the literary Boston people! But it is a wild ambition, and I fear I would not, even if I studied there. And there *are* interesting literary people in New York too. But Boston is the centre of such things.

To Hannah Whitall Smith   2 May 1882   Smith College
Miss Sanborn [Mary's English tutor] lent me Walt Whitman, and such an insufferable mass of conceit and nonsense I do not think could have existed. There are perfectly *disgusting* parts, but she warned me of them, so I was preserved from these. F [her closest friend, Florence

Dike] stumbled upon the worst one and was thoroughly disgusted and enraged with the book. I saw first:—Imagine a man writing 'I sat studying at the feet of the old masters/Now, if eligible, O that the old masters might return and study *me*.' This is a *mild* instance of his egotism, really and truly. But there is something almost sublime in it, it is so fearfully reckless and courageous and honest.

To Hannah Whitall Smith   3 May 1882   Smith College
F and Miss Sanborn say I should never speak a word about Walt Whitman ... for everyone would not know I had been warned to skip the bad parts.

To Logan Pearsall Smith   13 October 1882   Smith College
Don't persuade thy friends to read thy favorite books. Long experience has taught me this bit of practical wisdom. At first my faith in mankind was blighted—I felt myself to be a solitary genius walking alone on serene heights, far above the common rabble. *I* could read and appreciate (after my own fashion) *Les Misérables*, Emerson, George Macdonald*, Robert Browning and the rest of my heroes. Volumes of these I lent indiscriminatingly, expecting my friends to share my enthusiasm. Except in the case of Florence and Emerson I have been disappointed every time. . . . One evening, full of youthful enthusiasm I produced a volume of poetry and read some parts of Myers to an unsuspecting and innocent Bandersnatch†, expecting him to be lifted to the seventh heaven with ecstasy. As I look back upon it now, I admire the youth for his honesty. 'I don't see much in it' he said.

As time went on, Mary was first won over and then more and more captivated by Whitman's poetry, and Robert, to please her, invited the old man (though he had not as yet met him himself) to stay with the family at Christmas. Hannah, however, continued to disapprove fiercely of him, as did their Germantown relatives and friends. Alys was even prudish enough to cut all the shocking pages out of the copy of *Leaves of Grass* Whitman gave her. Robert would have followed their lead, but for Mary's spirited defence. In the end, however, the poet became a close friend of the Smiths, and even Hannah became more

* George Macdonald (1824–1905) Scottish novelist and writer of children's stories; friend of Hannah's.
† Bandersnatch was the family name for young men, whom Hannah believed to be uniformly dangerous. It was taken from the frightful monster in Lewis Carroll's *Alice Through the Looking Glass* and *The Hunting of the Snark*.

or less reconciled to him. For Mary he developed a warm affection. He called her his 'staunchest woman friend' and his 'Bright Particular Star'.

To Logan Pearsall Smith   23 January 1883   Smith College
I hope thee is marking thy volume of W.W.'s poetry—the places thee particularly likes. Or does thee like it? I find I cannot at all follow his advice and leave him—I read much, both of his prose and poetry, and hardly know which I like best. However I cannot expect everyone to be as enthusiastic as I.... Somehow I feel of late a new interest in things, even the commonest—a general desire for information.... The immediate cause is W.W.... I relieve my mind to Sadie and one or two others who know me well. Aunt Sarah and other people write me such dreadful letters that I dare not talk about him much—or at all.

To Hannah Whitall Smith   25 January 1883   Smith College
To tell thee truly, thy little leaflet on 'God as a Mother' does not appeal much to me.... Of course He must have had that side to have made thee, but isn't it displayed in *making thee*? Does thee see what I mean? And what does thee think of it? I can't help thinking of the remark 'God made man—and he returned the compliment' which seems to me to contain some rather keen criticism.... I like to write my thoughts just as they come this way to thee, without the slightest reserve.

To Hannah Whitall Smith   1 February 1883   Smith College
Dear mother, *don't* write as if I were on a 'fearful precipice'—*I honestly don't think I am.* But there is that within me which rouses itself up into opposition to having anybody state anything as if there wasn't 'another side', and I am apt to take the other side whenever I can.

To Hannah Whitall Smith   13 February 1883   Smith College
Thee writes in a spirit of *loathing* to what God has made natural in men, and in women too, which thee calls 'brutal lust'.... It is only the abuse thee ought to loathe, the want of self-control, not the feeling. If I should follow thee I should loathe nearly every man, because, as Walt Whitman says, 'wherever are men—are our lusty, lurking, masculine poems'. Thee says I know nothing about men—I trust at least that their minds are not all taken up with it—I *know* they are not. As far as purity and happiness goes I would rather side with Walt Whitman. ... I guess thee would say 'Ugh' at the thought of any young man feeling what seems to me a most natural desire to be near a girl whom

24

he liked, to hold her hand, to put his arm around her. I should be sorry to be forced to loathe so many of my friends. I know they do think of such things and would enjoy them ...

From his prose and other writings I know that he [W.W.] means here that the sexual act should never take place except with direct reference to the child who is to be the result. Thee will probably know more definitely than I how far this idea is ahead of most people, most married people.... Walt Whitman is more moral than John Whitall who condemns him. Pearlie [his wife] herself told me that she was sorry to have a child so soon. What an awful shame to bring a child, even *at all* unwelcome into the world!

To Hannah Whitall Smith   18 March 1883   Smith College
I wish it were possible to have W.W. one night with us ... still if we can't have him I shall go to see him often and take him flowers.... I have a great many things saved up to ask him, and I am looking forward with real pleasure to seeing him. Shall I ever forget the first time when we drove the landau, and I was so frightened and yet composed at the thought of meeting my Hero face to face? Théophile Gautier, when he first went to see Victor Hugo, fainted at his front doorstep. I did not faint on the marble steps of the little Camden house, but I shall never forget my feelings.

To Robert Pearsall Smith   21 May 1883   Smith College
I will try to be very careful about unnecessary expense. There are a great many little things I can save on. I got my spring and summer dresses before I knew that the mines* were as the flower of the field— when we were all feeling rich, and building castles in Spain. However it's not so very bad after all, since it is all my summer outfit and my best Fall dress combined, and is only $113.00. I feel quite in the humour of saving money, although I suppose I don't know very much about it nor what it really means. I am not quite sure to whom to apply for lessons—not thee I guess (!)

To Robert Pearsall Smith   3 June 1883   Smith College
Dearest papa, how are stocks? Thee will have to sell a few I am afraid, to send thy impecunious daughter some money. There will be my board bill for two months, my horse's bill for the year, the curtains for this room, a few books, and fees to the servants to take up the money thee may send

* In one of his euphoric periods Robert had invested a great deal of money in a silver mine which turned out to be worthless.

me.... I think $400 will suffice! It sounds pretty big as I write, and I realize what a dear daughter I am. But if thee grumbles, poor old papa, I will say 'Who brought me up to spend money?'

The family had moved out to Germantown, and during the following year Mary stayed at home trying to study. She had now fallen into a gloomy frame of mind, brooding on her own character and future, and writing long introspective letters.

To a Friend in England   12 March 1884   Germantown
[This was probably Evelyn Nordhoff, a college friend, whose brother, Walter, foreign correspondent for the *New York Herald*, was to marry Mary's cousin Sadie Whitall.]
I have been facing the spectres of the mind, Doubt and Despair.... It seemed like intellectual suicide to say to myself that I believed in God, Love, Evolution when so many of my emotions lead me to believe in Chance and Evil.... I remember once some of us had great fun making what we called a list of Literary Personalities—that is of the men who spoke to us personally through what they had written or whose strong individuality was more interesting to us than their works. My list was—Socrates, Swedenborg, Spinoza, Jacob Boehme, Emerson, Walt Whitman and Victor Hugo.... Sometimes I think I would like to be a doctor ... a purely literary life has great attractions for me too. Sometimes in moments of enthusiasm I feel as if I would like to give up everything to music. But I suppose it will be Reform of one kind or another that I will go in for finally.

To a Friend in England   21 May 1884   Germantown
I think it is a savage instinct in me that simply hates conventionalities in an unreasoning way and rebels against limits and restraints. 'Going where I will, my own master, total and absolute ... gently but with undeniable will divesting myself of the holds that would hold me.' These are the mottoes which accord with my original nature.

To a Friend in England   29 June 1884   Newport R.I.
I must tell thee of my last three weeks which have been spent at the home of my friend Edith Carpenter.... Yet even there, while I was gaining physical and spiritual health with every breath, I saw some of the saddest sides of life. The New England character is very different from any other. There is a sterling honesty and 'Yankee Grit'—but they miss all the poetry and sweetness of life. The men are bound

26

down to an honest earning of their livelihood, and have no time for the amenities of life—their wives are household drudges, with the tender graceful part of their nature destroyed. Do you remember mother's idea about the equal division of property between married people? I never half saw the necessity for it before. But two women told me they would give almost anything they had to have a settled income of their own, apart from their husbands'—'even if it were only a hundred dollars a year' they said.

That year Mary was 20, a tall handsome girl with fair hair, straight black eyebrows, blue-green eyes and her mother's indomitable chin. She and Logan both went to Cambridge, Massachusetts, in September, she to study philosophy at the recently founded Harvard Annex (later to become Radcliffe College for girls) and he as a Harvard undergraduate.

In August 1884 the British Association for the Promotion of Science had met in Canada, and some of those attending it went on to attend the American Association for Advancement of Science in Philadelphia, staying with local families. One of those who stayed with the Smiths was Frank Costelloe, an Irish barrister practising in London. He was a convinced and pious Catholic, and had studied classical philosophy at Balliol College, Oxford, where he became a favourite pupil of the famous Master of that College, Dr Jowett. He was nine years older than Mary, a solemn, rather short, bearded man, with political ambitions as a Radical, a deep sense of duty, and a devotion to philanthropy. He and Mary went out for drives together, and he promised to prove the existence of God to her by philosophical arguments, pouring scorn on her warnings that she had inherited her father's unstable nature. In a way, Frank embodied the synthesis of Hannah's ambitions for Mary in the world of philanthropy and Mary's own hopes of culture and philosophy. She was much taken with him, and took him to call on Whitman before he returned to England.

To Walt Whitman   12 November 1884   Cambridge
Logan and I will be home soon—for Thanksgiving. Papa said 'What shall we do to celebrate your vacation?' 'Persuade Mr Whitman to come over!' I said....

I had a letter from Mr Costelloe (one of the Englishmen who came over with me to see you), and he asked me to tell you that he read the little book you gave him to the passengers on the steamer going home, and both reader and audience enjoyed it sincerely, and were much

27

enlightened and strengthened by the 'wonderful faith and hope' that breathed through the poetry. You certainly *do* 'blow grit' into people!

Without telling her parents she began writing to Frank from Harvard. After some weeks he proposed—and was accepted—by cable. The news was broken to the family during the Christmas holidays, and it came as a severe shock. Not only was he a Catholic, and an Irish one at that, but despite his good record in philanthropy he lived in London, which meant that the family would be separated from Mary.
   Hannah and Robert made every effort to dissuade Mary from what they were convinced—not without reason—was a rash marriage she would soon regret.

To Hannah Whitall Smith   25 February 1885   Cambridge
My dearest mother, thy letter this morning was very lovely. I *will* try to be less savagely independent in the future, and more reasonable. This matter shall *not* make any breach in our confidence if I can help it. And thee is so good and forgiving and loving that thee pardoned me even before I asked it.

To Hannah Whitall Smith   7 March 1885   Cambridge
Dearest mother, I have written so much lately that I am tired of writing, and I am going to limit myself to postals for a time. I have already answered thy question as fully as I could about Mr C's father. Why doesn't papa write to Lloyd's guest, Prof Ramsay?* Mrs Ramsay introduced Mr C and said her husband had known him for years. There must be a letter for me now crossing the ocean, telling me more than I know at present about the form of his religious beliefs.

To Robert Pearsall Smith   13 March 1885   Cambridge
I am going to try my best to be reasonable and sensible about it all. I have a very high ideal of marriage, and if I cannot realize it, I shall never marry. If I can, I feel sure that thee and everyone who knows me, will be glad to have me do so. And I am sure that if I have time to judge and weigh everything carefully, to see it all in a clear light, that nothing can ever tempt me to lower my ideal, and that I can tell with a reasonable degree of certainty whether I can realize this ideal in the case which is now under discussion. We must leave it therefore until I

* Probably Sir William Ramsay, Professor of Chemistry at University College, Bristol, who spoke at this British Association meeting.

have some chance to judge clearly. I do not believe we shall gain much by writing about it—though I am glad to have thee express thy thoughts to me.

To Hannah Whitall Smith   12 April 1885   Cambridge
My darling mother, thy letter and papa's I got yesterday were a great pleasure to me. I sent them right off, and I also cabled Mr Costelloe that your opinion had grown more favourable. I did not think we ought to keep him for two weeks under the cloud of those other letters. I am ever so much obliged to you for writing them. I am sure when you come to know him that you will see my love and trust, which has seemed to you so blind and unreasoning, is amply justified. It may be that faults of manner which are still displeasing to you may remain, but these things have never been essentials to me.

To Robert Pearsall Smith   13 April 1885   Cambridge
It *must* be a painful awakening to find one's 'swan' hatched out into a hawk who is not content with sailing on the calm waters, but must needs swoop out into more dangerous untried elements, and try its wings against the breezes. I am sorry it came so soon—but of course it was inevitable to come at some time.

That summer, the whole family except Logan, who had reluctantly gone to work in the family firm, crossed over to England, where Frank met them. He was to contest a Parliamentary seat in Scotland later in the year, and after various visits the family went up to Glasgow to hear Frank speak.

To Aunt Lill [Robert's sister]   18 July 1885   Broadlands England
I find him in reality all and more than his letters indicated, ... I find that his Catholicism is liberal enough for me to sympathize with, and that his circle of friends is, as father himself said, the one which above all others he would feel happiest in leaving me in the midst of. The old promise about a year's delay has been quite superseded, as they see equally clearly with myself. We shall be married, I hope, some time next autumn, possibly in September or October.

To Aunt Lill   29 July 1885   Glasgow
After we left Broadlands we went to the Isle of Wight, and father and Alys and I lunched with Tennyson and his family at their beautiful place near Freshwater. He was exceedingly interesting in conversa-

tion, and took us up into his 'den' where he writes, and all over his lovely garden. He looks like his pictures, but his complexion is more swarthy, and the usual expression of his face is rather more humourous than one expects. His great horror is people who come to see him and then print newspaper accounts of it....

It was a most enthusiastic meeting, and he (Frank) spoke very brilliantly. Mother was delighted, for he came out strongly on the subjects of Temperance, Women's Rights and Moral Reform. He is working in London now with Mr Stead,* the editor of the *Pall Mall Gazette*, and Mr Bunting, editor of the *Contemporary*, [*Review*], to promote further moral reform and to improve the laws.... I need not say that I am very happy. But I would like to tell thee that Frank is one of the most earnest, sincere and religious men I have ever known, and that I am sure that my life with him will be a better life than it could be alone.

* W.T. Stead, journalist and social reformer, who conducted a campaign against child prostitution. Frank had supported him actively throughout.

CHAPTER TWO

Ideal Marriage

September 1885–December 1889

Frank and Mary were married on September 3rd, and the wedding reception was held in Balliol Hall, Oxford. It was presided over by Dr Jowett, and as the Smiths were strict teetotallers he was obliged to drink the bride's health in lemonade.

The Costelloes left the festivities early and spent their honeymoon canvassing in Glasgow and Edinburgh for Gladstone's Home Rule for Ireland campaign.

To Hannah Whitall Smith   9 September 1885   Glasgow
O mother, there could be nothing more healthy and natural and interesting and good and altogether nice [than] the life we are leading now. We are *too* blessed—but we mean to be worthy of it if we can, and I think God will help us.

To Robert Pearsall Smith   21 October 1885   Edinburgh
It is great fun even to be '2nd fiddle' ... as thee calls it, except that I won't admit that I am that, for we are *one*, not *two*. However, *if* we were two, I should tell thee that while my whole soul would rise in revolt against being secondary to someone who was not really more clever or able, I feel that in this partnership I am in my proper place as Junior Member. I couldn't, with all the opportunity in the world, make as good political speeches as Frank makes, nor would I be a 'fit and proper person'—with all the Women's Franchise conceivable—to oppose the Rt Hon G.J. Goschen*. But I am to have my time too— next Friday I am to address a women's meeting.

Frank did not win his election, and later in the year he and Mary moved into a house in London overlooking the Thames, near the
* George Goschen was a moderate Liberal opposed to Irish Home Rule; Frank Costelloe was a Radical.

Houses of Parliament. Mary had a miscarriage in December, but soon recovered and began to settle into her new life.

To Aunt Lill   23 December 1885   40 Grosvenor Road London
It *was* an inconvenient time to fall ill! The dining room was the only one in all the house which was not being papered or painted or both (except the kitchens) and we had a temporary bed put up at one end behind a screen. The house was full of workmen—over fifteen every day, I should think, and our furniture from America and Glasgow was hourly arriving in packets large and small. My servant was just going, and I had two new ones to engage. The kitchen fire would not burn, the nurse I had for a few days fell down stairs and broke her nose, and altogether it was such an experience that I feel now that *no* housekeeping trials can daunt me! I used to lie in bed and laugh to think of it.

To Alys Pearsall Smith   14 January 1886   London
He is so much *better* than I. He does what he ought and doesn't go about following out his own whims and desires regardless of the moral law. And that regardlessness has been the evil of my training, and is, I suspect, the evil of thine. It never used to occur to me to do anything from duty—and so, though by nature and circumstances I was kept reasonably straight, I got no training whatever in self-denial. But one can't be always a child, and things *must* come that are hard to do, and then one misses the training frightfully.

To Aunt Lill   31 January 1886   London
We are just beginning to feel almost settled down now, for things are more or less in their places, and our regular engagements on Committees and charitable work and things of that kind are fairly well arranged. There are so many things to do in London that it is almost impossible to avoid doing too much. A great many philanthropic people one meets are too busy to have any home life at all, or even to make real friends. It is very unwise to live so, and yet I can perfectly understand it, because idleness seems wicked where there is so much to be done.

To Logan Pearsall Smith   19 February 1886   London
Frank and I were 'at home' last night. We provided our friends with a grand combination of the Sit Down Agony and the Stand Up Bore of the most approved pattern. Between forty and fifty came to our first,

and we expect more next week when the Tragedy will be repeated. O the misery—the blank hopelessness, the double-dyed stony despair of entertaining English people. Everyone seemed to think it a success, but my heart is like lead when I think of a nawful girl in blue who sat in corners all the evening and of one who wore a purple sash and sat quietly in the middle of the room, and of various unattached and unattachable bandersnatches who were too awful to introduce *even* to the blue girl. And then—oh Logan! the matrons that yawned against the wall and the old gentlemen who wandered from room to room like lost spirits looking for wine but finding none.

To Alys Pearsall Smith   9 March 1886   London
As to equality, fair Loo*, methinks thee will find more English men than American men who go in for a strong programme as far as Women's Rights go. I scarcely meet any man who questions that. What the family said about the great difference in the treatment of women is pure *bosh*, as to the position of married women. Girls *do* have a fearful time, I admit. Most married women here are stupid and foolish to a degree that it is hard for an American woman to realize, and—frankly—they deserve the treatment they get. But a woman here *can* take any position that she is equal to fill, and an interesting and thoughtful woman can have a splendid time here.... I say this merely to remove the misconception under which thee is evidently laboring, *not* because I like England. For I do not. Sometimes I think I almost hate it, and I fly into continual inward rages at the Stupidity which forms, as Oscar Wilde said, the staple of English Society.... The one basis has been a long talk with Oscar Wilde, who, whatever you may think about his moral attitude towards the universe, is undeniably clever—the cleverest talker I have ever met. It chanced this way. For some strange reason I am understood to be, in a small way, a social success, and so a Mr and Mrs Hancock who are well-known lion-hunters ... gave us a dinner to which they summoned various social celebrities, including Mr and Mrs Oscar Wilde and Justin McCarthy. I had a fascinating time after dinner with the fair Oscar, and simply *revelled* in his witty aphorisms about America and England and Art and Novels and all manner of subjects. So engrossed did we become that we stayed till half past twelve, and parted with the hope of meeting again at one of my Thursdays.

* Alys's nickname was Lurella, or Loo, after the heroine of a novel by William Dean Howells called *The Lady of the Aroostook*.

To Hannah Whitall Smith   3 April 1886   London
Since I last wrote, my time has been chiefly spent in the slums
working for Mrs Barnett*, but I must confess I think I shall not do
very much of that kind of work in the future. It tires me and I think I
can do more elsewhere. But it bores me to think about it so I will
change the subject.

To Hannah Whitall Smith   April 1886   London
We haven't had our first quarrel yet. How can we? For when I get
cross, as I must admit I have once or twice, I can instantly see on his
face the expression which I know means that he is asking God to show
him if he has been really wrong towards me, and praying with all his
might to be shown how he can make me happy.

To Hannah Whitall Smith   27 September 1886   Schönwald Germany
I think thy prayers and all our wishes are coming true! I can't be sure yet,
but I thought I would tell thee the very first hope I had. I am three days
past my monthly time . . . and I can't help hoping! I will write thee from
day to day of the progress of events. This will bring it to about the middle
to end of June. . . . O if it could only be! How I shall love it.

She was indeed pregnant, and her elder daughter, Rachel (Ray), was
born on June 4th 1887.

To the Family   12 November 1886   London
On the inspiration of Logan's and Alys's letters I wrote a long letter to
dear W.W., whom I *hate* to think of as suffering and lonely. O do all
you can for him in the years that are left to him to live, for whatever
you may think of his poetry, he is a great genius and a genuinely good
and beautiful old man, and he deserves far more than the world has
given him. . . . I think that America in general, and every American in
particular, is responsible for him. He didn't invent himself, he is the
inevitable product of American civilization and we ought all to bless
him for being so good.

*To her Family   18 November 1886   London   (Hannah had sent Mary an
afghan knitted by her grandmother, Mary Whitall, after whom she had been
named, and who had died some years previously.)*
I remembered a great many things about her that I had quite lost
* Henrietta Octavia, later Dame Henrietta Barnett, a well-known philanthropist.

sight of. I remembered the first time I discovered her *ears*! I used to think she was quite a different sort of creature from most people, and as she always wore a white cap, I never imagined she had ears, just like everyone else. But one day, when she was sitting in her green-cushioned rocking-chair in the dining-room, reading her Bible to herself through her spectacles, and I was sitting on a little low chair making a pincushion for her, I looked up and for the first time saw her ears through the thin gauze of her cap. It was a terrible moment. I felt as if it upset all my universe, it was a sacrilege to look at them and yet they had a terrible fascination for me and my eyes were fairly *glued* to them, or rather to the only one I could see. I was terribly afraid she would find me out looking at her, and yet a horrible curiosity seized me to know if there was one on the other side of her head like the one I saw. But I didn't dare to stir, for fear she would discover my wicked thoughts. AFTER A LONG, long while in which I scarcely dared to breathe, I plucked up courage and stole round and took a peep at the other side, and there to my horrified wonder was *another ear*!

Hannah was still not happy about Frank. She argued with Mary about his religious views and feared that he was her pet aversion, an authoritarian husband.

To Hannah Whitall Smith   29 November 1886   London
Thee has fallen into Evans'* error of collecting quotations that seem to bear on thy view without understanding the fundamental definition of the terms ... and this inexactness in the use of terms is really the secret of all my 'Paganism' or 'Atheism' or whatever Germantown chooses to call it—for although I realize that I am in no sense a genius, and will probably never be even a thought-power in the world, yet I have a very keen mind for logical inconsistencies and for vaguenesses that cover inexact thinking. I am good at *destruction*, though not at *construction*, all my philosophic teachers have told me that.

To Hannah Whitall Smith   December 1886   [London]
He [Frank] does not believe in divorces; and in 'separations' only in *very* rare and exceptional cases, where there is wickedness on both sides. The one important thing then is to preserve the unity of the

* Thomas Evans (1798–1868) Quaker writer and compiler of quotations.

family and do your duty to your husband or wife. When a difference of opinion arises, it is the *duty*, of course, of the one who is in the wrong to give in, but if they both think they are in the right and are not willing to submit to the decision of a third party, it is the duty of the one with the highest moral nature to yield his or her own claims and if need be happiness, and submit to the only condition that will enable them to fulfill their solemn marriage vows, 'in sickness and in health, in happiness and in sorrow—till *death* shall separate them'.... In all this the position of husband and wife is entirely equal, and Frank thinks that they are equal ... the point that he makes against mother is that *legally*, as in contracts and bankruptcy and business arrangements, you must have a law that will work when people are *not* living from a sense of duty. The present law, with modifications, gives the ultimate deciding vote to the man ... and Frank, from his whole theory of the solidarity of society, thinks it is better to have some law, even when it presses at times very hardly in cases of exceptional moral obliquity, than to have no law at all.

To Hannah Whitall Smith   6 January 1887   London
I was a Whitmanite at Smith College—the individual was the only thing I took any stock in. Did I ever tell thee what I solemnly took as my motto? 'Henceforth I ordain myself loosed of *all limits* and imaginary lines/Going where I list, my own Master, total and absolute.' ... Thee can easily see that with such a view of the way I wanted to conduct my own life, I could not in justice refuse the same right to other people ... I used to defend suicide and divorce, and my idea of growth was 'revolution'.

To Walt Whitman   17 January 1887   London
Many thanks for thy card of the 3rd.... I am afraid by a curious fatality all thy biographers want to make thee out *too good* for thy liking! Has thee never thought of expanding the 'Specimen Days' into Autobiographical sketches? Then thee could tell the world thy wickedness to the full, which thy friends are so uncomprehending as not to see!... We have had nothing here but a succession of thick fogs, and today when I saw the flush of the real sun in the sky, I thought it was a fire! In pursuance of the course of reading I wrote thee about, I have begun to take Greek lessons and read Plato's Republic. In our spare moments (which are, alas! none too many) we are working out our idea of the ideal State, as a sort of supplement and corrective to Socialism.

To her Family   25 January 1887   London
It is quite hopeless to try to explain why BFCC [Frank] is the person calculated to help me best along the thorny road, but from the moment when he told me that to his mind the foundations of the world were the four corner stones of God, Duty, Free-Will and Immortality, and that (as was his wont) he was prepared to *prove* them to me, I knew he could help me.

Hannah finally determined to bring the family over to England to rejoin Mary, and by 1888 all the plans for the move were made. Alys was to stay out her time at Bryn Mawr College in Philadelphia, where she was now a student, whereas Logan was to accompany his parents, for he had rebelled against the glass business and persuaded Robert to finance him at Oxford instead, with a view to his becoming a writer.

To Aunt Lill   20 October 1887   London
The astonishing news from the other side has put almost everything else out of my head. When I thought I *had* to be separated from them, I bore it with as much philosophical resignation as I could muster, but now that they really are coming I am so wild with joy that I begin to suspect I must have been desperately homesick all the time without knowing it!

To Logan Pearsall Smith   24 October 1887   London
I know now what it is to be in a hurry. I used to think I knew, but it was a mistake. There can, however, be no doubt at all now. We are simply rushed to—I was going to say death, but I will say the extreme verge of possibility. Frank has 6 hours a day of his Commission work—and he ought to do more as they are pressing the enquiry on at a dreadful pace. His largest case, Parker and Bingham, will go to smash if it isn't finished before November, and he still has about a hundred bundles of old parchments (Wills, indentures, Charters etc) written in horrid crabbed hands in pig Latin, to examine. Besides this the Redcar people are angry with him for not going there, and want him to do the preliminary work there, and then the usual number of small 1 and 2 guinea cases are coming in to be attended to all the time and he has accepted *four* Vigilance cases*. Besides this the publishers

* The National Vigilance Association carried on much of its work for social and moral reform through Court actions.

are screaming at him for not finishing his German translation*, and we *must* get that under way—and papa has just written to ask him to write a review of his Copyright article!

To Hannah Whitall Smith   23 November 1887   London
It is partly political work that takes up my time. Since the Trafalgar Square disturbance† I have been to several meetings to protest against the conduct of the Government. Tomorrow I have a Home Rule Committee to attend, on Friday a Liberal Federation Committee, and next Tuesday I am to address a meeting in favour of Home Rule. I do not grudge the time I give to things of this kind, for it is a very good sort of educational training, and most appropriate to my future station in life, but it certainly does take a great deal of time! Sometimes when I am very tired I get really discouraged, and I almost wish Frank had been a native of Kamschatka, instead of an inhabitant of this fearfully complicated city at the centre of the world.

To Hannah Whitall Smith   18 January 1888   London
I went to Dr Garrett Anderson‡ on Monday.... She asked me whether I was pregnant again, and I said 'no', and then she asked me how I knew, so I told her that we had made up our minds not to have another child at once. Thee can hardly think what a lecture she gave me—I should think a woman would be ashamed to say such things. She said if I was *her* daughter she would warn me most seriously that such a way of life was wrong and wicked and all sorts of terrible things. I was more angry than when Dr Smith had given me a warning on the same lines, for I thought a *woman* ought to have more sense. So I asked 'Isn't it very bad for a woman's health to have as many children as she possibly can?' 'Certainly it is,' she said, 'but there are plenty of other ways besides abstinence of avoiding that!!' ...
It is a fortunate thing I married a man who agreed with my principles—I think it would almost have turned me to *hating* my husband if he had wanted me to use any of Dr Garrett Anderson's 'other ways'.... As to saying it is impossible—it is a flat lie. I am sure

* *Aristotle and the Earlier Peripatetics*, translated from E. Zeller's *Philosophy of the Greeks* by B.F.C. Costelloe and J.H.Muirhead (1897).
† A demonstration in Trafalgar Square on November 13th protesting against the suppression of free speech about Home Rule. It was broken up by soldiers and mounted police.
‡ Dr Elizabeth Garrett Anderson, sister of Dame Millicent Fawcett, the Suffrage leader, and one of the first two women doctors to practise in England.

our love for each other grows greater every day and that Frank's self-denial for my sake makes him love me more, and helps his own character in every way.

Mary changed her mind about birth control, as about many other things, in later years.

To Hannah Whitall Smith   13 February 1888   London
Thee is right in saying Frank is a good husband. He is perfect to me and there isn't anything that I could possibly complain of, even if I were not so much in love with him. I am perfectly happy in our love, I believe in ideal marriage more than ever I did, and the future looks very bright to me.

To Bernhard Berenson   28 February 1888   London
I have just heard from Mrs Burton* that you are in England now, and I cannot help hoping, since London is the centre of England, that there will be some chance of my meeting you. Will you come and spend next Thursday evening (March 1st) with us, from 9 to 11? Or if you are not free then, will you come to dinner with us next Sunday at 1.30? ... Gertrude says you are probably at Oxford. If you are, I am sure you must be enjoying it keenly. It is one of the loveliest places in the world. I wonder if America will ever produce a place like it?

To Hannah Whitall Smith   24 March 1888   London
Invitations to speak are *pouring* in upon me. I believe in a little while I could have an engagement every day if I wanted it. I am so lazy that I don't feel like doing it but Frank is always urging me on.... I see, however, that if for any reason I ever get very keen upon public work, there will be plenty of avenues open.

To Robert Pearsall Smith   7 May 1888   London
Frank and I are invited to some very grand parties this week. Tonight we are going to the Marquis of Ripon's, tomorrow night to a great Liberal Soirée, then to Lord Rosebery's and finally on Saturday to a Mrs Joicey's who is said to give very brilliant parties. There is to be held here an inaugural meeting to found a Women's Liberal Association for Westminster. I am simply overrun with invitations to

* Gertrude Hitz Burton, whom Mary had known at Smith College and Harvard, had been very taken with a young man called Bernhard Berenson, and when he went to Europe she asked Mary to befriend him.

39

speak for Liberal Associations, Home Rule unions, Education Reform Leagues and Temperance Societies. There are so few women who can speak in England. They have asked me to stand for the School Board, but I do not want to very much.

When in the autumn of 1888, she found that she was, after all, going to have another child, Mary began to feel desperate. The child, another daughter, was born in March 1889, and named Karin, but Mary was never, either then or later, able to summon up as much affection for her as for Ray. Her state of mind went from bad to worse, and by the winter of 1889 she was in deep depression.

Diary   21 February 1889   London
A woman who is going to have a child ought to be removed from all care and responsibility. I have had all kinds heaped on me, and Frank is too busy to take more than a spasmodic kind of care. It was *wicked* beyond words for us to dream of having a child if we were not prepared to give up something for it. He is not prepared to give up any of his activities or pursuits to help me lead a quiet, restful, healthy life—we had no Xmas holiday, we never had an evening, and he is always behindhand and worried with his work and of course I am dragged along in his wake. I cannot live a separate life. But this has been misery for many months back. I think I will never have another child unless conditions can be *entirely changed*.

Journal Entry   9 December 1889   London
In the present order of things (perhaps it will always be so) in marriage the man takes everything from the woman. Of course he gives some things in exchange, but not all.

He absorbs *the whole* woman's life and gives her love, support, a home, much of his time, but not his life, in the sense in which she gives hers.

He takes her to live where his pursuits lead him, she is to be the hostess for his friends and pay his calls for him—whether she loathes calling or not. Of course she can refuse, but if she has a grain of unselfishness in her, she cannot refuse. It seems to be churlish. Her pursuits, *where they do not naturally coincide with his*, are set aside. He absorbs all her time with his home and work and society and interests. . . .

Look at my own case. I feel quite sure that there could not be a more unselfish self-sacrificing husband. I am far more selfish in every way. Yet whose life is it we lead? *Frank's of course.* ... Up to the end of our third year, I still hoped to have a chance to study a little and fill up, if only a little, the dreadful gap in my desultory education. ... But my practical life has been so full I *could* not, and he has never lifted a finger to make it less full. After the most solemn promises, he persuades me to undertake fresh Thursday evenings, fresh political speeches, fresh duties and cares. *He* has had his splendid education— he cannot conceive what it is to be without it—and *constantly feeling the lack* ... As a matter of fact, it comes to this. What capacities for development etc I have which do not coincide with the plan he has formed for himself of his own life—may lie dormant—may die for lack of nourishment. I am told that I shall find my *true* development in casting myself generously, unreservedly into the march of his life. This, he says, is what the *union* of marriage means. (These two shall be one creature—and that one the husband) ...

To say I married too young a man who had already passed beyond the requirements of my age, that we have lived a life of *his* age and education since (which nevertheless my selfishness has from time to time rendered acutely miserable), that my occupations leave me no chance for the things I would naturally have chosen—all this does not help matters a bit. Here is the life to be lived, and I must try to live it. ... Therefore, woman, sink thyself and thy needs and empty hopes. They cannot be fulfilled. Join the army of those who exist to fill up the gaps in the interesting lives of others and learn, as most women learn, to consider it enough interest for thee.

CHAPTER THREE

Escape

November 1890–September 1894

During the summer of 1890, Gertrude Burton's friend Bernhard Berenson reappeared in London after some three years' travel and study in Europe. This time Frank and Mary invited him down for the weekend to their cottage near the Pearsall Smith country home at Friday's Hill in Sussex.

Bernhard, who spelt his name with an H until the 1914 war, and who was known to his friends as B.B., was then just twenty-four, and elegant and exotic in appearance and manner. He was a year younger than Mary and two or three inches shorter, nervous and sensitive, with dark hair, Slav features and wide-set grey eyes.

The Berensons had come to Boston from the Jewish Pale of Lithuania when Bernhard was a child. The family consisted of a short-tempered father, Albert, who somehow never managed to make good in the new country; his wife Judith, who adored Bernhard; a younger son Abie—like his father, no great success—and three sisters, all younger than Bernhard: Senda, who was to marry Professor Herbert Abbott of Smith College; Bessie, who did not marry; and Rachel, who was to marry Professor Ralph Barton Perry of Harvard.

Bernhard, brilliant and ambitious, made his way through Boston Latin School and on to Harvard. There he studied not only Greek and Latin, but also Hebrew, Sanskrit and Arabic literature, determined to make a name for himself as a writer. Upon graduating he failed to win the travelling fellowship he desired, but a number of his well-to-do friends, notably Isabella Gardner, a wealthy patroness of the arts, had faith in him, and financed his studies in Europe. In June 1887 he set off, and for a year pursued Art and Culture in Paris, Oxford, London and Berlin. When in August of the following year he reached Italy, he fell deeply and permanently in love with the country, and above all with its Renaissance art.

In Italy he met Giovanni Morelli, an Italian scholar nearly fifty

42

years his senior, who had developed a scientific method of art criticism and attribution. Morelli emphasized the importance of analysis and comparison of the paintings themselves, particularly the painters' treatment of such apparently insignificant but actually revealing details as eyes, hands, ears and drapery. Berenson was greatly impressed by Morelli and his method, and began to study pictures closely and tirelessly in the Morellian manner, wandering from church to church and gallery to gallery, making new and confident attributions as he went.

At their second meeting, Bernhard made an enormous impression on Mary. He seemed to embody all the culture and brilliance she had thought to find in Frank, and in the event had not found. She started out by deploring his lack of social conscience, but it was not long before she too was to shed the beliefs and duties she had begun to find intolerably boring.

Frank, too, enjoyed Berenson's company and conversation (though Mary's parents did not) and hoped to convert him to Catholicism. He did, in fact, become a convert the following February—largely, as he remembered later, in order better to understand the art the Catholic Church has inspired—but the 'vaccination', as Mary afterwards called it, did not 'take'.

Throughout that August of 1890, while Frank was at his legal work, Bernhard and Mary spent increasingly idyllic hours together in picture galleries and private collections. In September all three went to Paris, and when they separated, Bernhard and Mary began to write to each other daily, with more and more warmth of feeling.

At the end of December the three met again in Florence and Rome, and either in Rome or in London, whither Bernhard followed them in February, Bernhard and Mary became lovers.

To Walt Whitman   28 November 1890   London
Thy postal of ten days ago has just come. It is so good of thee to write. I am ashamed to think how long a silence I have kept—yet I have thought of thee very often. I have been so busy—'facilis descensus'— into politics!—and when once there it is hard to get out. Of course the one miserable thing occupying the political field is Parnell's incredible meanness. He has dealt the death blow to Home Rule in this generation, I am afraid. I feel so sorry for the many Liberals whose one cry and interest has been Home Rule. It is not so unhappy for me, because for several years *all* my work has been given to what seems to me infinitely more interesting than the machinery of politics—the

43

reform of existing social abuses, such as the overwork and underpay and the generally wretched conditions under which the poor live. The collapse of Home Rule will bring *these* questions much more to the front, but I think it means a Liberal defeat at the next election, as the Party is not prepared.

We are all so well—children and all. Frank and I are going to spend our Xmas holiday at Rome, if all goes well.

To Gertrude Hitz Burton   5 December 1890   London
I do feel that he [Bernhard] ought to take some thought for his future.... He feels, I think with reason, that a few more years of the enjoyment and appreciation of beauty in Italy would give him that exquisite and rare culture which only one person in a thousand could ever attain. Because it is so beautiful, he dimly feels that it *must* be of use in the world, merely the existence of a supremely cultured person, whether he does anything practical or not... The flaw is in his leaving out the moral and social elements, but how to make him see this I don't know.

To Ray Costelloe [aged 3½]   24 December 1890   Florence
I send thee a Christmas card which Santa Claus gave to Bernhard-berenson for thee, and Bernhardberenson sends it to thee with a kiss. We had a long walk today, and we looked at a great many pictures painted by a man named BOTTICELLI, make Grandma teach thee that name.

To Bernhard Berenson   Undated, no address   [Early 1891, London?]
Wednesday morning 8.30. The letters have just come, but none from my dear love. I was afraid the Naples letter would not come until tonight and I shall be away at Guildford. How my heart sinks when I think that by some chance it may fall into other hands... O my Darling, only a love such as thine could make me happy—it fills my whole world, there is no room for another thought. I am all filled with joy and love—oh! my dearest, dearest. Pray for me, so that pain shall never come to me through thee.... Remember my own, how I held thee in my arms, and know that it was only a poor symbol of the absolute, tender love I feel for thee.

To Hannah Whitall Smith   16 February 1891   [London?]
Tell Alys that B.B. writes to Frank constantly and to me less often, which she will consider a good sign. Not that it does in fact make the

slightest difference! One of the great advantages of marriage (if people take it right) is that it removes at any rate a portion of us from 'the weary strife of frail humanity' as to falling in and out of love, which agitates the unmarried.

To Bernhard Berenson   [Spring 1891 London]
Dear, I awoke at about 2 o'clock last night trembling—and I remembered and lived over again everything. How I love thee. I dream of it all the time. Thine.

To Hannah Whitall Smith   4 March 1891   London
Father was in an awful rage yesterday, but he appears to be in a better humour today. He seems to hate poor Berenson, but no doubt he will learn to reconcile himself to the inevitable, as people always do. It is such a pity to hate him, for if Papa took him right, Berenson could amuse and entertain him immensely.

To Bernhard Berenson   [Spring/Summer 1891]
My Joy. Thy letter came, and in spite of this terrible absence my heart is full of sunshine and gladness. O if I could say to thee everything thy dear letter says to me. I know so well that we love each other in just the same way. Sometimes I am tempted to think I love thee most and again that thy dear love is more, but I know that it is just the same. Yes—I worship thee, dear love. I almost pray to thee—at least my prayers are always so filled with thee and only thee that the angels would not know which one of us was uttering them. O what a pleasure it was to have thy letter.... O love, love, love. What bliss to know I shall see thee in 45 hours. I want to see thee so! Sweet, I have solemnly resolved that I will not outlive thee—and of course I will not outlive our love. If such a terrible soul—death came to me—(but it cannot)—I should kill myself. But I do not fear that ... Ah how I love thee and long to make our life really beautiful. I pray to God to keep me. I hope He doesn't really disapprove! I know so little about Him— but I do not want to apologize, even to Him. I was thinking what I should say if I went to Italy with thee. It would not be an apology. No, dear one, do not fear that.

Mary had conceived the plan of spending a year in Italy as Berenson's pupil, and Frank, unaware of the true situation and hoping that this change would cure her restlessness and relieve the strain on their marriage, tolerantly agreed.

She set off in August 1891, and throughout that autumn she and Bernhard travelled round Europe, looking exhaustively at pictures, with Enrico Costa, a friend of Bernhard's, as 'Chaperon'. Mary was very serious about art, and determined to make a genuine professional study of it.

By December they had settled next door to each other in Florence, in lodgings overlooking the Arno, and there they worked and loved.

Mary had not entirely severed relations with her husband, and there was still talk of her returning at the end of the year. Frank agreed to the two children going out to spend most of the winter and spring with her, and Hannah also came out to visit her, and to cast a maternal eye over her circumstances. Mary wrote to her mother, as she always did, virtually daily, and the letters, as always, were full and frank, though she did not, perhaps, reveal all the details of her new life.

To Hannah Whitall Smith   11 August 1891   The Hague
I want to make it as easy as I can for Frank. Do be as nice to him as you can, please. It isn't *really* his fault, and he is paying dearly for his mistakes. I am quite sure that the only thing for me is to be absent for a time, till I fill my life with pursuits, but I don't want to have people blaming him.... Nearly *all* the mistake was mine.

To Hannah Whitall Smith   26 August 1891   Dresden
I want to settle them [the children] in Florence about the end of October. By that time I shall have been able to learn a great deal, and it will be bliss to settle down to a winter of quiet work, with Ray having nice young companions. It will be hard on Frank, but still not really worse than if he had not been married—I mean not more uncomfortable. Still, if he wants to keep Karin I shall make no objection, because she is really too little to learn Italian, whereas Ray will learn it so that it will be as natural to her as English—Still all these things can be so much better discussed than written about ... then I will see the Angel too [Ray], without whom I am only three quarters happy. Sweet little Seraph—I wonder why I love her so?

To Hannah Whitall Smith   4 September 1891   Munich
I am hard at work, but not too hard. I feel as if I had just awakened to myself.... No one will know what the fortnight of solitude was to me, and what my comparative solitude and my complete independence are now! It was too delightful.

To Hannah Whitall Smith   12 September 1891   Verona
There is no use at all my taking up art unless I do it seriously. I should be unhappy if I permitted myself merely to dabble in it.... I feel sure I could write, I will not say a good style, but at any rate persuading and convincing books, if only I knew enough. But to say anything worth saying you must be able to say it in fifty ways, you must really know the subject to the bottom. Then you can choose your way of saying it. Now one thing I mean to do in Florence is to write. If I were entirely alone in the world I believe I should spend six or seven years merely studying before I tried to say anything at all. But in the circumstances, I feel as if I should in a sort of way justify my actions if I were able to write something.... Now this autumn I have a chance to study I may never have again. Berenson is not giving me information 'on the cheap', because in work like this you *have* to use your own eyes. In things connected with words it is not hard to borrow other people's ideas—no one has done it more than I. But in this work it is impossible. However his help is immensely valuable. It prevents me wasting time, which I am sure I should do to the extent of several years without him. No one has yet been trained as I am being trained to look at the really best things, and to *start* where other people have ended.

To Alys Pearsall Smith   16 September 1891   Verona
The churches here are full of lovely pictures—almost all Veronese, except for a Titian, a Savoldo and some Mantegnas. The sacristans are as a rule very nice, when they see you mean to linger. They pull the curtains and let in the light and then go away, leaving you to climb up and get a better view if you like, or arrange it as you please. The Museum 'closes' at 4, but I usually stay till 6, as the light gets very good in the later afternoon, and it is cooler.

To Hannah Whitall Smith   28 September 1891   Venice
I feel as if quite lately I had taken a leap forwards. It *may* be backwards according to some standards, but to me it seems forwards, and I seem to be getting an interior peace which is very different from the old tumult of bitterness and uncertainty in which I was raging when I was at home. Of course the danger is that I have (I think) no orthodox standards of any kind. Thee, who is such a rebel against orthodoxy in religion, cannot be surprised or shocked if I am a rebel against orthodoxy in conduct. Frank is quite right in saying that the one heresy leads to the other in the next generation at least. What he isn't right in is thinking that religious orthodoxy has much real

influence on conduct. A little impartial reading of history would show him that it has practically no influence at all. Well, just as thee depends on thyself and thy own sincerity in thy religious views, so I must learn to do in my own views about the relations of people to each other—how far selfishness and unselfishness should be carried, what 'duties' appertain to the individual in his various social relations. I have been thinking and thinking about it, ever since I came away from home. When I came away I was a violent 'individualist'. I have been modifying and changing since. The one thing that is certain (to my own mind) is that it does not do for me to take anyone else's views, Frank's or thine or anyone's. I've got to act from bottom convictions of my own.

To Hannah Whitall Smith   10 October 1891   Venice
Yesterday afternoon, on the express invitation of the sacristan of one of the churches (Santa Maria del Carmine) we went and washed and cleaned what turned out to be a most beautiful picture by Lotto, but which was invisible under candlegrease and dust and cobwebs when we first went to look at it. It was great fun having it come out inch by inch under our fingers.

Diary   28 December 1891   Florence
It was hard for me not to have a 'moral' prejudice against her [a Mrs Way, a friend of B.B.'s]—*so* hard, for she is the kind of woman—flirtatious and overmannered—from whom I have always fled. But when I am just, I know that flirting is only one of the escapes from ennui, like religion, or devotion to children—and not so very much worse in its effect on the world. . . . What interested me most was to see that even a person like B was not shocked with such arrant flirtatiousness, but on the contrary rather pleased with it.

When the children finally arrived, the reality was less attractive than the idea had been.

Diary   2 January 1892   Florence
Every girl ought to be made to spend six months taking care of little children before she marries. She would then think twice before having children of her own!! The nurse came at 11!! Children restless all night and I terribly unhappy at being absent from B.

Diary   5 February 1892   Florence
In the evening mother and I talked. Poor mother! Poor old people

everywhere who try to make over young people's lives according to their pattern—and poor young people! What an awful institution for hypocrisy and oppression the family is! Honesty is the one *personal* virtue—all one's other virtues are questions of geography and history. I shall *never* oppress my daughters.

Diary   14 March 1892   Florence
When we grow old, we won't look back upon our famous books, on the flattery we have had, but to our early loves, to our real *enjoyments*, perhaps often those in which the intellect has had little part. I shall never forget the charm of these days—not only for the awakening of my intellect— delightful as it is to begin to think freely—but because Bernhard looked in such and such a way, and spoke in sweet deep tones. . . . Ah how happy, how happy I am. Truly this is a marvellous year.

Diary   11 April 1892   Florence
A day of quarrels, alas: over plans and over the general tendency of children to engulf the personality of the mother—at any rate her intellect. I did a great deal of the quarrelling, perhaps all—but I thought better of it in the night. After all it is stupid of us ever to quarrel.

Diary   13 April 1892   Florence
She [Mrs Way] feeds upon the 'highly spiced' French novels, novels which do nothing but ring the changes upon the ecstasy of the supreme moment of sexual passion. This, I am pretty sure, is a fiction created by men novelists who no doubt are taken in by the cleverness of the people they hire (in one way or another) to give them so much rapture for so much pay. So they believe women feel as men do, and even more. I do not believe it—and I think Mrs Way is taken in by all this writing, and thinks there is such a thing for women to feel, and that, since she does not feel it with her husband, she might feel it with another man.

Diary   1 May 1892   Poggibonsi
Coming back we heard nightingales singing near an operatic Grotto— arches and ivy and clear water and all complete, and tried to experience the proper emotions. We were not successful, but probably the scene will arrange itself, emotions and all, in our memories.

That summer of 1892 Mary came back to England and made it clear to Frank that she was not going to return to him. Frank would not

agree to divorce her, but instead made her sign a Separation
Agreement by which she had to undertake not to interfere with the
children or their education, though she would be allowed to see them
for short periods every year. Mary was profoundly upset by this, not
least because she was made to see that he had the right to bring them
up in his religion, a religion that she was coming to hate more and
more, as she was Frank himself.

Hannah was also desperately upset. She could not understand how
a mother could abandon her children for whatever reason—let alone
for a man—and her letters begging Mary to return became more and
more urgent.

Diary   14 October 1892   Ravenna
It gives me a curious despair about the improvement in the lot of
women, since I, who am (presumably) in the van, find it such a
struggle to choose definitely between being a person and being a
mother. I know that all that is personal in me, all that means self-
development, real education, knowledge, enjoyment, is with Bernhard.
With Ray I could not help sinking to a mere instinctive motherhood—
that is with Ray and without Bernhard. Yet, even knowing this with
certainty, the struggle against the chains of womanhood—the *inside*
chains—is a terribly hard one. Still if the laws were just to women,
there would not be a quarter of the struggle.

Diary   25 October 1892   Macerata
We both seem rather cross these days and I am unhappy except when
I am at work. Each little thing I see keeps reminding me of Ray, and it
seems as if I *could* not give her up . . . Bernhard's patience is giving out,
too. I can see so well. He finds almost everything I do amiss, and
shows at every moment his contempt for the feeling I have for Ray,
which he thinks is a mere brute instinct, simply killing my personality. . . . It is very natural he should feel so—he has no family ties, life
is full of all sorts of marvellous possibilities for him—and a great deal
is spoiled because of *my* mistakes, because of my child, whom he
thinks a rather detestable specimen of humanity in herself.

Hannah and Robert were terrified of scandal, though Mary was
quite unperturbed. Some sticklers for convention now refused to
receive her, but Bernhard's unmarried men friends welcomed her,
including Charles Loeser, who had been at Harvard with him and
was now hoping to become an art expert himself, and Carlo Placci, a

sociable and volatile Italian, who became one of their closest friends. Florence was full of unconventional expatriates, too, such as Vernon Lee (the pen-name of Violet Paget), a gifted English writer and brilliant talker, who lived with her dear friend Kit Anstruther Thompson at Maiano below Fiesole.

A number of old friends also kept in touch, such as Professor William James, the philosopher and psychologist, brother of Henry James and for many years a family friend of the Pearsall Smiths. There was also Eugénie Sellers, a friend of Logan's, who later became the assistant head of the British School of Archaeology in Rome, and a strange pair of ladies, aunt and niece, called Katherine Bradley and Edith Cooper, who lived together and wrote lyric poetry and lurid 'Jacobean' drama, jointly, under the name 'Michael Field', Katherine being 'Michael' and Edith 'Field'.

Bernhard and Mary spent a great deal of their time, as ever, in travelling and looking.

To Robert Pearsall Smith   14 January 1893   Florence
I have seen Prof James several times. He is certainly charming, but he is so utterly out of place here, that it detracts from his charm. He *will not* look at anything except as an illustration of his a priori theories about art. He would be furious if anybody took Psychology that way, from a priori theories about the soul. What can you think of a man's intellectual method when he applies it only in spots?

To Ray [aged 5½].   21 January 1893   Florence
I know very well that people would tell thee I was not a loving mother. They cannot see into my heart, or they would not say that! But thee promised to keep it in thy mind to believe me, and not them. Because *I* ought to know, ought I not? Whether I love thee. And I do know, that I love thee dearly, dearly, my precious Ray.... I love thee more than anybody else in the world, except myself. Gram will be surprised at me for saying this, because people do not usually tell the truth and say they love themselves most of all. It is the fashion for people to think that they love other people better than themselves. And *sometimes* they do, but it is very rare. People as young as I am, very seldom do.... Now that I have found studying of my own I really like to do, I do not want to give it up in order to stay with thee all the time. If thy father would let me have thee always with me, I should be perfectly happy.... But he wants you in London. So I go away, and only come home now and then, so that I can go on with my studying.

51

To Hannah Whitall Smith   9 March 1893   Florence
I called on the Jameses yesterday, to take the *Spectator* (for which many thanks) and found Prof James simply *furious* over Vernon Lee's last book *Vanitas*, which contains a long and minute character study of Henry James, almost mentioning him by name. Prof James says it is the most indecent, indelicate, utterly incomprehensible affair imaginable, for his brother and Miss Paget have been very good friends—or at least seemed to be. Yet all the while she was taking cool impersonal notes upon all his peculiarities and little habits and ways of thought and life. William James considers her a 'most dangerous woman', and he is going to write and tell her that after this book she must not be surprised if he declines to continue the previous friendly relations. All this indignation sounded very funny to me, I must confess, from the brother of the author of *The Bostonians*, which contains such an evident study—even caricature—of dear old Miss Peabody, who was the James's old family friend during Henry's youth. Yet he declared that he did *not* mean Miss Peabody, and on the whole I can believe him, as I understand how readily a novelist can forget the individual who suggested the type to him. In the same way, I have no doubt, Vernon Lee is half unconscious of having drawn Henry James to the life.

To Gertrude Hitz Burton   15 March 1893   Florence
I do not know whether I told thee that he [Frank] and I are formally separated and that I wish to have it known by everyone who ever devotes a moment's recollection to me. So now I am 'on my own hook' with the satisfactory feeling that everyone I know entirely disapproves of me. Still there are a few exceptions; that makes up for the rest, and in the end, if I really succeed, as I mean to, I think that even my family will acknowledge that I had a right to take my life into my own hands.

To Hannah Whitall Smith   1 April 1893   Florence
Thy letter* brought tears to my eyes, in fact it made me cry right out
* Hannah had written: 'I fully believe thy desire to see me happy in my last years is genuine, although thee does not always seem to act it out.... Thee will not think, darling, I am sure, that I do not sympathize with thee from the very depths of my being. My heart aches for thee and with thee continually and I would gladly lay down my life (though that is a *small* thing to do) to make thee happy. It seems an awful thing that one should be able to wreck their life in a few rash and blinded moments! I want to do all I can to help thee and to make things easy for thee, and am only too eager to spend and be spent for thee and for thy poor precious little daughters. But I seem powerless to do anything, alas!'

like a baby. How I do hope things may be endurable to thee. I am young and the joy of life is strong in me, so that I can quite well bear a good deal of anxiety and real sorrow and deprivation without feeling that it is more than the ordinary lot. I have such very great pleasures, and I feel my interests enlarging every day. Above all I am young, and that makes me happy in itself. But it is different for thee.

To Hannah Whitall Smith   25 May 1893   Bergamo
We ['Michael' and 'Field' were staying with her] have been wandering about in carriages way off the beaten track. At one place, Massa Fermano, they still preserved the tradition of an Englishman who had come there 10 years ago—a sort of strange visitant from another sphere. What the legend about three English ladies will grow to in ten years is laughable to imagine, particularly 'Miss Mike' [Katherine Bradley], with her frowzy flowing hair, who insists on wearing a heavy fur about her neck on the hottest days 'to keep me cool'. I told the people they were Poets like Dante and Ariosto and Tasso, and they were immensely impressed.

To Hannah Whitall Smith   21 August 1893   Munich
It is dreadful to shut yourself out from anything that has given great pleasure to cultivated people, and my conscience has long been uneasy about Gothic. Now I have seen it at its best, and feel more satisfied. Its real home is France, and that is the place to see it. I cannot say I care for it as much as for Renaissance architecture, but still I feel I know what it is. The historical side I know very little about. Art has a curious growth of its own, an evolution which can be studied apart from history. But that is technical, and I am sure you never have a *real grip* on any phase of art, until you know the contemporary history of the human spirit—which is its real interest.

To Frank Costelloe   10 October 1893   Venice (Draft)
As to your remarks about my having no right to interfere in your household, I must remind you that ... I have every right to interfere if I consider that unsuitable arrangements are being made for them. This right no threats of any kind shall induce me to give up.... Nothing that touches the children is indifferent to me. Very much your best policy would be to be perfectly frank to me in any plans you may make that affect them. It would save us both a great deal of annoyance.

To Robert Pearsall Smith   16 November 1893   Florence
I see the way open to me, with the start I have had, of becoming really a scholar in all that pertains to the art of the Renaissance. One advantage of this study is that so many paths are still unexplored, and so many sources of original investigation are still open. I haven't very great ability, still I have a certain facility and plausibility which will ultimately gain me a hearing, and if to this I add, as I mean to do, an absolute accuracy as to the facts and the occasional contribution of perfectly new matter, I am bound to make a certain place for myself, particularly among continental scholars who are more interested in scholarship than the English.... If in the course of years I can thus gain an impersonal position as a serious student and an agreeable writer, I shall have plenty of interesting friends. I have a few, even as it is, people who know the situation.

To Hannah Whitall Smith   21 November 1893   Florence
'Michael' writes me a rather jubilant note this morning, congratulating me on not having a poet's heart, for 'a poet's heart' she says, 'is at best a healthy wound.' I *am* glad I haven't one! All the same, I have a suspicion that I have quite as much heart as 'Michael'! What turns the so-called heart into a wound is very often vanity—unless of course there is some serious loss, which 'Michael' is not suffering under.

To Robert Pearsall Smith   24 November 1893   Florence
I am anxious to publish it [*A Guide to the Italian pictures at Hampton Court*, compiled by Mary and Bernhard during the summer of 1891] because it will give me an *independent* standing among professional people, who now of course know me, if they know me at all, as a pupil of Berenson. It is important for me, therefore to stand on my own feet as soon as possible ... Thee remembers the essay on Venetian painting which I gave thee to read a year and a half ago. Well I offered it to Putnam then, along with the badly arranged Hampton Court material. He said he liked it, and if it could be combined with something less cumbrous and of more general interest than the Hampton Court stuff, he would print it. As I was not in possession of sufficient knowledge to do anything else with it, I gave it to Berenson and advised him to make lists of all the genuine works of Venetian painters. This he did, and I submitted it to Mr Putnam last summer and he accepted it at once. My idea of course was to have both

names because I thought and still think that the best way to answer scandal is to tell the exact truth as openly as possible, namely that we have been doing serious and scholarly work together.* Mr Putnam wanted both names, but mother opposed it so decidedly that I yielded the point and asked Mr Putnam to leave out my name. This I thought was only fair, as the smaller part of the work is mine, and then I am using his notes for the Hampton Court book which is to appear in my name. It is going to be a useful little book for those who care for the subject. But human nature is queer! One thinks one isn't ambitious and is only anxious to have peace to do quiet scholarly work no matter who gets the credit, yet I find myself much more interested in the possible publication of the Hampton Court affair than in the *Venetian Painters of the Renaissance*, although I hope that may have a small success, which is the most to hope for a book of that character.

Mary wrote very frequently to her daughters, often in the form of a continuing story, and generally illustrated with spirited drawings.

To her Children   7 April 1894   Florence
Dear Chicks—that *was* a nice letter you sent me! I have read it over and over until I quite know it by heart. The back was wonderfully crowded with kisses, but I have kissed them all and found them very sweet.... I am very much interested in your drawings and I keep them all carefully, and hope you will send me as many as you can. I always show them to some of my friends and we talk a great deal about them. For there is this very funny thing, that *all* little children, no matter what race they belong to or where they live, American, English, French, German, Italian, even Chinese and Japanese, all draw almost exactly alike. Funnier still, even grown-up people, before they were so well educated as they have come to be in modern times, used to draw just like this, and indeed you still find peasants and savages drawing in the same way.

To Hannah Whitall Smith   25 May 1894   Florence
The amusing Oscar Wilde is here, and I have seen him several times. This afternoon I am going to take him to call on Vernon Lee's

* *The Venetian Painters of the Renaissance*, the first of the four books which were to make up *The Italian Painters of the Renaissance*, was published in 1894, Bernhard having supplied the lists and collaborated with Mary on the final version of the essay.

55

brother, Eugene Lee Hamilton, who, by the way, has just published a very decent volume of poetry called 'Sonnets of the Wingless Hours'. Oscar says such extraordinarily clever and subtle things, I can't help liking to talk to him, but he is so untrustworthy, on the other hand, so utterly lacking in any kind of character with which I have sympathy, that it is a 'mingled cup'.

To Hannah Whitall Smith   26 May 1894   Florence
It was a great success. Oscar talked like an angel, and they all fell in love with him—even Vernon, who had hated him almost as bitterly as he had hated her. He, on his part, was charmed with her—he likes people without souls, or else with great peace in their souls, and when he met her before he found her restless and self-assertive. But yesterday he admitted that she had grown less strenuous.

To Hannah Whitall Smith   14 September 1894   Dresden
Of course I have considered the question of 'scandals' arising about me—have considered it I think, from every point of view. As thee knows, for myself it is a matter of *absolute indifference*. I can always, under any conceivable circumstances, have all and more than all the interesting friends I want. The only points, therefore, which I have to consider are 1) the children, both how it will affect BFCC [Frank] in letting me be with them, and how it will affect their relation to me, as they grow up. 2) thee and father—particularly, of course, thee.

   I have thought it all over very carefully and my actions are based not upon caprice or impulse, but upon a thought-out plan. But it will take time to work out. I am now convinced that, with time and freedom, I can become one of the most important people in my own profession, as well as one of the most interesting women to cultured people. I mention this because this is the point I rely upon to attract the children when they arrive at the culture-seeking, intelligence-appreciating age.... As thee knows there are no women from whom I could learn anything in my kind of work, and comparatively few connected with art in any intelligent way—though there are plenty of minor artists. The idea of my requiring a chaperone, or refusing for lack of one to associate freely with the people with whom I work or who can help me on, is very insulting, and belongs to a world with which I no longer have the slightest sympathy—except always in so far as it is a world that can give *thee* pain, or the children. For the moment, however, thy mind may be quite at rest. Berenson is in

America, Costa in South America, Obrist in Munich, Hapgood* in Venice and I here with Christina†. With Frizzoni‡ I scarcely think even the most malicious person would try to make up a scandal, but he is in Milan.

---

* Hutchins Hapgood, American writer and journalist whom the Berensons called 'Fafner' after Wagner's dragon, and greatly liked.
† Christina Bremner, an English writer friend of Mary's.
‡ Gustavo Frizzoni, pupil of Morelli, collector and connoisseur and friend of Berenson.

CHAPTER FOUR

Diversions

September 1894–November 1897

Mary was now beginning to achieve her ambition to be known as an art historian in her own right. One of her articles had appeared in the influential *Nineteenth Century*, a skilful exposition and defence of Morelli's—and Berenson's—method. She had been able to place reviews of books on art in various magazines, and in the summer of 1894 her *Guide to the Italian Pictures at Hampton Court* was finally published, only a few months after Bernhard's *Venetian Painters of the Renaissance*, the book about which she had written to her father in November 1893.

The *Venetian Painters* proved more successful than either of them had dared to hope. It was favourably reviewed, and its publication led Isabella Gardner to renew her acquaintance with Bernhard, and to accept his help in obtaining pictures for the great collection she was to assemble in her Boston palace, Fenway Court. Thus began a partnership which was to be highly profitable to both of them and to last until Isabella's death, thirty years later. It made possible the beginning of the life of cultured luxury which Bernhard and Mary were to lead.

Throughout the spring, despite these happy developments, Mary remained restless and disturbed, still torn between Bernhard and the children. In May Hermann Obrist, a young sculptor and embroidery designer from Munich, came to Florence. He was a tense, argumentative young man of dashing appearance, full of fiercely held psychological theories, and both Bernhard and Mary liked him. Bernhard enjoyed his serious conversation and admired his energy and his work. Mary found him fascinating. Emotionally susceptible, as always, she soon believed herself to be in love with him and began an affair which she concealed from B.B. He was still unaware of the state of affairs in September, when he went to the United States to consolidate the reputation he was beginning to acquire from his book and from a number of short pieces which had been appearing in the *New York Herald*.

I feel as if I did not need to say how much I love thee—thee knows it by now, and my yearning to express it is not what it was in the days when we spent all our time writing round and round about it to each other. It is none the less real and ardent now, but has passed beyond the need of words.

To Hermann Obrist   1 October 1894   Friday's Hill
You see, after all, you haven't committed the 'unpardonable sin' of marrying me, so you can afford to let me have these insights into your real way of feeling, without dreading either that I will be hurt by them, or will cherish them up and brood upon them. Already when you tell me, I feel as if it were the real beginning of a frank human relationship, where each one of us can afford to be quite natural, and can report faithfully what we find upon our explorations into those 'Dark Continents' we call ourselves. Yours is perhaps not so dark a continent as mine.... Mine is still inhabited by monkeys but I am clearing a few footpaths, and constructing a few habitable huts. At any rate, *since* you told me that you felt quite unfriendly for a while at Dresden, I felt far happier about your real affection for me. For I knew how you felt, by instinct, without knowing why or how. Now I see that such coolings are part of you (like your moustache) and must be taken for granted.

Meanwhile Mary's sister Alys had become engaged to the young Bertrand Russell. Since he was seventeen he had been a frequent visitor to the Pearsall Smith house at Friday's Hill, falling in love with Alys at first sight, so he reported, but making no move until he was twenty-one.

Alys was five years older than Bertie, very pretty, with dark curly hair and blue eyes, a Bryn Mawr graduate and a virtuous daughter, though by aristocratic English standards far too independent. Bertie's family disapproved of her, and he was sent to Paris for a three months' separation in the hope of breaking the engagement. Mary now made a closer acquaintance of her young and brilliant future brother-in-law, and in her somewhat emotional state of mind could not resist flirting with him. Forbidden to see Alys, he found Mary excellent company; in November they stayed at the same hotel in Paris for ten days, sharing a sitting room, while Mary awaited B.B.'s return from America.

To Bernhard Berenson   5 October 1894   Friday's Hill
Berty's idea is to have the state provide 'procreation tickets' of a certain colour, and have heavy fines for those who dare to have children with those whose ticket doesn't correspond—thus eliminating disease. The congenial ones could marry all the same, even if their tickets weren't right, but must use checks.... They are both against marriage, in the present sense, altogether. Alys has a little penny pamphlet containing pictures and prices of half a dozen varieties of check, all safe and harmless, from one shilling to 2/6. The doctor has undertaken to distribute them in the village. Shall I send thee one?... Among all his friends, Alys says, these questions are hotly discussed ... At one of their Cambridge meetings, one of Bertie's friends read a paper on the following subject, 'Is it wise to cohabit with a woman one loves psychologically?' ...

I used to be so bored and miserably dull, before thee came and saved me. As the sapient Logan was saying yesterday; people brought up spoilt, as we were, need a strong intellectual enthusiasm, a goal it takes *hard work* to reach, to keep them from deadly ennui. Alys, for instance, confesses that until she fell in love, she was bored nearly to death, and regarded life with indifference—and she will again, when she ceases being in love, if she isn't careful.

To Alys Pearsall Smith   8 November 1894   Paris
He [Bertie Russell] certainly has an A no 1 'Thinker', and I consider it is an immense thing for thee to marry such a truly intellectual, thoughtful man. He has an *all round* brain, that works well on every subject. I look forward to years of real joy in his companionship, of genuine 'stimulation'. Higher praise I could scarcely give, because I consider a really fine brain implies a fine character. He is a brick. And *such* a dear.

To Hannah Whitall Smith   23 November 1894   Schliessheim
How grateful I am to thee for many of the ideas I was brought up on—as for example, that you always get your due of love and liking. I see people continually jealous, exacting, restless, demanding more, making themselves and everybody else miserable, and I could not do that simply because thee taught me so young that I always got as much as I deserved, and the only way to get more is to *deserve* more.

60

To Bertrand Russell   24 November 1894   Munich
Dear Berty... You must pull yourself out of bed very early and meet the Orient Express at 8.30—or no! I will come and breakfast with you at 9 on Wednesday morning.... I shan't leave until 1 o'clock so we shall have time for a short talk. And if possible we must have Thursday evening. But I don't know when Berenson is to get to Havre... *How* I look forward to seeing B.B. again and talking shop—and no more personal problems. Perhaps you cannot understand it—but I like to sleep well and eat regularly and feel that I am getting on professionally, and not be occupied in trying to force the 2+2 of human relations to come out 5, or 4½!

I look forward to seeing you again, *mon cher enfant*—and I wish it were to be for longer. Yours Mariechen*

By now Mary's infatuation with Obrist had died down, and when she met Bernhard there was an emotional scene of confession and forgiveness in Paris, after which she spent Christmas with her family, and he returned to Florence.

To Bernhard Berenson   25 December 1894   London
I rather hate to feel so much. It brings one's heart up into one's throat in a most uncomfortable way. Still, thy letter has come at last. I can swim out into peaceful waters again. I don't know why I was so excited—I suppose hating to part with thee after so short a time together, and the fear that assailed me that, when thee thought it over thee would feel my behaviour had been too 'feminine' for thee to stomach and thee would just keep silent out of slow disgust. Or something of that kind. But thee need not, dear! I shall wipe off old scores, and thee must too.... I shall indeed be very careful now, I have had a lot of pain from all this, a lot of disquiet and disturbance. I don't like it, I shan't endure it again. Join hands and let us go together into a peaceful, regular life, full of work and enjoyment of impersonal things.

To Bernhard Berenson   5 January 1895   Friday's Hill
I had an interesting little talk with Ray last night as I was brushing her hair—children's confidences come in fits and starts. She said one of the girls in the school said the reason her mother stayed away was

* Mariechen (pronounced Mareeken) was another of Mary's nicknames given her by a German nursemaid when she was a baby.

61

because she was a drunkard. 'But I explained to her how it was' Ray said, 'and I told her when *I* grew up, I would lead my own life, and not be a burden on my daughter.'

Mary and Bernhard had now moved up to the hillside below Fiesole, where they again lived a few doors apart. Mary shared her villa for a time with a friend of Vernon Lee's called Maud Cruttwell, a red-faced, somewhat mannish Englishwoman, who claimed to be an expert on Botticelli, and who acted as housekeeper and sometimes as her 'chaperone' on various trips with Mary.

To Hannah Whitall Smith   28 January 1895   Fiesole
My days pass like this: wake at 8, with lots of hot water. Hang out of the window for a while for the sunrise light on the mountains; coffee at 8.45, a cigarette and a little literature—Pater or Lamb or Hawthorne. Then writing—at present the *Beaux-Arts* article* (it has to be translated, so style doesn't count). We lunch at 12.30 and generally have someone.... Then I 'have the afternoon to myself', for a walk and galleries, the two often combined, for it's a great climb to get here. We dine at 8 and read English poetry until nearly 10, and then I have an hour for letter-writing.

To Gertrude Hitz Burton   3 March 1895   Fiesole
Poor Bernhard becomes every year less and less expressive about personal matters, as he dives deeper and deeper into ideas and work ... I know so well how dumb he grows when he feels he ought to say something personal—how it drives him to absolute silence. It is not lack of feeling, but partly inability and partly reluctance to express it ... We are living here at least as quietly as thee can be ... and I like it very much. Books, pictures, photographs, writing—my daily correspondence with the children, and a few professional letters—a small class of students once a week who gather round Bernhard's table and ask questions and study photographs.... Maud Cruttwell manages the house without a creak in the machinery, and very economically— we have almost no callers and pay no calls.

To Karin Costelloe   8 March 1895   Fiesole
My darling Karin. When thee gets this thee will be 6 years old! To

* The French art journal, *Gazette des Beaux-Arts*, to which both Bernhard and Mary were frequent contributors. This article, which appeared in the May edition, was a review of Bernhard's latest book, *Lorenzo Lotto*.

think that nobody on earth can stop thee, or keep thee little—thee *will* go on getting older and older, and more and more grown up! Isn't it funny? If we just *killed* ourselves with trying, we couldn't make thee 5 again, once thee is 6! Well, I wish I could see thee and give thee these 6 kisses, instead of sending them. We should have a grand hugging and kissing and a 'wm—wm—wm' just as long as thee wanted.

To Hermann Obrist   13 April 1895   Paris
I set out to have that finest of all human relations, a relation of *perfect honesty* with B.B. There was everything in its favour—and *I* failed at the first serious temptation. It is too late to remedy it now. I simply must bear the disgust I feel for myself at my failure. If he and I cannot rely on each other, it makes the world a rather lonely place, for if we, who have no false ideals of 'ties' or anything to hinder our being ourselves together—if we can't do it, who can? I hate to think I broke the compact. I ought to have been more courageous. It was hard for me in some ways, and he did not make it easy, but all the same, I did fall back into that detestable woman's way of lying and managing and concealing.... The failure has sapped my courage and my confidence a little—has left me with less hope and enthusiasm, has made me feel that perhaps I scarcely deserve to be an 'exception', such as I have ventured to try to be. For—think!—on the first temptation I fell back again into the usual feminine deceitfulness. I couldn't have been worse if I'd been an ordinary married woman.... Then for what did I sacrifice my feeling of honesty, I ask myself? Ah, dear artist, there is the bitterest sting of all. If I could have kept my love, it would have carried me through everything—nothing else would have counted. But I have not been strong enough even for that. And *so soon!*

To Hermann Obrist   30 April 1895   Fiesole
To refer to a problem you set in one letter—if B.B. fell in love with someone else, what would he do? Whatever he did, I am pretty sure he would not deceive me. And I, on my part, would be oh! how different. But it doesn't solve the question to discuss that... I can't, for the moment at least, feel even tender about my past feelings. When I think of a year ago (we were at Cagli) my first sensation is shrinking back and wishing I had been different. Fortunately I kept no journal. *Basta!*

Mary and Maud Cruttwell had a number of guests at the villa: Bertie and Alys Russell, who had married in December 1894, in spite of his family's disapproval; Logan, who was working hard at polishing his prose; his somewhat censorious friend, Eugénie Sellers, and 'Michael Field'—'The Mikes'.

To Hannah Whitall Smith   15 May 1895   Fiesole
The Mikes went away last night, and Maud and I began to breathe freely again—literally and metaphorically. Their dread of *draughts* has condemned us to close stuffy rooms, and the monstrous delusions about themselves in which they live have condemned us to the worst stuffiness of hypocrisy.... They think they are a Great Poet—unappreciated at present, but certain to be famous and adored in the next generation—and they think that their souls are united and that it is good for them to be together. As a matter of fact, the utter mistake of both these theories is 'obvious to the meanest intelligence'.... Michael makes constant demands for sympathy, and it has been hard to preserve even a decent appearance of it. To anyone less resolutely obtuse my feelings would have been only too plain.... But after all there's something rather attractive about them. And Maud and I feel we have been great brutes. But really it was too awful when I was at breakfast to have Michael come tripping in, as she did every morning, and say 'And how has little Mary slept?' and chuck me under the chin. No, never, never again shall we have them here.

Diary   17 June 1895   Fiesole
All this time at Fiesole grappling with the Book*, and enjoying it very much. Every day we saw deeper into the 'why' of real art enjoyment. Practically the whole will come out in Bernhard's books, but I do wish I had kept a record of our discussions from day to day. However I was lazy and did not—and so I have missed the detailed memory of one of the happiest and most *growing* months of our lives.

To Hermann Obrist   24 June 1895   Fiesole
You happen to be wrong about B.B.... he would not steal your ideas. I have never known him do such a thing consciously, and in this particular case he is so serious and earnest as to be next door to *impersonal*. Furthermore the book is already almost written. It is on the

* Berenson was now at work with Mary on *The Florentine Painters of the Renaissance*, the second in the series on the Italian painters. This book, less historical and more psychological than the *Venetian Painters*, was the one in which he propounded his theory of 'tactile values'.

Florentine painters, a companion volume to the Venetians. In it he takes occasion to discuss the essence of our aesthetic pleasure in figure-painting both at rest and in movement, and *hints* at landscape and line ... I know well, from having worked all spring with B.B., the hard, sweating intellectual labour it takes to simplify the thing and get at the bottom ... What happiness for me, who cannot originate, but can take pleasure in real thinking!

To Bernhard Berenson   1 August 1895   Friday's Hill
Bertie and I are at it hammer and tongs, over thy theory of 'pleasure' which he begs to dispute *in toto*, basing himself upon the more recent psychologists.... Bertie doesn't want to be forced into a constructive definition of pleasure, but I can see he leans strongly to the view that the pleasure we undoubtedly do take in the realization of the object is to be grouped under the pleasure of knowledge rather than the pleasures of increased capacity for realizing objects.... I wish thee were here to thrash it out thyself with Bertie ... I am doing my best since thee isn't here.

In their efforts at reconciliation and the restoration of their mutual honesty, B.B. and Mary decided to analyse her affair with Obrist.

Diary   1 November 1895   Fiesole
In the evening Bernhard and I read over the correspondence between Obrist and myself ... I must confess, it was much duller than I thought it would be. It bored us to death. Besides this, it was obviously hollow and not ingenuous.

Diary   7 November 1895   Fiesole
I am utterly and entirely beaten and discouraged. Reading the last of those horrible letters has broken me. Bernhard was very, very angry, and hated me bitterly for many moments together. There seems nothing left to start fresh with—nothing.... To be a person who is fickle in soul—to have loved once, as I really loved Bernhard, and then to waver, to be unable to hold fast to the good thing. So selfish, too—not to think of the pain to him—and yet he should be my first thought, as I know I am always his. When I left BFCC [Frank] I thought my love for Bernhard was *forever*. And then I couldn't hold firm, but yielded to the delight of feelings that sprang up (for it *is* wonderful to be 'in love') ... And yet, if it had been Bernhard, should I have blamed him? Sometimes I think not, for Love in whatever form

it comes is a God, and even if it destroys all one's so-called 'moral nature', it remoulds the world 'nearer to the heart's desire'. Why should we put faithfulness above it?

To Bernhard Berenson   4 January 1896   Friday's Hill
Thee mustn't say that it is because I don't care to write to thee if my letters are dull. The children simply tire me to death, and leave nothing interesting to be said. And it is not only that. Mother does not realize that my meat and drink has become the possibility of escaping to impersonal interests, and at every moment I am pulled down into the most revoltingly sordid and to me almost heartbreaking worries— this and that going wrong with the children's bringing-up—too burdensome to tell anyone about.

To Bernhard Berenson   5 January 1896   Friday's Hill
O Bernhard—if thee *should* get to hate me, or not want me, and I came back here, not even the children could in the least make up, not for thee, but even for the life thee has given me, almost as free as life can be from what is sordid and mean. I mean to come back to thee more than ever determined to 'unsordidize' ourselves.

To Bernhard Berenson   10 January 1896   Friday's Hill
I hope now that chances *have* come to thee, there is not going to be apparent that curious little defect, which one sometimes sees in people at the point of success, which prevents their realizing any advantage. Don't let it be! Buckle down to the work and do it. Thee can well enough.

In the summer of 1896 Mary had a minor gynaecological operation in London. News of this came to Frank, who believed it—wrongly—to be an abortion, and was furious. Hannah, who had been trying to placate Frank in order to maintain some hold on the children, was terrified and wrote to Mary that she thought he would divorce her and stop her access to her children altogether.

To Bernhard Berenson   [May?] 1896[1] *Nursing home, London*
In the day I think of nothing but thee. Everything else had dropped off. Thee is the only thing that made me want to live. Yet I never knew thee until those last days in Paris. When I think of the ways I have made thee unhappy, I flush down to my shoulder-blades. Nurse after nurse asks me 'What is it?' Unhappy thoughts.

66

To Bernhard Berenson   12 June 1896   Fiesole

I had a truly torturing night, unable to sleep, going over in anticipation all the pains of tearing Ray and Karin from my heart. But I am really prepared for the worst; and have thought a great deal, too, that maybe it would be like a surgical operation and restore real health. We should be married and live where we chose.

To Bernhard Berenson   13 June 1896   Fiesole

I have just received thy comforting letter, and the enclosed from Mother. Also a telegram from her saying 'Mistaken'. All that misery for nothing. It seems cruel of her, but I am sure she had no idea how I would suffer, for of course she does not realise all he *could* find out and all he could say.... However the danger has blown over and things will go on, no doubt, at their ordinary pace. I am tenderly amused at what thee says about thy present clinging to respectability. Truly if it were not for the children that would weigh little with me.

Diary   9 July 1896   Fiesole

Miss Sellers came up to spend the night. She was full of kindly lecturing, and she has a fine outspokenness, so that she really gave me what is so rare, a perfectly friendly adverse criticism of Bernhard and myself. She thinks that to take people up with such enthusiasm and to drop them with such indignation as we do is undignified.... Bernhard has the reputation of being a man who cannot bear other men, as he is furiously jealous of their reputation. We are both supposed to be very unstable and changeable in our opinions and enthusiasms.... I see the justice of her remarks. Especially when I think of myself and Obrist, how I 'magnified his name'—but did not glorify it forever.

To Bernhard Berenson   15 July 1896   London

I am also sorry thee teased me about my fat. That danger I have taken in hand. I shall never eat another potato ... I shall not drink at meals. I shall have a cup of tea brought to me in bed, to quench my thirst, and eat gluten bread and an egg for breakfast.... I am really serious over it—the more so as I notice that when I get fat I look like Father. Too horrible!

To Bernhard Berenson   13 August 1896   Friday's Hill

I am terribly bored, dearest Bernhard, and sick with disgust at the stupidity and boringness of most people. The impossibility of talking—the dreariness of the platitudes we all utter—the vanities and weaknesses of us all. It is horrible. Bertie is the only person whom I thoroughly like and get on with, and Logan in spots.

To Bernhard Berenson   22 August 1896   Friday's Hill
I am in turn, surprised at your answer to my question about *l'Homme au gant**. It was scarcely necessary to tell me that the presentation of character is not the same thing as line, colour, tactile values, movement or composition. What I meant you to think about, when I asked the question, was whether this presentation of character was not more direct, more vivid and more pleasure-giving than we should be likely to get either in literature or in life itself? Whether this instantaneous communication of the significance of the personality was *not*, in short, an artistic pleasure. Just as in Masaccio, the spiritual significance is not an element added to and different from the artistic, but is an integral part of the artistic impression.

Diary   8 October 1896   Ancona
Bernhard seems so nervous and cross that unless he had told me out and out that it was not so, I should not have been able to help thinking that he dislikes me intensely. Everything I say or do gets on his nerves, whenever he looks at me it is to tell me I am fat, or red, or hairy, or slouchy or untidy—and all these remarks he makes—and others on my Americanisms and my general stupidity, in bitter tones with a frown and not the slightest appearance of finding anything nice in me. It may be one way of expressing affection, to be greatly concerned with another person's faults, but it is not the happiest way. It makes me very unhappy.

To Alys Russell   12 December 1896   Fiesole
I have the Signora Triulzi every day to work for about 8 hours, mounting the photographs†, and I am trying to catalogue them—there are 12 or 15 thousand, and I think it will be months before they are finished. In the midst comes an urgent command for a third edition of the *Venetians*. Like Father's favourite snake which casts off its bright skin yearly, so we cast off old attributions to take on new ones. There are hundreds of changes to be made, and all the new

---

* Titian's painting in the Louvre.
† Photographs of paintings—only just becoming available—were an invaluable tool of their trade, and Bernhard and Mary were gradually building up an enormous library of them.

collections to be added, and I feel at my wits' end. The worst is, we nearly always quarrel while we are working over the lists.

Diary   2 March 1897   Fiesole
A miserable day for me owing to Bernhard's losing his temper several times while working with me in the morning, and simply furiously in the afternoon because he thought I was cheated by the men who brought a book from the railway. Perhaps I was, but it is scarcely worth making a disgusting scene about. I feel very miserable about it—such things upset me terribly—and if he is like this now, what *will* he be as an old man? It isn't a *deep* fault, but it is perhaps more wearing than a really worse thing would be.

To her Children   24 March 1897   Fiesole
After lunch he [Placci] took me to call on Mr Hildebrand, who is, I think, the greatest living sculptor. He lives in a beautiful villa on the other side of Florence, with his lovely, lovely wife and a huge family of daughters and one little son. Some of the daughters are just getting grown up, and I couldn't help wondering what you would be like at their age. We talked a lot about it on the way back, for although those girls are brought up what I call perfectly, Placci says he doesn't like them! They are brought up in just the way I should like to bring you up if I had you all to myself—they have never read anything but the finest books (in all languages), never seen anything but the greatest works of art, never heard anything but the best music. And they like all these things—fine books, great art, beautiful music—very very much. And yet, and yet—it isn't the same thing to have it all *given* to them, as if they had fought for it and won it for themselves. I have often noticed this with perfectly brought up children, their taste is good, but it is a little tame. So I consoled myself for your awful books of adventure and the dreadful art your blue eyes gaze upon and the trashy music your little ears hear, thinking that when the day comes for you to take hold of things *for yourselves*, you will make everything you learn glow with your eagerness.

To Ray and Karin   30 March 1897   Fiesole
I have had such fun today with an enormous dog, a boarhound . . . He belongs to a man named Wilfred Blaydes, who lives nearby. I had a walk with the master of the dog this afternoon, and I made a few shy advances to Reno (the Dog).

Wilfred Blaydes, a somewhat dilettante young Englishman, was evading his father's efforts to make a lawyer of him and writing a book on philosophy. He sent Bernhard and Mary one of the chapters, called 'Epicure and Death'; they both liked him, and once again Mary became infatuated. Their affair was even shorter than the one with Obrist, but this time Bernhard found it harder to forgive. Mary hopefully reminded him of his magnanimity at their earlier reconciliation, but he punished her throughout the summer, which he spent in St Moritz among the rich and fashionable, by long descriptions of his flirtations there.

To her Children   5 April 1897   Fiesole
Today as I was walking down to town in the sunshine, I had a dreadful attack of melancholy, so that I hardly knew how to bear it, melancholy at not being with you in these delicious years of your childhood. I saw some other children and I could not bear it that they weren't you. I just sat down on a stone and cried and cried and then had to go into town and do my business with red eyes.

To Bernhard Berenson   29 July 1897   Friday's Hill
Last evening, as I was dressing for dinner, a sudden sense came over me of thee, as thee was ten years ago, when thee first came to Paris. Of course I didn't know thee then, but thee has told me enough to make it possible to reconstruct thee. This I have often done, but never so sensuously as last evening. I did not see thee, but I seemed to feel just what thee felt then, how new to life, how hopeful and yet unhopeful, *à la fois*, how sensitive, how foolish and how sensible. All thy possibilities seemed to dawn upon me, giving me a feeling of infinite *tendresse*, a sort of lovely twilight feeling, that brought bitter-sweet tears to my eyes. I leaned a long time on the window-sill, listening to the wind in the trees and thinking of the young thee. And I felt an awful tightening of the heart, with a fear that I may have killed, or (I hope only) nipped with frost some of the best of these possibilities. Dear Bernhard, we must not let it be so. I feel that the worst thing thee has to bear now—is it not so?—is the not to be put by sense that there is no more mystery or surprise, or sacredness about me—*que je suis une chose connue, et qui vaut très peu la peine d'être connue.* Thee feels I act on motives mechanically, and thee knows my mechanisms—and despises [them]. Now please read what follows as carefully as thee can—it is all I have to say on the matter which is past. Can thee remember thy state of feeling that night which thee now so much

regrets, when thee was brought to acquiescence in a state of things from which thee now revolts? Thy feelings (I am not now speaking of judgment) were heavenly that night, thee must remember. Thee said it was worth all conceivable pains to feel so, if only for a moment. Now, Beloved, if, *while thee felt* so, anyone had come and denied to thee the value and importance of those feelings, thee couldn't have admitted that person was right—could thee? The thing, however mistaken, judged from the point of view of the whole of thy life, was genuine and exquisite (at the moment)—foolish as thee has come to think it since. My only excuse, or rather explanation for my *inexcusable* behaviour to thee, was that I had allowed myself to feel under the influence of an emotion, genuine and sincere from its own point of view, which for the moment shut my eyes to every other point of view. I was not deliberately wicked or unkind or deceitful or anything else thee thinks me, any more than thee was, that night, deliberately idiotic. I had to say this to thee once, and I hope thee will really understand it. From the point of view outside the feeling I did things that cause me to turn hot and cold all over, but from the inside point of view, well they were quite different.... and I have given thee a formal *business* promise that I shall never again (if it continues to matter to thee) take another excursus into my own inside point of view, apart from thine. Ecco!

To Bernhard Berenson   4 August 1897   Friday's Hill
O Bernhard, Bernhard, if thee will only relax a little and be nice to me and grow happy I shall be happy, dear, and *so nice* to thee. Please try relaxing thy mind and heart the way Miss Fairchild* showed them how to relax their muscles. I'm sure if thee tries thee can find, *à la longue*, the physical movements that will make thee feel less hard towards thy loving Mary.

Throughout his life Bernhard was a touchy and quarrelsome man. He quarrelled at this time not only with his old friend Carl Loeser, but with Vernon Lee, whom he had admired and whose company he had enjoyed for years, accusing her of plagiarizing his views and language in a recently published article 'Beauty and Ugliness'. Both quarrels lasted for many years, despite Mary's efforts to mediate.

* A friend of Logan's who urged all her acquaintances to relax by lying on the floor.

To Bernhard Berenson   20 August 1897   London
It would be a mistake for us to quarrel with Miss Paget. It's a mistake
to quarrel, the thing to do is just to drop people quietly, and then a
person accusing another of stealing his ideas and printing them is
always in a ridiculous position. It is true, it certainly is what she *has*
done, she and the Anstruther, even to the very phrases; and the only
recognition she makes is in a snubbing little note where she carefully
omits giving the name of the book. But I am *sure* thy best pose is a
dignified approval of their work, a sort of taking-it-for-granted that
these are the commonplaces of aesthetic criticism—for so they are.

To Bernhard Berenson   21 August 1897   Friday's Hill
But I grow truly frightened about the Grazioli*. How dull life will
seem when thee leaves her! I am sorry for that. But I suppose it is
better to have known her? She sounds awfully fascinating.

To Bernhard Berenson   24 August 1897   Salisbury
I passed the (our) White Hart going to the Close yesterday afternoon.
But until I see thee I shall not tell thee the thoughts and memories it
brought up. It was curious, I remembered even the tiniest details of all
kinds—even the 'crab croquettes' we had for dinner—and other things,
many, which I will perhaps remind thee of—perhaps not, depending
upon where thy thoughts are, whether with me or the Grazioli.

To Bernhard Berenson   25 August 1897   Friday's Hill
A week from today I shall see thee! Shall thee be glad? O Bernhard
what a fiend—or rather worse, what an idiot—I am to have made it
possible to ask such a question with a corner of true doubt in it?

To Bernhard Berenson   26 September 1897   Cambridge
Bertie was *very* affectionate, and I didn't quite know what to do. But I
think I managed all right by taking a perfectly natural tone of
friendliness. I do not want to put it into his head that I notice
anything, because then he would get the idea that I thought
something more intimate *was* possible, however undesirable, and I do
not believe he really has thought of it.

Diary   12 November 1897   Fiesole
Wilfred Blaydes sent me two telegrams from Siena—the letter I wrote

* Nicoletta Grazioli, an Italian duchess, one of the St Moritz ladies.

to him on Tuesday got lost somehow. I am very unhappy and distressed at the thought that perhaps he finds, after all, that he does love me, in spite of everything, and that this is making him wretched. But perhaps I am wrong, for he told me again and again that his love was dead.

Diary   14 November 1897   Fiesole
A telegram came from W.B. asking me to meet him in the Duomo at 3. I did. He said he loved me more than anything, even 'niceness', and he wanted me to go to Naples with him in the evening train. I had already written to him the reasons why we must not see each other any more now, and nothing he said changed those reasons, or could change them. So I left him after half an hour, and came up here to weep. Dear Bernhard comforted me very much—and he could not help saying it was an original situation for *him*. But he was equal to it. The train came and went, and Wilfred was gone. He said I should never see him again.

CHAPTER FIVE

In the Market Place

December 1897–December 1899

In January 1898 Bernhard and Mary moved their households again, halfway down the hill to the village of San Domenico, where they still lived almost side by side, but more and more luxuriously as their finances improved. They settled down to work again as soon as possible. B.B. had published *The Central Italian Painters of the Renaissance* in 1897—the third of the series—and was now beginning *The Drawings of the Florentine Painters*, his most massive and scholarly work. He had also written a number of influential articles which revealed him as one of the most knowledgeable men in the field.

Mary, too, was continuing to make a place for herself in the art world—as Mary Logan, since Frank objected to her using his name. She had become something of an expert herself, and B.B. was happy to rely on her opinion of pictures seen in his absence.

There was, nevertheless, some feeling against them in the art world, particularly in England, where Bernhard was considered arrogant and Mary too partisan. Among the most unrelenting of their critics was Arthur Strong, an Orientalist, art historian and Librarian of the House of Commons, whom their friend Eugénie Sellers had married.

Many friends found their way to the new villas, including Robert Trevelyan—'Trevy'—a poet in the classical style, and a delightful eccentric.

Diary   15 December 1897   Fiesole
Logan and I went in to shop, and bought a superb Aubusson carpet and some china. I enjoyed the spending of money *immensely*! But I feel that I shall never enjoy it again quite so much. They say the taste grows, but I think I can never again feel the same closeness to the dread of not having enough, the contrast which makes the first taste of the superfluous so delicious!

To Bernhard Berenson   [early 1898?]
They [the children] can't imagine what sin is. Well, neither could
Oscar, his wife told mother, not even when he made her give him
every penny of her income, telling her it ought to have been settled on
him, not on her, and that he had a *right* to it all. He used to leave her
without even enough to pay the household bills and the children's
schooling. She believed him innocent up to the last.

Diary   5 March 1898   Volterra
In the evening we discussed the meaning of the word 'decadent',
Logan contending, quite rightly, I think, that it means a person who
takes hold of important things by the handle of personal sensations,
like Whistler, who, commanding a gun-boat in S. America during a
rebellion, decided to join the party that had the best view of
Valparaiso as the ships were manoeuvring, or a man who becomes a
Catholic because he likes the smell of incense or the look of vestments.

To Hannah Whitall Smith   17 April 1898   San Domenico
The telegram [telling her of her father's death] has just come. The
wind is howling about the house, and the rain falling steadily and
heavily on the roof, and I am haunted by the feeling that poor
Father's unloved and lonely soul is maybe blown desolately about,
cold and shivering without its bodily covering. It is strange how all
the old commonplaces become alive and vivid when a serious thing
like this happens. I should hate to think he had just stopped existing,
who was so wrapped up in life a few hours ago, and I should hate to
think he wasn't happy. It would be nice to believe in Purgatory, and
climb up to Fiesole Cathedral through the rain and wind, to burn
candles for him and have long prayers said. But as thee would say 'He
is in God's hands' whatever that means, so I suppose he is all right.
. . . Poor Father! He did not win much love in his life, and what he won
he could not keep. I suppose no one will feel existence the poorer for
his death, and yet one has a great deal of human emotion over such an
event. We shall soon remember only what was engaging about him—
and the *habit* of him will be hard to break. I can't help feeling as if he
were taking a great interest in the disposal of his body, trotting around
himself to give the last touches.

To Logan Pearsall Smith   28 May 1898   San Domenico
I read Shaw's plays, which Alys lent me, and now I am furious at
having wasted time over the stuff. If Ibsen is bad (and he is) what *can*

75

one say of Shaw? And his 'problems' are no longer new. We went to see the Duse in *Hedda Gabler*, and were horrified with her, it, and ourselves for wasting our money ... She is living with D'Annunzio at Settignano, poor thing, she desperately in love with him, he merely calculating that if she acts his wretched plays he will make more money out of them. He stuffs her head with the idea that he and she are The Latin Renaissance!

Bernhard was now buying lavishly for Mrs Gardner, and by 1898 had obtained for her, among other things, Titian's superb *Rape of Europa*, a Rembrandt self-portrait and a *Philip IV* by Velasquez. These triumphs inevitably took him into the financially rewarding but morally dubious world of picture dealing, and it was not long before he was made aware of its dangers.

Early in the year, Mrs Gardner wrote that her husband, who disapproved of the scale of her expenditure, had been listening to disparaging stories about B.B. and was now questioning his honesty. Her letter was disturbing for the accusations were not entirely without foundation, owing to a special arrangement made by Bernhard (without Mrs Gardner's knowledge) with Colnaghi's, the prominent English dealers, and Otto Gutekunst, their director. Mrs Gardner continued buying, however, and Mary and B.B. grew less apprehensive during the summer.

Diary   23 June 1898   Milan
Our last week at Venice was one of great anxiety—business complications with Mrs Gardner—Bernhard was simply awfully worried and felt at times almost suicidal. The only bright side to it was that it brought to the surface certain tender and devoted feelings that I have for him, which do indeed form, as I am now quite sure, a firm and unshakeable basis of affection. Then, besides all this, which is so deep that only serious affliction brings it out, he is the only really interesting person in the world to me. His mind is a perpetual delight.

To Bernhard Berenson   24 August 1898   Friday's Hill
Uncle Horace*, in one of his 'happy fits', is here, and we are all occupied in rushing from room to room to escape his incessant flow of

---

* Horace Smith (1837–1906), Robert Pearsall Smith's younger brother, who suffered even more severely than he from the family manic-depression.

talk. He can't even eat, he is so busy talking. Each thing he says is rather good, and he has burst forth into a racy Americanism that is truly delicious—but like the Psalms, this is too much! This important element in aesthetics must not be overlooked!! . . . Uncle Horace is too much. This is the third room he has followed me into to talk about reformed cookery, pigeons as war news-carriers, the number of notes a pianist strikes a minute, telepathy, the press—heavens! I am thoroughly distracted.

To Bernhard Berenson   26 August 1898   Friday's Hill
I had an amusing talk with Alys and Bertie last night. Alys says she hates men and despises conversation as a waste of time and thinks smoking is a 'filthy habit'. But she adores Bertie, and so has fashioned her life to be occupied chiefly in these three things. But it is quite true, I fancy, and it accounts for the queer icy streaks one comes across in her every now and then. She even prefers sewing to whist. I wonder if, *à la longue*, even Love can bridge over such fundamental differences between her and Bertie. Bertie says that he has resigned himself to being *always bored* after he is about 30. 'At home, even?' Alys asked. 'Especially at home' Bertie answered remorselessly.

To Bernhard Berenson   30 August 1898   Friday's Hill
Trevy's book has come and I shall try to write to him about it today. It is 'poetry' in the sense of being the finest sort of material for poetry; it produces a 'poetical impression' and a serious one, too. He has a great many adjectives that are real *trouvailles*. But I am afraid he is not one of the great poets—except in those rare flashes of character which thee has told me about. Probably these will never come to expression.

I have tried to read Michael Field's last, but really I cannot! One line is amusing: 'Life is so vulgar! Let's leave it to the crowd.' But it is the very, very worst thing they have done, poor dears.

In September Mrs Gardner wrote again of her husband's suspicions, and this time the situation was serious. B.B. was terrified, for there was danger that Mr Gardner might discover a discrepancy in the price of three Rembrandts she was then purchasing. With Mary's moral support and practical advice, however, Bernhard poured out flattery and apology, and a crisis was averted for the time being.

To Bernhard Berenson   12 October 1898   San Domenico
The danger has done that—it has revealed to me how inexpressibly dear thee is to me. I could go through everything with thee, and it would not be more than a surface trouble, if I still had thee. I was glad all the time of thy having Bertie, for I knew it would distract thy mind. Otto [Gutekunst] I am *sure* will stand firm, and this danger may blow over. Then a new system must come into operation—thee will have thought it all out. Yes, I hope, but remember if it all comes out, and the worst happens, I shall stand by thee more lovingly than ever before.

To her Family   All Saints Day (1 November) 1898   San Domenico
I am hearing such a funny sound, it comes to me like a moaning and wailing, but it really is Aunty Loo practising her voice-production. Mr Power is coming tomorrow to give her a lesson, and me another singing lesson. You must make her do it for you, you have never heard anything so funny! You make your mouth into a great resounding cave, and just roar forth sounds that echo and re-echo.

To Alys Russell   24 November 1898   San Domenico
For the first time yesterday my 'real voice' came out. It is a very low, rather powerful—and I may add, indescribably hideous contralto. It is just the voice I *didn't* want to have. I wanted a light clear voice to sing nice little tinkling things, and lo and behold I have an 'organ' suited only to the bellowing of passionate moving songs. I should not have begun had I known.

To her Family   7 December 1898   San Domenico
I meant to write after the post came, but the day turned out so lovely that I simply put some lunch in my pocket and went off for a day in the woods. It was as warm as summer, but all the odours of the woods, the sharp smell of the earth and the decaying leaves, and the aromatic fragrance of the pines showed that it was autumn (really winter, though in this weather I cannot believe it). But there wasn't the least bite of chilliness in the air. I lay for hours in the moss reciting poetry to myself and thinking of the people I love, you first of all. Ah! if you had been there. Moments came and went when the odours of the woods made me feel as I used to feel when I was your age and now and then I was cheated into imagining that I too was still at the dawn of life. The happiest moments one knows, as one grows older, are those when one recovers something of the way one felt as a child. If I

could be you and myself in one, you with your fresh nerves and your buoyancy and natural hopefulness, and I with my power of noticing and enjoying my own sensations, and of understanding beauty—that would really be heaven! But to one person in this world is given the needle, to another the thread.

Eugénie Sellers Strong was a difficult friend, emotional, opinionated and self-centred, although scholarly and brilliant. Mary deplored her new husband's influence, and at a recent meeting they had quarrelled, not only about B.B. but also about Eugénie's tactless criticism of Logan.

To Eugénie Sellers Strong   9 December 1898   San Domenico [copy]
Our last long talk ... seemed to me to reveal a very, very great difference in our point of view, our interests, our associates, our ideals. Before your letter came, which in accusing me of attempting to bully and blackmail all the world into siding with Berenson (I quote) put a violent end to our friendship; even before that letter came I had made up my mind not to risk passing another hour so very unpleasant as the one you gave me with you. Your conversation, if you can recall it, was a scarcely veiled sneer at the life we are living here, an insinuation that Mr Berenson had been misrepresenting to Mr Reinach* his whole position in London, as regards access to pictures, Mr Mond's gallery, and so on, and it ended, I remember, with an expression of the deep commiseration you and your husband felt for what you considered the 'intellectual tragedy' of my brother's life, and an attack on his 'third-rate' friends. I am sorry I remember the conversation so well, but it certainly gave me the feeling, which further events did not dissipate, that in your present way of thinking, we were anything but congenial companions. In fact I left your house feeling as if I had been pricked all over with pins.... I am sorry to bring up old things which are unpleasant. I do not dwell on them at all, but on the charming times we have had in Italy together—never to be repeated, I am afraid, as you have chosen a life which bears you far away. I am sorry for that, and yet I am glad you are so happy, and I send my sincere wishes that it may always be so.

I am glad, too, that you cherish some pleasant remembrances of me. Let us keep these intact, until the time comes when we have been able to forget the others.

* Salomon Reinach, prolific French Jewish writer on art and archaeology and long-term friend of Berenson and Mary.

To the Children [Ray, Karin and their three American cousins]
6 February 1899   San Domenico
Dearest children, I am quite enchanted with the Elephants, which reached me today—each one of which threw me into a special and peculiar fit of laughter [see p. 88]. Ray's Elephant has a timid frightened look, as if he were aware that the wild dance he is executing with his legs is not very graceful!—doesn't my copy of him make you laugh too? Val's Elephant, on the other hand, looks cross and scornful, as if he thoroughly despised his keeper who is standing on his whiskers—I beg your pardon—his tusks. Karin's Elephant—which I must say I think is the most like a *real* Elephant—looks as if he were on board ship in a very rough sea—though the little boy who comes out of his mouth is a rather surprising effect of sea-sickness! Pug's Elephant looks as if he were just going to burst into tears, as if he were thoroughly disgusted with this wicked world. Harold has sent me two, and of the two I prefer this one, who is smiling in such a genial way. And here is the best Elephant I can make, who brings you my compliments!

To Hannah Whitall Smith   17 April 1899   San Domenico
Mr Davis* is coming up today, and Logan hopes he will buy for £100 a picture he has just bought in Siena for £20. He has already sent word that he wants to buy another picture. I have one which cost me £80, but I shall not let him have it for less than £1000, and I don't believe he will pay so much. But I can wait—another year he will pay it, and in the meantime *I* enjoy it!

To her Family   20 April 1899   Venice
The exciting story I meant to tell you, and never found time, was about the Madonna Logan bought in Siena. It was a great beauty, but one night, after studying it carefully, I came to the conclusion that the edges of the blue mantle that draped her head were repainted. So I got a rag and some—well I am ashamed to say, spit—and began to rub. A little of the blue came off, and Logan and Percy [Feilding] were so excited that they took their handkerchiefs and with the same primitive moisture began to rub the other parts. More and more blue came off, and we were seized with a kind of fury. I rushed into my room and got some ammonia mixed with water, and we began to clean. With a

* Theodore Davis, American millionaire copper magnate, then collecting pictures in Italy.

mixture of triumph and dismay, the whole mantle began to come off in our hands! They relied on me and I said 'It's all right' in a tone much more assured than I felt, and presently the whole blue came off and revealed underneath a charmingly drawn, delicately pink mantle. The blue paint was in fact a modern daub, which hid the best of the drawing, and the Madonna looks far more beautiful without. The truth is that ammonia does not touch pure tempera painting, but only carries away oils, and as this original picture was a very early one, done before oil painting was invented, our cleaning was really safe enough. The only danger was that it had been entirely ruined underneath, so that we should find nothing but bare wood when we had removed the blue.

To her Family   10 May 1899   San Domenico
I feel very greedy and dissipated, for I have just eaten—a piece of bread! My first in a fortnight. How good it tasted! You who eat it every day cannot have any idea how delicious it is. Thy warning, Gram, about the risk of spoiling my digestion in the process of thinning down, rather frightened me, and I am in consequence making little modifications of my hard fare.... I'm going to begin massage on Saturday and have a nurse pound away at the fat parts of me, for the funny thing is that I'm only fat here and there, not all over. (I won't mention the fat parts, but if you remember how I look, it isn't necessary!)

Diary   8 June 1899   Venice
We called on the Antiquario beside St Mark's and found more excellent Sienese forgeries, which gave us doubts about—most of Bernhard's pictures!! The Antiquario confessed they *were* forgeries, and we offered him a hundred pounds if he would show us the man who did them.... By hook or crook we must get to the bottom of it. If Bernhard's pictures are forgeries then of course it is clear his science— and no one's—can distinguish. As to beauty—they are lovely! But *there are too many of them.*

The previous December Mr Gardner, Bernhard's accuser, had died, but his death did not end the trouble over the sales. Mrs Gardner became aware of a discrepancy in the price of a pair of Holbein portraits she had agreed to buy and attacked both Bernhard and Colnaghi's, even threatening to sue. Once again Bernhard was in despair, and Mary full of ingenious suggestions.

The moral price Berenson had to pay for the larger and larger sums of money he was making was one which continued to weigh on his mind all his life, as (with whatever good intentions) he penetrated further and further into the equivocal world of the picture trade. It was already too late, however, for him to withdraw into a life of pure scholarship.

When it came to buying and selling on their own account, Mary took to it all with considerably more zest—and less conscience—than he, delighting in the perils as well as the rewards. One peril was the prevalence and immense skill of Italian forgers, and another was the need to smuggle the pictures out of Italy. Export of works of art judged to be national treasures was forbidden by the State, though corruption was so rife that vast numbers of such works were in fact smuggled out, and Mary, in conjunction with the equally enthusiastic American 'robber baron' millionaires, delighted in foiling the customs authorities.

To Bernhard Berenson   9 June 1899   Friday's Hill
Thee must argue and argue with her to prove that Colnaghis are *invaluable* for her gallery. Take her to Agnew's miserable show which is the best he could have done for her in all these years and compare that with the Titians, the Crivelli, the Botticellis, the Pessellinos and all the other things *they* have got for her! ... Tell her how thee is trying to get Frizzoni's Bellini and probably can't unless thee should be able to bribe his friends to urge him to part with it and so on ... Above all things, show no sign of thy inward agony.... Thee must tell her straight out that thee has had to use lots of money bribing etc almost always, but that *on the whole* it has cost her less than if she had been in the hands of anyone else.... All this thee must say, not write, for I am convinced she is extremely amenable to personal influence. It is some emissary of Agnew's who has put her on her present tack.

To her Family   20 June 1899   Venice
You will be glad to hear that I have made a gain of about £800 on that picture whose photograph I sent. I feel a wild temptation to spend a lot of it this summer having a great spree with you—but I am going to invest it and lay it up for a time when you will really care about money and need it more.

To Bernhard Berenson   July 1899   Friday's Hill
Above all don't be afraid. If thee has to acknowledge having done

wrong, do it frankly, and explain what reparation it is in thy power to make. It is an awful time, and my heart just *aches* for thee, but I know thee can pull through it. And I do love thee so, Bernhard. Never so much or so truly, so consciously.

In the end Isabella was won over, and there were no more rifts in their long association.

To Bernhard Berenson   13 July 1899   Friday's Hill
Here it is pretty dull, for, as we get older, we are growing apart. Alys cares for Philanthropy, Bertie for Mathematics—Logan and I more or less hang together—but general conversation can't be much but gossip or facts. And we are in this impasse, that we loathe Alys's friends (who loathe us back) and they don't care for ours, so there is scarcely a soul we want to invite here. But of course I don't care when I have the children.

To Bernhard Berenson   18 July 1899   Friday's Hill
We are just recovering from a terrible fright. Karin was thrown off the pony this morning, and although she didn't *seem* hurt, she seemed 'queer' and presently went off into convulsions and entirely lost consciousness. . . . I couldn't help feeling thankful beyond words that it wasn't Ray. There is an unspeakable difference in my feelings to them. I wonder if mothers generally have these strong preferences. Karin is awfully sweet, and I hate to see her suffer. But Ray—it is another world.

To Bernhard Berenson   27 August 1899   Aix-les-Bains
I perfectly hate it here [Mary had taken her mother to a rheumatism cure]—it is dull and hot—it is a maddening thought that the children are now at Friday's Hill, and I am not there . . . Sometimes a kind of hot impatience comes over me, so strongly that I can hardly force myself to speak politely to Mother. She is an awfully fine person, and I admire her and in some ways love her above *everything*. But we have so little in common that constant companionship is a certain strain on me. Her whole inner life—as far as thoughts go—and thoughts are what one speaks from—is built on the hideous *'subtilités d'un barbare'* apropos of the Bible, and they drive me nearly crazy. Yet it would be too unsympathetic to shut her up on her favourite subject. I tell thee all this, so that thee can fully realize that I am not staying here for *pleasure*.

83

Diary   4 October 1899   [San Domenico?]
We have run our forger to earth—but a very easy matter it was—for
'he' is a rollicking band of young men, cousins and friends, who turn
out these works in cooperation, one drawing, one laying in the colour,
another putting on the dirt, another making the frames, and some
children with a big dog keeping guard over the pictures that were put
in the sunshine to *'stagionare'**. A real Renaissance group of jolly
workers, intent on sport, *burlo*†, and their trade, which they never
think of as art. Their chief is Federigo Ioni, a rakish-looking man of
30, very free and easy—a good fellow. They hide nothing.

No legal action seems ever to have been taken against Ioni, and
Mary took to employing him to search out real works of art for her to
buy.

To her Family   12 November 1899   Fiesole
The great excitement of the day was a telegram from an agent I sent
down to Umbria to look up a splendid picture I heard was secretly for
sale.‡ He suddenly wired that if I could send him twelve hundred
pounds *at once*, he could snap up the picture.... So I had to rush to the
Bank and persuade them into lending me the money, and telegraph
England for securities and all sorts of things. The money was *just*
being paid into the Banca d'Italia as it was Saturday, and I caught it
in time.

To Ray Costelloe   14 November 1899   Fiesole
The great excitement of yesterday was when I stopped at the Bank in
the morning, and found a telegram from my picture agent saying that
as he had taken a false name, he couldn't draw out the £1200 I had
sent him ... I have telegraphed to my agent to come back, and the
Bank was wired for the money, and altogether things are in a confused
state. But the picture is worth all this trouble and more, for it is very
beautiful and very valuable.

* Dry out and season.
† Rowdiness.
‡ This picture, now in the Isabella Gardner Museum, is known as '*The
Annunciation of the Gardner Gallery*' and the painter is known as 'The Master of
the Gardner Annunciation'. At the time it was thought to be by Antoniazzo
Romano, and has since been tentatively identified as a Gandolfino or a
Roreto.

To Hannah Whitall Smith   17 November 1899   San Domenico
The great picture business is at a standstill so far as news is concerned. The Agent went to Assisi taking his own packer and restorer. Secretly, inside the monastery, they were able to make a case for the picture, and glue down a little blister, and wait till midnight and then drive away in a cart with the picture out of the old Papal States (whose laws are very strict about exporting works of art) and get on the train at some Tuscan station. No one in Assisi was to know they had gone, except of course, the friars. It is a fearful plot ... Quite as exciting as the life of a smuggler of old in the caves on the coast.

To her Family   23 November 1899   San Domenico
Since I wrote, I have seen *the* picture. It is hidden away in a back upstairs room in order to have the cracks mended. It is a PERFECT BEAUTY, one of the very best pictures painted in the fifteenth century and worth a very very great deal. I am enchanted with it and hope to grow quite rich by it.

To Karin Costelloe   25 November 1899   San Domenico
I promised to tell you how *the* picture is to be taken out of Italy: but first I must say that I don't consider this wrong, because here in Italy the pictures are apt to go to ruin from carelessness. This one, for example, I got *just* in time to save it, for the panel on which it was painted had cracked right down the Madonna's face and figure, and the paint was all but falling off. Her dear beautiful nose and one eye were nothing but a huge blister of paint, and to bring it here strips of fine muslin had to be pasted over it in a dozen places, otherwise the paint would simply have fallen off. Now it will probably go into one of the big Museums and be well taken care of, and delight hundreds and thousands of people who could never have seen it otherwise. I *hope* it will go to the National Gallery. However—as to the way they get it out. They take it to the Overseer at the Gallery here, packed in a large box, to get permission to export it. That is, they're supposed to, but in reality they take another picture, some worthless daub of the same size. The Inspector looks at it, and of course says they can do what they like with rubbish like that. He then gravely seals up the box and puts the mark on which serves to carry it through. But all the time the box is cunningly made to open where he would never think of putting a seal, and they carry it home, open it in this secret way, and substitute the good picture for the bad. Myself I think the Director knows all about it, and he knows it is hopeless to enforce the law, but

85

of course he cannot go openly against it. So for dealers with whom he is *good friends* (i.e. who bribe him), he doesn't look too carefully into how the boxes are made!

To her Family   3 December 1899   San Domenico
In the Italian Parliament there has been a great outcry against the strangers who come to Italy pretending to write but really robbing Italy of its 'artistic Patrimony'. No doubt all the Senators who shouted in applause of the speech against these indescribable wretches had themselves sold or helped to sell pictures and bronzes, but the more they had sold the louder they shouted. Sensible Italians are very indignant, for no one buys anything out of public galleries, and what good does it do the public to have pictures shut in private houses? Besides they are always offered first to the State.

While all these exciting things were happening, news came to Mary that Frank was very ill with cancer of the ear.

To Hannah Whitall Smith   9 December 1899   San Domenico
If we find that he [Frank] is really, seriously, hopelessly ill, I shall try to *make* him let me come home and take care of him. It would save the children a great deal, and it might make things easier to arrange. Besides, I am *awfully* sorry for him ... only I do not want to complicate matters if he is going to get well after all.

To Bernhard Berenson   12 December 1899   London
He has a cancer, and he has known ever since September that he could not live long. So he has spent his time, Father Brown says, making things as disagreeable for us as his lawyer's skill could devise.... Yet it is very pitiful to see him lying there, with closed eyes, tossing about and murmuring incoherent snatches of things. The nurses say he isn't really suffering, but he is a terrible wreck ... Father Brown says he considers the Will grossly unfair and unkind—and probably futile as well, for he says the children can't be alone, and there is no one but us to take them. He is quite on our side.

Frank's Will stated that his daughters were not to be left in the care of Mary or her family, for reasons which he said he believed would be admitted as valid even by Mary herself. He appointed five Catholic guardians—one of whom was Father Brown and one James Britten,

Karin's godfather, with instructions that the girls were to live with their governess and be brought up as Catholics.

To Bernhard Berenson   14 December 1899   London
The situation is the same, except that for a few minutes this morning, when something broke and the pressure on his brain was removed for an instant, he grew lucid and spoke to the children and to me, but without, I think, recognizing me.... He is suffering no pain—what luck! for this is usually the *most painful* form of cancer. Of course there isn't a shadow of hope (or fear) of his recovery—but I dread his lingering on and on ... *Later.* I have just been summoned in. He is fully conscious, and we had a reconciliation scene. He kissed my hand. I am now in hopes that he may be able to make a new Will. I have sent for the doctor and Father Brown. They will join me in urging it.

To Bernhard Berenson   17 December 1899   London
I am suffering from a most unusual oscillation of emotion. When I see him it is awful—that weary wreck, all his life and his ambitions come to nothing, and the horrible pathos of leaving no one to mourn his going. When I do not see him I feel such anger and indignation and hatred on account of his Will that I could almost echo Bertie's wish to restore him to life and torture him for ten years. Thee can't conceive how painful it is to be swinging from one feeling to the opposite. But on the whole a sort of sickened pity predominates.

To Bernhard Berenson   21 December 1899   London
The moment he is dead I shall establish the children at No 44* and grandma will take a cab and within the hour will be the guardian appointed by the Court of Chancery. We have decided to do everything in *her* name, because against me there are, as thee knows, things that might be said, which it isn't worthwhile to bring up, and against Alys and Bertie can be urged their rather rampant irreligious-ness, and the report that Alys preached 'Free Love' in America.

To Bernhard Berenson   22 December 1899   London
He died this morning at 5 o'clock, without any struggle. The breath just stopped.

* 44 Grosvenor Road, Hannah's house, four doors away from the Costelloe household.

Frank's Will had not been changed, and there was in fact a considerable legal battle with the three guardians who remained obdurate (James Britten alone sided with Mary and Father Brown). In the end, however, Hannah won guardianship on condition that she brought the girls up as Catholics, and this Mary had to accept.

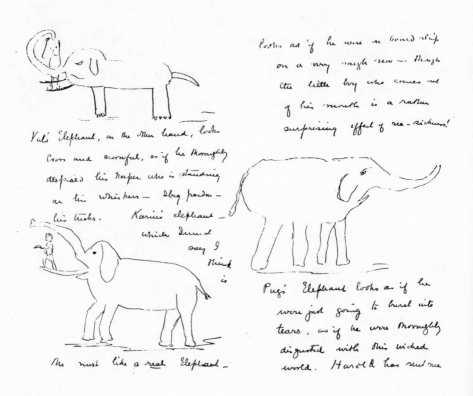

Vali's Elephant, on the other hand, looks cross and scornful, as if he thoroughly despised his keeper who is standing on his whiskers — I beg pardon — his tusks. Karin's elephant — which I must say I think is

the most like a real Elephant —

looks as if he were on board ship on a very rough sea — though the little boy who comes out of his mouth is a rather surprising effect of sea-sickness!

Pug's Elephant looks as if he were just going to burst into tears, as if he were thoroughly disgusted with this wicked world. Harold has sent me

CHAPTER SIX

Holy Matrimony

January 1900–December 1902

Bernhard and Mary decided to get married at the end of the conventional year of 'mourning'—though it is possible that Bernhard was less enthusiastic about the prospect than Mary.

B.B. was still involved in the formidable amount of research and concentration required for his *Drawings of the Florentine Painters*. He was dogged, however, by recurrent dyspepsia—a misery which persisted all his life, and for which no one was able to find a sufficient cause. Marriage would enable them at last to combine their households, and during the summer Mary found, and was able to rent, a villa called I Tatti, on a hillside between Fiesole and Settignano. It was at that time a very simple house, and needed a lot of work to make it fit for their increasingly luxurious requirements, but it was well situated and there was a good deal of land with it. It remained their home for the rest of their lives.

While Mary moved into the new house to supervise the alterations, Bernhard stayed, until the wedding, with their friends Henry and Janet Ross, who were now their nearest neighbours at Poggio Gherardo, a medieval castle on the next hill. They were much older than B.B. and Mary; Henry was a retired banker from Egypt, a man of great charm, and Janet was a very formidable old lady, who as a child had sat on the laps of almost all the famous writers of the day. Her biting tongue was much dreaded, but she and Mary became very fond of each other.

To Bernhard Berenson   1 January 1900   London
Of *course* it is a happy New Year, Bernhard, and I take the wishes thee was too tactful to send. I *am* happy, perfectly joyful at the thought of being free to do my utmost (it won't be half enough) to make thy life happy—and oh! un-preoccupied with worries so·that I can *live* in our interests. I feel like a god when I think of it—my heart is *inundated* with joy. O thou dear!

To her Family   15 March 1900   San Domenico
I now have a great piece of news for you—the PICTURE is safely out of Italy! The agent is going with it all the way to London to put it in safe hands. Did I tell you my invention for getting it out? We had a huge trunk made with a false bottom in which the picture was safely packed away. To explain the size and shape of the trunk I had a lot of *dolls* made, and Signor Gagliardi went as a commercial traveller in the doll trade. They were, though, large, cheap and worthless dolls, or I should have sent one to you. He went on Tuesday, and sent a telegram yesterday morning from Basle to say it was all right. When I get back I really must take you to see it.

To Hannah Whitall Smith   23 March 1900   San Domenico
I have had word from the picture, too, which has arrived safely in London. The famous dolls were left in Paris. The Italian who took it on says that at the frontier everybody was looking at the enormous trunk and speaking about it, and cold shivers went down his back, but when they saw the dolls inside, they were satisfied. But it was a risky business.

To her Family   7 April 1900   San Domenico
I am just about taking another Villa, a much more beautiful one than this, and costing £40 less a year! It is very near Mrs Ross. I have longed for this particular place for years, but the man has just died. We are going to it today. I have to stay and see it through, for fear it is snapped up by someone else, as it is the nicest place left in these parts. You shall see it someday.

To Hannah Whitall Smith   13 May 1900   Rome
I am feeling (temporarily I hope) rather poor, because Mrs Gardner has given up buying. The trustees do not sympathize with her, as her husband did, and they refuse to let her have any money. As they are also her heirs this is perhaps natural. She does not want *the* picture— at least she wants it but cannot raise the money for it*, and it may be some time before another buyer turns up.

Hannah was appalled at the thought of a woman lucky enough to become a widow being so foolish as to marry again, and made all sorts of objections.

* The famous smuggled picture; Mrs Gardner did finally raise the money to buy it and it became one of the glories of her collection.

To Hannah Whitall Smith   22 June 1900   Venice
Thee would be right in fearing that possibly marriage might create
some inward barriers except that the peculiarities of the circumstances make such a fear groundless. . . . He has never tried to come
between me and the children, for he recognized and often says that, in
spite of the natural longing he has as a man to get 'perfect devotion', it
is right and inevitable that my children should be closest to my heart.
To my feelings there is no possible human emotion that can compare
with a mother's love. I could not change this if I were torn to pieces by
wild beasts for it.

Once the plans for the marriage were announced, Mary started
writing to B.B.'s mother, and continued to do so every week until she
died in 1938.

To Mrs Berenson   1 July 1900   Venice
Just as soon as his work will allow it, I mean to come with him to
America, and I think he will have less nervous dread of the voyage if I
am with him. I should love you to have some of the *real comfort* in your
son's company that I feel when I am with my own children. I hope
that I can make Bernhard happy ... and I think I can if only his
health will let him be happy. I have been very devoted to him all these
years and I love him more than ever now, so that we ought to be very
happy together.

To Bernhard Berenson   17 July 1900   Friday's Hill
Bertie is teaching them Euclid, but alas my beautiful dream of their
coming in contact with a 'first-class mind' is upset by the sordid fact
that this first-class mind doesn't know how to impart its knowledge,
and the poor things are in a perfect maze of miserable bewilderment.
For their first lesson he gave them *fifteen* propositions, and they
scarcely understood one, poor things! Mother tried to speak to Alys
about it, because of course it is an *awful* way to teach, and it makes the
children hate the subject. But Alys wouldn't listen to a word, and it
was useless.

To Bernhard Berenson   25 July 1900   Friday's Hill
I want thee once to see just a little of the children, for thee will, I am
almost sure, find them inoffensive, and it may even be that thee will
actually *like* them. . . . But if it turns out that they do annoy thee, and
bother thee, I will try my best to make them *as little* bother as possible.

To Hannah Whitall Smith   9 September 1900   Paris
He [B.B.] says we ought to be 'correctly' married when the time comes, in church (Catholic) with a few prominent Catholics present— very quietly, of course, and without a High Mass, but in such a way that none of the guardians or Catholic friends of the children can have a word to say against us. What does thee think of it? It would rather take the wind out of their sails, wouldn't it?

To Hannah Whitall Smith   29 September 1900   San Domenico
B.B. was feeling awfully poor (it is a purely psychological question with him) in view of the *enormous* changes at the villa he will have to pay for, when yesterday a London dealer dropped in and bought three of our pictures—the three I care least for.... This cheered him up, and indeed I am sure he will have plenty of money, even for our extravagant ideas in the way of beautiful surroundings.

To her Family   30 September 1900   San Domenico
The new butler, Roberto, is the funniest looking of men, and his voice is a tiny frightened shriek. These are not whiskers as you might think, but real moustaches, and it seems they are *de rigueur* in Archiepiscopal circles (he was valet to the Archbishop of Fiesole for 14 years) for the same reason, I suppose, that non-clerical people like clean-shaven men servants, namely to be different from their masters. Priests, being clean-shaven, require hairy servants.

To Hannah Whitall Smith   3 October 1900   San Domenico
Thee will be relieved to hear that there is no possible doubt whatever of B.B.'s being an American citizen ... there is no need for a 'Separation of Goods' for in Massachusetts Law they are as separate as they are in England.... Poor B.B.! He is so miserable and ill, he looks quite worn and with a strange look almost of fright. It goes to my heart, and I am awfully glad I shall soon be able to take better care of him. It makes you very fond of a person to become necessary to them (if you like them to start with), and he says he would really give up the bad business of living if it were not for my good health and spirits.

To Hannah Whitall Smith   26 October 1900   San Domenico
Thee needn't think Logan and I persuade, browbeat or hypnotize B.B. into spending money. It is often quite the other way, except that all the money for paying passes through my hands, as he doesn't want

to be bothered. But he is even worse than Logan, in some ways, and I'm not a famous brake, where money is concerned. However I cannot feel worried about it, for we are sure to make a great deal. We have several schemes on hand now.

To Hannah Whitall Smith   11 November 1900   San Domenico
Berenson will of course not stay with me. He never does. He will go to the Rosses on Dec. 1st, and will stay there till the fatal day arrives. He says he can't consider *anything* till his chapter on Michelangelo is finished, so I can't fix any date for the ceremony. It will be towards Xmas, but the later the better, as a household is much easier to organize without a man in it.

Mary fixed the date for the end of December. It did not pass without incident: against Bernhard's wishes she insisted on having Hannah, Logan and her daughters out for the occasion, endeavouring, as always, to convince herself that he would come to enjoy the company of the children.
    A more ominous arrival during the weeks before the wedding was a romantic character called Mounteney Jephson, an English explorer and a friend of Isabella Gardner.

Diary   19 November 1900   San Domenico
Mr Mounteney Jephson came to tea. He told us about his exploration with Stanley, a whole year in the jungle, lost, 5 months in prison under sentence of death with Emin Pasha. It was fascinating to hear him talk.

The wedding took place on December 29th 1900. There were two ceremonies, a civil one in the Town Hall, and a Catholic wedding two days later—to confound the Guardians—held in the small chapel belonging to the new villa. Logan was suffering from acute toothache, Mary towered over her small husband, and Hannah made a strange figure, in her Quaker's bonnet, among the sophisticated Florentine guests. The children treated the whole thing as a joke, declaring that Mary was too middle-aged for orange blossom, and making her a wreath of oranges instead.

To Hannah Whitall Smith   13 January 1901   I Tatti
This house continues to be as it were under the Star of Bethlehem with Kings of Antiquity (or at any rate of Antiquities) winding in

procession up the hill bearing precious gifts in their hands. This morning, and it is only ten o'clock, we have already had three Antiquity Dealers here, from one of whom we have bought what we never thought to get hold of—a *real Perugino*!* Logan will open his eyes at that. It comes from Castiglione Fiorentino near Arezzo, and is, alas, in a deplorable state of ruin and repaint. But when we are able to spend a couple of hundred pounds to have Cavenaghi thoroughly clean it and mend the cracks, it will be one of the most valuable pictures in the market.

To Hannah Whitall Smith   16 January 1901   I Tatti
Thee would be *surprised* at the mildness of B.B.'s temper. I lost some of his photos and he actually said 'What is the use of worrying. Don't bother about it, I'll write for others' and not a word of rage. Logan will hardly believe this.

To Hannah Whitall Smith   23 February 1901   I Tatti
I hear the sound of disputing voices out in the hall—the *'Capo di Famiglia'* and half a dozen antiquarians who are disputing over the price of another Monsterpiece, a really very fine old picture divided into Gothic compartments. If we buy it, it will be to sell again, perhaps at Christie's. We still have every day a regular procession of Kings of the East bearing precious things. This picture arrived on a cart just as we were starting for town, and at the tram we met two other antiquarians coming up. As we very seldom buy anything from them, I think it shows great persistence of them to keep coming.

Many friends, new and old, came to stay in the new villa. Among these were Mrs Baldwin, and her fascinating daughter, Gladys Deacon, whom B.B. had met on one of his summer excursions to St Moritz when she was just seventeen, and confessed to have fallen in love with. She was an eccentric and unpredictable character, but said to be the most beautiful woman in Europe, with Grecian features and huge blue eyes.
    Guests of a very different kind were 'Trevy' (Robert Trevelyan), who had just got married, and Israel Zangwill, the Jewish author and

* The picture was the *Madonna and Child with Bird in Hand*. It was smuggled out of Italy, left in Logan's charge and offered to Isabella Gardner for £4,500. She did not buy it, and it hung in the Pearsall Smith drawing room until 1909, when it was sold to John G. Johnson for £2000.

playwright, whose acquaintance Mary had made in England, while Gertrude Stein and her brother Leo, then visiting Florence, came to dine.

To Hannah Whitall Smith   2 March 1901   I Tatti
Our Parisian guests [Gladys Deacon and her mother Mrs Baldwin] ... are very beautiful, fairly agreeable, and easy to get on with. The girl is rather wonderful, but she is, it seems to me, considerably spoilt by living in that milieu. They are dreadfully rich, the sort of people who change all their clothes, nightgowns and sheets, *every day* (a mother and 4 daughters!) and have some famous actress or singer or musician at five hundred or a thousand francs two or three nights a week, when they give dinner parties. *Why* they came here is a mystery to me, but I suppose it is always better than staying at a hotel. Mrs Baldwin, who is the famous 'Mrs Deacon', weeps on my shoulder and tells me all her troubles—and indeed she has a most horrible story. Married at 17 to a dissolute madman of 45, she had 3 children in 2 years and was then practically abandoned by her husband. But by her immense beauty and wealth she got taken up in Paris society and was a very great belle. Her husband told her he was sick of her and *advised* her to take a lover, which finally she did, having fallen madly in love with a Frenchman. She was tormented to death by her conscience, but her worldliness prevented her getting a divorce. Suddenly her husband appears on the scene, and she is warned that he looks crazy and wicked. He is reading in her salon when her lover is announced. With a 'humph' he goes out. Presently he comes back with a pistol. The lover rushes out of the salon and she shrieks to him to escape through the bedroom. Instead of going away he hides behind the sofa, where the husband finds him and kills him on the spot. As he had long been urging her to get a divorce, she thinks he hid there to practically make a divorce inevitable. At any rate he died without a word. *No one* stood by her. The husband took all the children except the youngest, whom he repudiated as not his, and divorced her. A couple of years after he went raving mad and is now shut up in an asylum, believing himself to be a nephew of Moses. This pretty, silly lady, whose whole life was bound up in society, and who was desperately in love, found herself deprived of lover and society together. Whenever she speaks of love she weeps. She has had lots of chances to marry again, but refuses them as she still loves this man. It was 9 years ago.

To Hannah Whitall Smith   4 March 1901   I Tatti

I am glad Mrs Baldwin and her daughter came, they interest me greatly. To start with, in figure, in hair and hats and dresses, they are *exactly* like fashion plates, and in face too, only more beautiful. You feel that underneath those gorgeous dresses are all the marvellous lace petticoats and underclothes and stockings which come in the next pages of a fashion magazine, and finally that they are clients (as they are) of all the doctors for the hair, complexion, nails, eyebrows, etc, all the swell masseuses, all the perfumery, glove, jewel, cosmetic shops advertised in the back pages of such a magazine. It gives me quite a 'sensation' to look at them and to go into their rooms and chat while the marvellous toilettes are going on. Compared to such an elegant creature we are all miserable clod-hoppers. But they pay too much for it! Although they have hearts and brains under these frills, they have no leisure to cultivate them. Mrs Baldwin remains a lovable but excessively silly woman, who has ruined her life, and is trying to ruin her daughter's. The daughter is naturally gifted to an unusual degree, but erratic, whimsical, incredibly extravagant and undisciplined, and happy only in virtue of that blessed possession, youth!

To Hannah Whitall Smith   18 March 1901   I Tatti

The Trevys arrived yesterday. They hadn't sent word in time of their train, however I went down on chance to the probable train and there they were, he unshaven and all his clothes unbuttoned and dropping off, but yet awfully nice—she ugly and not very neat and, apparently, all right and a good enough wife for him, but without colour, without charm, without animation. She seems simple, easy-going, devoted to him, heavy, dresses worse than any woman I ever saw. She has however a nice direct look from her eyes. I don't find her disagreeable. But she is no addition to anything so far as I can see. Trevy was delightful in the evening, talking of Polyphemus and Galatea and Ulysses as if they were far more *real* than his acquaintances of today.

Diary   28 April 1901   I Tatti

I have let the months run by. Bernhard and I were married at the end of December, first at the Municipio . . . and two days after, here, in our own chapel by the Priore of Settignano. . . . I have given no idea of these months, but how can I? I am happier than I have ever been. Our house is beautiful and we get on *au mieux* . . . It is marvellous to be so happy—I cannot understand how I came to be so blessed.

Smith family home, 1881–1888, Germantown, Philadelphia

Smith family group, Fernhurst, 1894: *left to right* Alys, Logan, Robert, Hannah, Karin, Mary, Ray

Alys Pearsall Smith, 1892

Hannah Whitall Smith, 1886

Bertrand Russell, 1894

Mary Whitall Smith aged 19, 1883

Bernhard Berenson, 1891

Frank Costelloe, *c.* 1885   Mary Smith Costelloe, 1886

Hortense, Contessa Serristori

Isabella Gardner, 1888. Portrait
by Sargent

Carlo Placci in about 1895

Karin, Mary and Ray, 1896

Hermann Obrist, 1895

Israel Zangwill, *c.* 1900

Gordon Craig, *c.* 1907

Gabriele D'Annunzio

Gertrude Stein, *c.* 1910

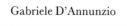

Mary Berenson, *c.* 1910

Bernhard Berenson, *c.* 1909

Joseph Duveen

B.B.'s mother, Judith Berenson,
c. 1910

Ray Costelloe in 1909

Karin Costelloe in 1914

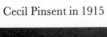

Cecil Pinsent in 1915

Geoffrey Scott, *c.* 1912

Diary   18 May 1901   I Tatti
I had a music lesson and called on the Rosses. Mother has sent a verse of congratulation to Mr Ross on his swiftly approaching death—'Joy, shipmate, joy' but he returned the prosaic answer that a bird in the hand is worth two in the bush!

Worried by B.B.'s indifference to his family, Mary arranged for Judith Berenson and her daughter Bessie to spend a holiday in England with the Pearsall Smiths, where they could see B.B. The visit duly took place, but it was not an entirely successful experiment; B.B. was chilly, Judith disappointed and Bessie depressed.

To Hannah Whitall Smith   12 June 1901   Milan
I have already got lodgings for B.B.'s mother and sister. They are very quiet simple people and not at all exacting. I felt it was B.B.'s duty to have them, as his mother adores him, and he never will go to see her.

To Bernhard Berenson   3 September 1901   Friday's Hill
I want to keep his [Jephson's] friendship and to share it with thee, so I am sending thee this letter, the most affectionate he has ever written me. I feel sure thee will think it is all right.

From their first meeting Mary had been fascinated by Jephson and his enthralling stories, and she had spent many hours with him, first in Florence and later—during the summer—in England. At first B.B., deeply involved in his work, had not been disturbed by this, but he became suspicious and resentful as he watched Mary's preoccupation grow.

To Bernhard Berenson   9 September 1901   Friday's Hill
Thy love is not quite genial enough—though I know all thy generosity—to completely thaw me out. I struggle, and this is the whole truth, under the sense of being too coolly 'seen through'.

To Hannah Whitall Smith   22 September 1901   Cadenabbia [Lake Como]
Life is so empty and idle for all these Lake dwellers, that curiosity to see me (imagine, *me*!) impelled most of the owners of Villas in this part—Prince Trivulzio, the Duchess of Terranova, the Duchess Malfi, the Marchesa Trotti and so on, to come up too, so there was a rabble there, and the usual Götterdämmerung of languages. It is a great '*déception*' as French people say, getting to know all these swells. I

97

used to come here as a simple tourist, and make dreams to myself about these wonderful great people who bore these historic names and lived in these beautiful pleasure palaces along the shores of the lake. Now alas, I know how they actually do put in their time—they stand on their terraces with spy-glasses and try to make out the passengers in every boat or bark that puts out on to the waters. The rest of the time they gossip—but not witty *spirituelle* gossip (such as you hear at Fernhurst and Settignano!!!!) but dull *terre-à-terre* remarks.

To Hannah Whitall Smith   1 October 1901   Gazzada
The company has grown much more animated since Donna Laura* came. She yells and gesticulates like a wild beast, and shrieks everyone down, upsetting glasses and smashing cups and making everybody furious. But (though I don't like her) I can't help recognizing that she has very good brains and uses them too. I have not often met a woman so intelligent, nor so intellectually perverse when she gets an idea into her head. But at any rate she makes a lot of stir and movement wherever she goes, and in a world of Bores this is something!

To Hannah Whitall Smith   14 October 1901   I Tatti
It really isn't a question of B.B.'s 'generosity', because my children are really his responsibility in part, for he prevents me being with them and sharing thy household expenses. Besides there is no real division between us of the money we earn. If I make a lot out of Wireless Telegraphy I shall give him what he wants to round off his steel investment, and a little later he will give me money to make another investment with. There is really no distinction. He never spends anything or invests anything without taking me into it, and I can't, on my side, do otherwise.... B.B. is, in fact, absolutely perfect about money—only, perhaps, too generous to outsiders.

In December Mary discovered that she was pregnant, and returned to London for an abortion. B.B. was adamantly set against having a child and he was also deeply suspicious of Mary's honesty as well as of her behaviour.

To Bernhard Berenson   14/15 December 1901   London
Poor old dear, I wish thee felt half as jolly as I am feeling now that the

* Donna Laura Gropallo, a learned but crusty psychologist and writer.

Anxiety is removed ... And yet thee will be horrified, it opened a door on me that I thought was closed and sealed. Some time—maybe?—what does thee think? It might be a good provision against dreariness in old age? Thee might like it, Bernhard, it might give thee a stronger hold on life.

To Bernhard Berenson   30 December 1901   London
Jephson isn't my lover, never was, never will be, there is absolutely no question of that, but it is true that the thought of him has taken up too much of my attention, and has been a sort of silent barrier between us.

To Bernhard Berenson   3 January 1902   Friday's Hill
We do not understand each other. Shall we ever? I am coming back to try my very, very best: but I am not sure I can rouse myself out of my easy-going surface ways enough to live up to thy standards in all respects ... but evidently we are not at one about the very basis of life. I don't much mind lies, I should not be indignant if thee told them to me, thinking to spare my feelings, or avoid an unpleasant discussion. They would not destroy my confidence. I should in fact ask myself *why* thee told them, whether it was that I was trying too hard to impose my ideas upon a nature different from my own.... As I have told thee, I shall try to submit my inmost nature to thee, since nothing else will make thee happy. If I can, I will, I can't speak fairer than that, Bernhard, and I shall not withhold from thee any of my difficulties.

To Bernhard Berenson   4 January 1902   London
I see thee is very anxious, and of course I know two reasons for thy anxiety ... one my miscarriage, the other Jephson. I wired to thee for I was so afraid thee *might* think I had been shamming illness in order to stay in London, which is not at all the case.... Jephson came to supper last night ... he says to show thee any letter of his which thee may not have seen—there are very few—and never even to think anything I am not willing to share with thee. He said he thought it was in all women's natures to be deceitful, and he had been pained at the thought that I wasn't perhaps out and out frank with thee. In fact he is entirely of thy opinion about everything, and was very nice and cheery. Of course he cares for me very much, but he says thee cannot mind that, for he tries to do so in the nicest, most loyal way he can. I said that it was quite possible thee might decide it was more sensible for us not to see each other any more—but *enfin* it was to be left to thee.

To Hannah Whitall Smith   10 January 1902   I Tatti
I find B.B. better than I feared. He slept beautifully last night and he
is very happy to have me back again. Life to him means simply me
and his work. It is strange that it should be so, but people are made
differently. Although it is a tie, I believe I would not have it otherwise,
would not have it fade into something more commonplace. And this is
after eleven years of close friendship and companionship, as well as
several attacks of 'inflammation of the heart' on both sides! So I
suppose it will last, and that whatever life brings, there will always be
that poetic thread running through it.

To Hannah Whitall Smith   11 January 1902   I Tatti
Almost the first thing I saw when I went into B.B.'s study—in fact the
very first thing—was a life-size statue—a Madonna—in Istrian
marble, a perfect beauty (in my eyes). B.B. didn't say a word, but
waited for me to speak. 'Why you have a Laurana!' I exclaimed—
Laurana being one of our very favourite Renaissance sculptors, a
rather mysterious artist who is unequal but always fascinating. Then
B.B. grinned for joy, for it wasn't an easy Laurana to conosh*. He got
it for £160 but it is worth at least £1000.

At this time the Berensons became involved in another quarrel. Roger
Fry had long been a good friend of the Pearsall Smiths and of the
Berensons, but the quarrel which now arose between him and B.B.
was never entirely resolved, despite Mary's efforts. B.B. felt that Fry
was making use of his learning and experience without acknow-
ledgement, a sin he was always prone to suspect, as in the similar
cases of Charles Loeser, his old Harvard contemporary, and Herbert
Horne, another connoisseur friend, as well as in the case of Vernon
Lee, and was never able to forgive.

To Hannah Whitall Smith   14 January 1902   I Tatti
The quarrel with Roger certainly won't come from *our* side. But the
situation is that he is coming down to prepare, with our books and
photos, above all our knowledge, for his next course of lectures, and a
man in earnest about making his way won't be put off with 'a little
tact'. The first thing he will ask is whether he may use our
photographs. If we say no, under whatever tactful terms, he will be so
disappointed that he can't help being furious with us. The quarrel

* 'Conosh' was their word for the practice of connoisseurship.

100

with Loeser began with 'tact' simply because we turned the subject whenever pictures came up. And of course if it is your information a man is after, he feels acutely when he is baffled in getting it. But B.B. suggested, and perhaps we could carry it out, lending them this house—to show our perfect personal friendliness, while we are away in Sicily, but secretly weeding out our photos, so as not to leave much unpublished information there. It would take me at least a fortnight's hard work and another week to put them back in order, but perhaps it would be worthwhile. They couldn't decently turn into enemies after living free in our house (and yet Mrs Strong has!). Of course we want to keep friends with them, partly from interest, but more from real affection.

To Hannah Whitall Smith   1 February 1902   I Tatti
I waked up this morning thinking of all sorts of pleasant things—and one of the most rejoicing thoughts was that I still have *thee*, and that is a blessing that most of my contemporaries are without—their mothers. Some of them, I confess, don't want them back, but that will never be *my* case! Thee can't imagine what solid comfort lies in the thought, which is always, always present at the back of my mind, that *thee is there*.

To Hannah Whitall Smith   10 February 1902   I Tatti
I am afraid she [Ray] is like Logan, and hates to 'tell all about it'. She told me she did, in some of those talks. She said she *hated* to be asked about her feelings, or even about her doings. I am sorry for this, but little by little I mean to point out to her how much nicer it is for other people if she is more open and expansive: but it is an affair of temperament, I fear, that can never be *much* altered. In this she does not resemble her Mother.

Diary   14 February 1902   I Tatti
Bernhard is less well, I am afraid, but his temper is softened and he is dear and considerate and loving. I really can't think what has made my fancy go wandering. It is certainly no defect in him—it must be native inconstancy in me.

To Hannah Whitall Smith   17 March 1902   I Tatti
Well, Gladys dawned on our horizon again last night. Thee is wrong in thinking there is the least pose about her. She is perfectly natural, and is a frightening mixture of extreme youth and very dangerous

womanhood. I wonder what will happen to her. It frightens me to think of it.

To Logan Pearsall Smith   22 March 1902   Viterbo
Gladys Deacon continues to be amazing and surprising, frightening; but I feel a great gulf of years between us; years and long habit of thought and valuing things. She is unfortunately too much of a Circe to be satisfactory, she turns one's head with her beauty and her vivid personality and one's old intellectual plodding ways seem irrelevant. The most serious person shoots out butterfly wings at the touch of her wand, but they are, alas, too frail to carry the heavy body. Or else the serious man simply 'falls in love' and then becomes whatever sort of animal he really is. Thus she has no chance of knowing people, and she passes like a brilliant, terrifying vision. Circe was lonely too I daresay.

Diary   30 March 1902   [I Tatti?]
I am worried over two things, first that Bernhard isn't resting, that he exhibits such alarming marks of fatigue: also that I fear he is laying up trouble for himself in caring too much for Gladys—and I do want him to be happy.

To Hannah Whitall Smith   2 April 1902   Siena
Yesterday in the little villages we visited she [Gladys] had a train of nearly 200 children, and most of the grown-up people. She played 'Pied Piper of Hamelin' and they followed her nearly two miles down the road. She snatched one little boy's red scarf and dashed ahead waving it ... leaping high and singing, looking wonderfully beautiful. ... You will be surprised to hear that B.B. joined this, running, shouting, leaping, and even playing with the children. (I think it did him a lot of good.) It was a truly surprising spectacle, and one I can never forget.

To Hannah Whitall Smith   8 April 1902   I Tatti
Gladys ... found the Duke of Marlborough's mother and sister in town, and went to spend the afternoon with them. The sister, Lady Norah Churchill, travels with four pet frogs. One of them she has trained to jump into her mouth from her hand when she calls 'Hoo! Hoo!' This is her great card in society and several men are supposed to have fallen in love with her from watching this performance!

102

To Hannah Whitall Smith   26 April 1902   I Tatti

The last time we went down to dine with Davis he showed us with pride a picture he had just bought of a Mr Cobb, which we at once spotted as a forgery. I thought it was our Sienese friend Ioni, but B.B. was doubtful about the author. However we insisted that it was a forgery, and Davis wrote the next day sending us a photograph and asking us to prove what we said. The happy idea came to me to send for our little restorer, whom we came to know through Carlo the cook, and as I was writing to thee he came in. I asked him if he knew of a Filippino that had been for sale in Florence. Certainly, and he drew me the sketch. 'Who painted it?' 'The young Constantini.' 'How do you know?' 'I saw him do it, and he asked me if I would bring it to the Signor Berenson. I refused, as I said the learned Signore would recognize it at once as a forgery.' 'Will you write this down and sign it?' 'With the greatest of pleasure.' So now I am writing to Mr Davis enclosing Coppoli's statement. It does seem incredible that these American millionaires, so sharp and cunning in most business matters, should fall victim to the dealers ... It must be that the very notion of art mesmerizes them, for they would be penniless if they carried on the rest of their business like that!

To Hannah Whitall Smith   10 May 1902   I Tatti

This book [*The Drawings of the Florentine Painters*] is really a 'Great Work', I am myself surprised at it. Nothing like it has ever been done about Art, for it is not only concerned with Drawings, but wanders off continually into the most interesting and suggestive general speculations. He has really achieved a thing to be proud of—and I know pretty well what the literature of the subject is.

Diary   13 May 1902   I Tatti

In the evening [Leo] Stein brought his sister to dine—a fat unwieldy person, the colour of mahogany, but with a grand, monumental head, plenty of brains and immense geniality—a really splendid woman.

To Hannah Whitall Smith   15 July 1902   Friday's Hill

We have had a charming visit from Bertie, he never was more genial and witty, and we saw him go this morning with great regret. He is certainly the most brilliant man of our acquaintance and he is worth all the 'humouring' that he might desire. I say *might*, because I think, as a matter of fact, he is very reasonable and easy to get on with.

To Senda Berenson   6 October 1902   Friday's Hill
I am trying to feed up poor Zangwill, like Bernhard, on eggs and Benger's Food. He is awfully run down and miserable, but still he is lovable. I'm afraid we neither of us care much for his work; but we both love him, poor, pathetic, unselfish, saintly, miserable grotesque that he is.

To Isabella Gardner   10 November 1902   I Tatti
Bernhard has asked me to write to you about the Constantinis, and I shall venture to take this occasion to say what I have wanted to say to you ever since we were married, but have not quite had the courage to say. It is simply that Bernhard feels a most genuine devotion to you, and that he has made me (to some extent) appreciate all you have been to him. It is not only that when he was young and unknown you confided to him heavy and honourable respon- sibilities, it is the way you did it—as different from most people who have sought his advice as a Queen from a petty Merchant! He loves the splendid way in which you have carried out your ideas, and is proud that you associated him with it, and really burns to be of use to you.... You have that power—to call up chivalrous devotion. Our charming friend, Mounteney Jephson, was always speaking of you, somewhat as B.B. does, although with less under- standing of your impersonal love of Beautiful Things—but with an intense devotion.

To Hannah Whitall Smith   21 November 1902   I Tatti
I must tell thee the 'Zangwill Legend' that is growing up in the servants' hall. The servants are bursting with laughter all over the house, his absurdities are *so* absurd and so genial. Although he has been here a week, he doesn't yet know the way to his room, and Leonide tells me he often runs and stumbles up to the top floor and gets to the very end of the corridor before he realizes there is anything wrong. Last evening Roberto came up shaking with repressed amusement saying 'Il Signore' was below saying he wanted to 'spazzare' (sweep) with B.B., but Roberto discreetly opined that he meant 'andare a spasso' (go for a walk). Last night Roberto begged me to tell Zangwill that it was dangerous to sleep with the *scaldaletto* in his bed. It appears that Z, finding that big machine with a hanging basket of coals in the midst of it, calmly got in, curled him- self about it and went to sleep. He said he noticed a sort of smell of charcoal. It was almost enough to have finished him off like

Zola.* ... He is the most awful pig anybody can imagine. Yet he is so saintly and good-natured, so *large* in his mind, that one is willing to forgive a good deal.

To Hannah Whitall Smith   8 December 1902   I Tatti
B.B.'s ambition is to have enough *income* to carry us through without windfalls. This means at least £3000 a year, counting £400 to the children and £500 to his family. I think we may easily end by having it if things go well.

* In September, the French novelist Émile Zola had been found asphyxiated in his bedroom.

CHAPTER SEVEN

Acclaim

January 1903–March 1904

Ray was now fifteen and old enough, Mary thought, to start to benefit from the cultural atmosphere of I Tatti, as she had planned, although the child was not proving as open to her influence as she had hoped. Ray and a schoolfriend came out at Christmas 1902, and Edmund Houghton, an English friend of the Berensons who delighted in driving a car, took them all on a sight-seeing trip.

B.B. had finished his massive work on the drawings of the Florentine painters of the Renaissance, but the phenomenal effort of concentration and memory involved in dealing with so much material which had never been photographed had brought on a real breakdown of his health, and more particularly of his nerves. The Berensons had planned a visit to America together for the spring of 1903, but on medical grounds this was postponed until the autumn.

Alys's marriage had met with disaster in 1902. Bertie fell completely out of love with her, and came to find her more and more intensely irritating, though there was as yet no other woman in his life. Alys, however, still loved him, as she continued to do all her life, and hoped against hope that his affection would return. She suffered a severe breakdown during the summer, and was deeply depressed again at Christmas, while she and Bertie were visiting I Tatti. They had agreed not to separate, and stayed together for the next nine years, in increasing misery on both sides. While it was obviously clear that something was seriously wrong, Alys had confided in no one—least of all in Mary, whose discretion she did not trust.

To Hannah Whitall Smith   5 January 1903   I Tatti
Presently a discussion arose whether my way of taking them [Ray and her friend] to see only a few masterpieces, or Houghton's way of

106

browsing round among all the curiosities of a museum, was better, and they spoke up with great warmth for me, and said I had been perfectly right on our trip to give them a few strong impressions that they would remember all their lives, rather than a confused recollection of a lot of things they hadn't had the time to take in. I was quite touched to find they had thought about my system and appreciated it... Well, of course it is true, that they *could not possibly* be seeing Italian Art under better auspices. When I think how I've toiled and moiled it would be a pity if I couldn't give them some results.

Diary   9 January 1903   I Tatti
Alys had just recovered from her terrible depression, which had lasted since Xmas, so she was very gay. But what an awful curse it is—she has only a few days every month free.

To Hannah Whitall Smith   13 January 1903   I Tatti
Isn't it funny, mother, that Alys and I have married men whose view of the world is *almost the same*? They seem so different, but really conversation between them amounts to one or other saying something and receiving the answer 'Of course!' B.B. says they agree too well to discuss much, except of course they can exchange views on historical matters and so on. The chief difference in attitude to life between them is that Bertie is much more philanthropic, believes more in the possibility of doing good to large masses of people.

To Hannah Whitall Smith   25 February 1903   I Tatti
What made me busy was, to start with, replying for B.B. to his publisher, Murray, who is in a great state about the failure of some of the plates of the book, and wrote a 'kind' letter to B.B. to reproach him with having shirked his responsibilities by running off to Italy and depriving Murray of his expert advice.... Thee can't think how it upset B.B.... He raged up and down the room, 'cussing and swearing awful' and I was to write a letter full of fire and brimstone.... Poor thing—he is overcome with remorse for his irritable temper. I found him in bed the other day, quite overcome. 'I am so sick of being cross with you, Mary' he said, 'but there is no one else I *can* be cross with, and I've such a lot of crossness in me.' Fortunately I don't mind it a bit, for I know it is tired nerves and I always laugh at him.

107

To Hannah Whitall Smith   1 March 1903   I Tatti
We are all enchanted with Gilbert Murray*, only B.B., who always takes his pleasures sadly, is raging at not having known him *ever* so long ago. He is the most congenial man, except Bertie, he has ever come across. It's really delightful having him.

To Ray Costelloe   5 March 1903   I Tatti
So Maths continue fascinating and Latin palls. O Ray, Ray, isn't thee going to be interested in the beauties of civilization? However mathematics are a part of civilization too.

To Hannah Whitall Smith   8 March 1903   I Tatti
They came, D'Annunzio and the Duse, in a closed cab (it was raining and we thought they would not come at all) and we watched it labouring up the hill, speculating if the Great Persons were inside... The Duse, a sad, interesting woman looking about 50, dressed in black with a grey veil waving about her head, *à l'Américaine*, swept in saying she could only stay a minute. Dandified, hideous, vulgar little D'Annunzio followed smirking in her train. He has Sidney Webb's figure, and a head like a white worm—intelligent though—he looks like a 'full grown lamb', very weak. The Countess Serristori† who had come to see the show, and whom we know as a very intelligent, fascinating, talkative sort of young boy, suddenly, under D'Annunzio's glances, turned into a languishing female, making eyes, coyly looking down, full of suggestive silences etc. It was the funniest transformation. I had heard that he fascinated Italian women as a snake fascinates birds. I was amused to see the process. Afterwards she said that just to hear him ask for tea was a delight, and when he said two lumps it was Rapture! Pure 'suggestion', for although he talks beautiful Italian, his voice is not as musical as Placci's. They suppose themselves to be the Apostles of Art, but they really cared nothing for our pictures, although Placci insisted on showing them round. They managed to get through a few conventional phrases, and then settled down to the real business of the afternoon, D'Annunzio to boast about his genius and his poems and plays and to flirt with the Serristori, and the Duse to work with Norman Hapgood‡ for all she

* Gilbert Murray later to become Professor of Greek at Oxford had been sent to the Berensons by Bertie Russell.
† Countess Hortense Serristori, a Spaniard married to an Italian, who remained a close friend of B.B.'s throughout his life.
‡ Norman Hapgood, writer and brother of Hutchins Hapgood.

was worth to advertise herself as actress and D'Annunzio as playwright in New York. They stayed two hours, and departed highly pleased with their afternoon's business. They both struck me as very common Italian people of the lower class, raised by intelligence, talent, power, but not refined and not thoughtful. Neither B.B. nor I were attracted in the least, but Logan fell under the Duse's charm.

To Robert Trevelyan   16 March 1903   I Tatti
He [Gilbert Murray] threw a bomb into our midst last night by saying that the far-greatest poets of England were Chaucer, Shakespeare, Shelley and—Tennyson!! Keats and Milton were 'not in it' in his estimation. It was a thrilling moment, which was relieved by his exquisite reading of 'Maud'. This, however, failed to convert us to Tennyson's poetic gifts. Logan and I held ourselves in in the noblest manner, and B.B. opened gentle angel's wings (!!) and brooded over the assembly, and after several hours of illuminating discourse, which never rose to argument, we separated with a strong desire to resume the discussion. Murray is an angel, it is charming to discuss differences of taste with him. One night he defended Dickens.

Diary   19 March 1903   I Tatti
Logan and I drove to la Doccia to meet the great Edith Wharton. We found B.B. there already, it was clear, loathing her. We also disliked her intensely.

To Senda Berenson   22 March 1903   I Tatti
The Duse and D'Annunzio came last night to listen to the music. Bernhard and I found him exceedingly interesting. He had no one to flirt with this time, so his vanity dropped off, and he talked most intelligently. She hardly said a word, but looked tenderly on him—she is evidently overwhelmingly in love. He treated her as most clever men treat their wives—with affectionate contempt. She looked sad and tragic and old, getting rather fat. B.B. says she would bore him to death, and so he imagined D'Annunzio is bored.

To Bernhard Berenson   Easter Sunday 12 April 1903   Friday's Hill
Alys made a very unfavourable impression on me the other day. She has gone back to her deadly philanthropizing—partly under Lady Mary[Murray]'s influence, I think—and everybody is rubbed a little the wrong way... And the children scarcely like her at all, she has become so critical and lecturing. She says queer rude things

109

sometimes ... Altogether I feel as if she weren't at all right, somehow, and I do feel awfully sorry for Bertie.

To Hannah Whitall Smith   1 June 1903   I Tatti
Thee says I neglect the children, passing only two or three months with them a year. Last summer, which I hope is a normal sort of summer, I was at home from June 4 to October 17, four months and a half. This year I have had to stick to B.B. because—I never mentioned this before—the doctor told me he was not at all sure he could pull him through, there seemed to be such a failure all round. Now whatever his defects and follies, B.B. has a touch of genius, and not only my life, but actually Ray's and Karin's will be raised to a different plane by having him, than if we were left to ourselves. When they are old enough to take advantage of it, a great deal of the most interesting and cultivated society in Europe will have open doors for them, and this is surely no slight advantage to young people.

The visit to America Mary now undertook was designed to encourage wealthy Americans—who were increasingly attempting to demons-trate their culture by acquiring works of art—and to convince them that the things to acquire were Italian pictures, and the man to advise and assist them was Berenson. Both enjoyed their stay among the extraordinary fleshpots of the people Mary called 'Squillionaires', and although they did not find another patron like Isabella Gardner, they made a considerable impression on the circles they had aimed at.
    Their first stop was the Newport home of Theodore Davis, whom they had got to know when he was buying pictures in Florence.

To her Family   12 October 1903   Newport, RI, USA
I am surprised to find how really interesting Mr Davis is in his own house, when you have the patience to let him take his own rope. He is a man of power and character, who has observed a great deal. ... He tells me that the rich people here amuse themselves in every conceivable extravagant way. This summer Mrs Fish* got a theatrical company to come up for the night. She made them close their theatre in New York, where they were playing, paid the damages (including a broken contract), put up a theatre in her garden and installed ten thousand dollars of electrical plant *for the night only*. They sometimes

---

* Mrs Fish, wife of Stuyvesant Fish, president of the Illinois Central Railroad, a prominent New York and Newport hostess.

bring all the N.Y. organ-grinders and their monkeys for a barrel-organ contest. Another friend of his was giving a big dinner and ordered two hundred and fifty dollars worth of 'incubated turkeys' for an entrée. And so on. It makes one's head reel, this casual way of talking of 'a hundred millions'. Well, well, I hope a small share of this river of gold will flow into our pockets.

To her Family   19 October 1903   Green Hill, Brookline, Mass, USA
Here we are at last in the house of the marvellous 'Mrs Jack'. But only in her country house, not in Fenway Court, her museum, which she refuses to show us until December, being a very imperious lady, and determined we shall remain in Boston longer than we meant to! She wrote us that she lived here in the country the life of 'an ascetic hermit' but we supposed this was a mere boast (like *some* hermits I have known!), but we have come to find it true. In two days I have lost an inch round the waist, between a plain spare diet and freezing cold. She is a person who cares absolutely nothing for physical comfort, so long as she has fresh air. She eats dry toast, but unlike poor Mrs Maitland 'who dried herself up on toast, ma'am' she flourishes upon it and remains as young at nearly 70 as if she were 25! She keeps all her sense of 'fun' too, all her spirits, all her love of adventure. Perhaps the only difference is that she now feels free to do exactly what she pleases, to see whom she likes, to live as she likes. She has no door-bell to her Palace, so that nobody can disturb her, and her telephone has no call bell.

To her Family   27 October 1903   Newport
Mrs Gardner's pet hobby seems to be a hatred of spending money on light. She saves up all her old candle ends, has only one light in her drawing room and none anywhere else, not even in the halls. Her bedrooms are supplied with gas, but the moment we leave them some one rushes in and turns them not down but *out*! It is really comic.

To Hannah Whitall Smith   31 October 1903   Northampton
I have just had an invitation to lecture at *Yale*, (where we go on Monday to see the Jarves collection). I think I shall accept all these invitations, partly through a desire to set young people on the right track about old pictures, and partly because one never knows how it may turn out to one's advantage to be well known in one's profession. It ought at least to increase the sale of B.B.'s books and help his publishers to set up carriages and horses!! My lecture here seems to

have been a success. The girls were whispering in American slang 'She can have me', and I have had lots of notes.

To her Family   3 November 1903   New Haven
Then there was a Berenson gathering, and they are all so good and so worried about each other, and so out of health, that it got on my nerves, and dreadfully on poor B.B.'s as well. 'If only they knew that the one thing I dreaded on this trip was a further intimacy with my family!' Senda you know—she is very nice—Bessie is improved, and Rachel I *thoroughly* like, but as individuals. As a Family, with their family worries and self-sacrifices, it is more than I can stand. The truth is that B.B. is so far ahead of them all, that he has given them a vision of something they are quite unable to realize for themselves, and this makes them discontented with the really very comfortable positions they have been able to attain.

To Hannah Whitall Smith   6 November 1903   Boston
Also at Wellesley I am to lecture. B.B. has persuaded me not to take money, as we are after bigger game, and although an occasional £5 or £10 would be very nice, I daresay he is right for the long run. I can prepare the ground for a Lecture Tour in case steel goes smash.

To her Family   17 November 1903   Boston
The whole thing [Mrs Gardner's museum, Fenway Court] is a work of *genius*. You can't think how disgusted people have been since, at hearing us say so. They do long to hear evil of her and her works. Half a dozen people have taken us confidentially aside and said 'Now tell us what you *really* think of it—you are quite safe with us!' and they *ought* to pardon her anything for the beauty of it and her generousness in making it to leave to Boston. It is the biggest gift Boston has ever had. Yet all they think of is envy, and small spites; and she remains a very lonely and unloved person. We really adore her, in a way, and stand up for her everywhere, *not* 'in a way', but all round.

They were delighted to see at Fenway Court the great Botticelli picture, *The Madonna and Child of the Eucharist*, which Berenson had obtained for Mrs Gardner, but not so delighted by the neighbours she had given it.

To her Family   19 November 1903   Boston
We were absolutely petrified with horror and disgust to find hanging

112

opposite to it a picture which explains Mrs Gardner's refusal to take some of the things B.B. has recently offered to her. It is a very poor picture of the school of Botticelli which belonged to the Duca di Brindisi, and which was offered to us about 2½ years ago. Besides being really poor, by *no* means one of the more attractive school pictures, the price was prohibitive, three hundred and fifty thousand francs (£15,000). The idea that after all he had done for her and the splendid things he has got she should *not even have asked for* his advice about this, but have paid goodness knows how much more for this thing; that the glorious things she has have educated her so little that she can believe it a Botticelli and hang it opposite to a real one—all these thoughts and the idea that *he* would be held responsible, came over B.B. and he nearly fainted away. Mrs Gardner saw it and said 'What is it?' so he said 'Why that is a picture I know and refused for you 2½ years ago.' She was furious, and resorted to her usual device, lying, and said 'No, it can't be, I've had it at least five years.' So we went on along the corridor. I confess it took away a good deal of one's first glow of enthusiasm; but still I find she has been pretty faithful, *considering*;—the considerations being her irresponsible wealth, her caprice, her ignorance, and the fact that every dealer in the world, professional and amateur, has been *at* her all these years...

Mrs Gardner came to lunch wearing lots of her jewels, at least a million dollars worth. She said one of her friends had been robbed by her butler of all her jewels, and this had frightened her so she made up her mind to wear them all. She was a blaze of diamonds and pearls, and I think she had on sets of sapphires and emeralds under her dress, which looked very lumpy in spots.

The quarrel with Roger Fry was renewed over the question of the *Burlington Magazine*, a recently founded English arts journal with which Roger Fry had become closely connected. Bernhard had written the lead article for the first issue and soon thereafter had become embroiled in a bitter dispute over editorial policy. Fry, though he would have liked B.B. to continue as a contributor both of articles and of money, found himself caught in the crossfire of infuriated rival experts, and failed to give B.B. that degree of support which he believed to be his due.

To her Family   *10 December 1903   New York*
Thee will see that after telling us that Sidney Colvin and Claude Phillips are willing to believe any monstrous lie about B.B.'s intrigues,

he [Roger Fry] coolly proposes to leave the management of the reconstructed magazine [the *Burlington*] largely in their hands, leaving B.B. entirely out. Now he must have known, after all our talks, that B.B. would not go on, unless he were certain of being consulted about the Italian things, and I do think it is very stupid of him to calmly kick us out of all authority and yet expect to make use of us. I wrote him that we wished well to his enterprise, but of course under the arrangements he proposed we could only be outsiders, and that B.B.'s name must not appear. Nor are we keen on getting money to support it; although if it poured in, of course, he should have some.... There is, however, no need to quarrel over it and we shan't, I'm sure. But it is clear as daylight, even to me now, that we can't really work with Roger, nice as he is. He is not really clever, he won't face a situation and take an open position. Nor will he for an instant try to see what B.B. really means.

To Hannah Whitall Smith   31 December 1903   New York
Ever since he came, he has felt that people took him kindly instead of suspiciously and with jealousy, as in England.... They take it for granted that he is honourable and learned and sincere, whereas everyone in England, from Roger down, take the opposite for granted: and of course in Germany and Italy and France he is much more loathed than liked. To be always on the defensive is extremely disagreeable, if you care at all, and he seems to care.

To her Family   3 January 1904   Chicago
We find that she [Mrs Gardner] is *determined* to have no one else in Boston but herself buy Italian pictures through B.B.! We came upon traces of her 'undermining' everywhere. At first it was annoying but now it is amusing, for we countermine. It is part of her nature to be intensely selfish, and to wish to be the *one and only*—it goes with her superb achievement, the motive power of which has been vanity.... She has done her utmost here to keep us from meeting the collectors, and to prejudice people against B.B., or to warn them from approaching him 'in his delicate state of health'. There is no lie she shrinks from.

To Hannah Whitall Smith   10 January 1904   Chicago
The last few days have been a sort of triumph, 'gratifying', but *au fond* absurd. There is no one but me to tell you about it, so I must do so, although it wears the appearance of blowing my own trumpet!

My speech on Wednesday at the Art Institute was, it seems, a great success, and it got talked about all over Chicago, to such an extent that when Friday came, and I had to speak to a fashionable Club, it was absolutely *packed*, not only with women, but with business men, who have never before been known to desert their pork-packing and their trust-manipulation in the middle of the day! What they crowded round me to say to me afterwards, I cannot, for very shame repeat.... Yesterday.... I gave another talk, this time on 'How to tell a Forgery'. It was the first of my speeches at which B.B. was present. He said that my delivery was the best he had ever heard, simple, confidential, but dignified, humourous and winning (*I* have to tell you, or no one will!) ...

We came home, rested, and then went out to a grand dinner given in our honour by Mrs MacVeagh.* There were about 30 people seated at a table covered with gorgeous tulips. One of the men calculated for my benefit that the 'interests represented' at that table were about nine hundred million dollars. Alas, human imagination (all except Mrs Gardner's) is so poor that all they can think of doing with all that vast sum is to eat, night after night, the most elaborate, deadly, wildly expensive dinners, and to let their wives blaze out into jewels and wear dresses so frail that one evening's use finishes them.... Quiet little Uncle Bernhard was really so witty and so very, very amusing that I assure you I felt a sort of pang at the thought of confining him again to the poky, dingy society of Settignano. He really has unsuspected social gifts! I, in the meantime, was talking chiefly to the son of Abraham Lincoln, who, as the head of the Pullman Car system, 'represents' nearly a hundred million. He does not seem to bear any resemblance to his father, but he looks an important man—a little the old Prince of Wales type. Mrs Gardner sat on the other side ... She was gorgeous that evening. She wore on her head two immense diamonds, about the size of the *Kohinoor*, sparkling and quivering with every movement. They were like a butterfly's antennae.

To her Family   14 January 1904   Detroit
You will be glad to hear that we have succeeded in selling Roger's picture for him. He said once that B.B. tried to bribe people into supporting him by doing such a lot for them. I suppose he will think

* Mrs Frankline MacVeagh, wife of a wealthy wholesale grocer.

115

this another instance! But really we know what trouble he was in, and used our *utmost* efforts to get his things sold. I am so glad.

To her Family   *1 March 1904*   *Boston*
And so things go—no *denaro in tasca**, but I do think every reasonable hope that this trip may turn out to be the beginning of a fortune. But we shall never find another great person like Mrs Gardner.

To her Family   *4 March 1904*   *New York*
Now that our trip is nearly at an end, I must tell you that it has been *great fun*. It has been an exploring visit, which is always fun, and we have found so much to like. Then we have amused ourselves so much together, talking it over—it has been a real lark from beginning to end.

* Money in the pocket.

CHAPTER EIGHT

Allegro Vivace

April 1904–August 1906

Mary enjoyed the next two years enormously. Her daughters, now seventeen and fifteen, were beginning to reveal definite characters of their own, and Mary turned the full force of her attention on to them. Both girls, first Ray alone and then the two together, were 'brought out' in Mary's far from conventional fashion.

Motoring was an important element in both these undertakings, and indeed was one of Mary's greatest pleasures at this time. It was a new art still, and much subject to disasters of all sorts, which in no way discouraged her. B.B. felt that it would be an extravagance to own a car, so Mary had either to hire one or rely on her friends, notably the vague but delightful Edmund Houghton and Carlo Placci, with his nephews, Albert and Louis Henraux.

To Hannah Whitall Smith   2 April 1904   I Tatti
Well, we are having a splendid time. Never did anything look more beautiful than this house when we arrived on Thursday in time for tea. Everything was exquisitely clean, and the house was filled with flowers. Uncle Damien [the coachman] was at the station weeping with joy, Roberto in an embroidered shirt and coral pin, and Ugo (gardener) with the contadino to get the trunks. We just wandered through all the rooms *enjoying* them till dinner, and after dinner sat about the fire (for it was cold) and laughed and talked.

To Hannah Whitall Smith   2 April 1904   (Later) I Tatti
We have had a most riotous evening, Karin keeping us all in fits of laughter. She really is too amusing. I think she must have a touch of genuine 'Irish humour'. The subject of the fun tonight was a little lecture I gave Ray and Winnie [a schoolfriend of Ray's] about their sitting so silent in company and never exerting themselves for conversation. So Karin determined to 'converse' at dinner, and did so

117

in such a way that our sides fairly ached with laughing by the time we rose from the table. Even old Ray joined in....

To get them up is like drawing teeth! They all have chocolate together in my bed, with the windows wide open, and this heavenly, heavenly view. The garden is full of flowers, and so is the house.

To Hannah Whitall Smith   *13 May 1904   I Tatti*
B.B. and I deserted our guests and went off to lunch with Mrs Ross to meet Mark Twain. He is a grand-looking genial old man, with ... beautiful happy eyes. He talked the whole time, long stories, very elaborate and droll, and quite lived up to his character. It was delightful.

To Hannah Whitall Smith   *26 May 1904   I Tatti*
Thee will laugh to hear that I am now nearly through my first week of an anti-fat diet*.... I must walk at least an hour—two if I can manage it—and have rigorous massage 4 times a week.... There is no doubt I needed this discipline, for I begin to *feel fat*, to be too heavy to enjoy walking, to feel buried somehow in flesh. It's no longer the vanity of looks that spurs me on, for I gave that up on my fortieth birthday.... The first day it was awful, and the masseuse expected to find me black and blue. But I wasn't, and the awful suspicion occurred to us both, that I made more fuss than most people would ... Can this be true?

To Hannah Whitall Smith   *14 June 1904   I Tatti*
The Countess Serristori, who was here yesterday, in a black mood of life being all a mistake and the only pleasant thing being to go to bed (this as *I know* is one of the symptoms of being married to a man who bores one!), found it almost *dégoûtant* that I feel so well and jolly and interested in everything, but B.B. told her he didn't think he could really go on living if it weren't for that.

To Hannah Whitall Smith   *25 June 1904   Bologna*
Those days in Houghton's automobile were simply ecstatic. I assure thee I felt 20 years younger, and as if I were perfectly new to Italy and it was all too wonderful—that delicious *exploring* feeling we used to have in the West, but even more so, for there were quantities of lovely works of art at the end of every expedition along those seductive

* Mary's love of good food prevented her from keeping to any diet for long. She made repeated attempts to battle with her increasing weight, but they were entirely unsuccessful, much to B.B.'s despair.

roads. It has simply opened a new life to us—we really didn't know that such raptures were in store for our middle age!

To Hannah Whitall Smith   26 September 1904   Conegliano
The roads are quite perfect along here, and sometimes we spin along at 40 miles an hour, which is too fast for me, as one *can't* really enjoy scenery at that pace. Placci's nephew, who drives, is very careful and steady and the chauffeur sits by him on the lookout: so there seems to be no danger in spite of our fierce speed. We seem to fill people's hearts with rapture as we go by—the small boys leap into the air hurrahing, and even grown-up peasant women dance and wave their arms with delight as we rush by. They feel that a new world is being conquered for man—or rather the old world is being more completely subjugated to his uses. The children sing out '*O hé i Signore!*' as if we really were Lords of the Earth and Air, who deigned to reveal ourselves to them for a moment.

To Ray Costelloe   19 October 1904   Gazzada
Gram says she read thee what I wrote before thee was born, that I had 'wild dreams for thee' if thee was to be a girl (which it appears thee is). I was still terribly in earnest over the Woman Question, and my wild dreams were to have a child who would overpass the usual feminine limits and prove conclusively that the female brain, if properly trained, could surpass (as I firmly believed it could) all the achievements of the inferior male brain. I thought of thee as putting Shakespeare to the blush, or pushing the name of Newton into oblivion. I was a goose *du premier ordre!* It wasn't so much of my daughter I dreamed but of the Cause of Woman. How much of this Cause has descended to thee as birthright, who can say? I myself have spent most of my time since studying and enjoying the achievements of the despised male section of humanity, and (I confess) my crest is lowered upon the question of the potentialities of women. All I dare say now is that they ought to have their *fair chance*. And maybe if thee should devote thy life to helping them get this fair chance in regard to Education, thee will, after all, come as near to realizing my 'wild dreams' as human actions ever do come to executing the dreams of Utopia.

To Hannah Whitall Smith   18 November 1904   I Tatti
B.B. and Santayana went out to walk.... On their walk they had, B.B. says, lots of talk, which has left B.B. feeling as if Santayana's

mental state were even more remote from his own than even an Italian's! Santayana has no 'vague yearnings', no unclear but ardent aspirations. His universe is ordered. It admits no room for those dark dusky corners in which the spiritual life most of us have is carried on. B.B. says it gives him the same sort of mental chill that he gets when he comes into real contact with Eastern thought—and it makes him a little uneasy lest after all Santayana may not be right, and he, B.B., be nothing but a hopeless muddlehead.

To Hannah Whitall Smith   29 November 1904   I Tatti
B.B. and I went for the most glorious two hour walk. . . . I never, never felt in better health. I could do nothing but make the most absurd jokes (not witty) and laugh and laugh as we went along. I am getting TOO jolly. Last night I woke myself up laughing so hard that I simply *couldn't* stop, I roared until I had to bury my head in the pillows for fear of waking Senda who sleeps above me. I dreamt that I was at a very swell dinner of all B.B.'s St Moritz friends, and that he sort of slunk in very late. After a while I noticed that he had on a large check tie under his ear as well as a white one, and this began to make me laugh. He saw it and turned to me with his most reproachful 'Mary!' and then he stood up and I saw he had forgotten to put on his trousers. He simply looked too funny for words, and everybody burst into peals of laughter, and I thought 'Poor B.B. Everyone will think kindly of him for giving them such a hearty laugh, but he can NEVER look at it that way.' Then I woke up shouting. But what a goose I am to take up all my letter telling such a silly dream.

To Hannah Whitall Smith   6 December 1904   I Tatti
I finished my article for the *Gazette [des Beaux Arts]* this morning and took it in to B.B. to read. The miserable man, who himself made me write it and wouldn't let me have any peace until I set to work on it, listened to it as if I were holding a basin under his head on a Channel crossing, groaning and showing signs of horrible disgust. This was very mortifying to my vanity, just at the moment when I was flushed with having got it written; but it turned out in the end that what excited his horror was not what *I* had written, but the idea of writing on art at all, and especially of writing about such a deadly thing as attributions. He said (and I think rightly) that all the stuffings I had put in to cook the thing into a readable article were perfectly nauseating, that the only dignified thing to do was to publish the two photographs and a few lines to say 'If you don't see that these are by the same hand, study

them until you do.' Although I agreed with him on general principles, it was difficult, at the moment, to see it. However, I said that I was delighted and would publish them as he said: of course the *Gazette* would not take such an article, but I was sure that either Reinach or Don Guido* would be delighted to publish the two photographs. Then ensued a funny struggle in his mind, for he wanted me to have the small kudos that attaches to publishing such a thing in the *Gazette*, yet he was attracted by the idea of not doing anything journalistic about it, but standing aside and letting the facts speak for themselves. I watched the struggle with amusement—one's life companion can be a very diverting study, if you take it that way—and forbore to offer any opinion. In fact at that moment of crisis, young Visconti Venosta was announced (for lunch) and the thing was left undecided.

This young man stayed until four, talking, as young people love to do, about himself, and being listened to, as old people love to listen with indulgence, and then B.B. decided to take a nap. As I covered him up (he says he must put up a monument sometime to the man who first invented marriage!) he said 'Mary, you had better finish up that article and send it off.' 'To the *Gazette*?' I asked; and he grinned. So I suppose it is decided. To tell the truth, I feel so jolly and good-humoured that I like doing one thing as well as another, and feel as if I could go on doing articles for years, or never do another one, with equal pleasure.

To Bernhard Berenson   7 January 1905   London
This is *our* day, and I wish I were spending it, and the night too (a part of it) with thee. Strange that such a thing as 'falling in love' should lead to so happy a life as we are learning to live together.

To Hannah Whitall Smith   24 February 1905
It is such a comfort to have a cook whom one can absolutely depend on— and this cook is really very good. He gave us a most delicious creamy tomato soup, then some little birds stuffed, on polenta, then nice young asparagus, then tender roast beef with new potatoes and salad, and finally coffee ice-cream and cake. We all ate a great deal too much.

To Hannah Whitall Smith   2 March 1905   I Tatti
I asked the doctor today if there was a name for the disease I have,

---

* Don Guido Cagnola, wealthy art collector and founder of the magazine *Rassegna d'Arte*, to which B.B. and Mary frequently contributed.

which is being too happy, happier than my circumstances warrant. He said it was the first time a patient came to him with that complaint—but it is called in Asylums *Euphoria*!

To Hannah Whitall Smith   9 April 1905   I Tatti
I am going to devote myself to making her [Ray] 'see life'. Houghton has promised not only to take her on an automobile trip, but to teach her to run it.... I am planning *all sorts* of things.

To Hannah Whitall Smith   16 April 1905   I Tatti
I can imagine how thee will miss Ray, for I see she is a creature to count on ... It would have done thy heart good to hear her talking ... about thy influence upon her, especially in regard to not getting 'offended'.... Ray also has a great admiration for Karin who is, she says, the very cleverest girl she has ever known, simply head and shoulders above the other girls in her class. She says that Karin is not yet awake to the responsible side of life, but she thinks that when she does wake up, with all her brilliancy, she will be something wonderful ... so let us hope that the time is not far off when that rather thoughtless young animal will become humanized. She says it is true that at present Karin has too little tact, but I am sure that, with her brains, she CAN get it, when she is awake to its importance.

The companion provided for Ray's 'coming out' was a young American cousin, Willie Taylor, who was visiting Florence; a rather callow youth, who appealed more to Mary than to Ray.

To Hannah Whitall Smith   24 April 1905   I Tatti
I'm afraid she is not much taken with Willy, but I hope she will get to like him better. To B.B. and me he seems the most wonderful of youths, so true and sincere and full of sound sense, besides being absolutely first-rate mentally. But Ray cannot take our middle-aged point of view. We don't mind Willy's conceit, his absurd self-confidence makes us smile indulgently, for we see it melting away by the sure action of the years, but Ray, of course, regards it as final, and she is very severe on it. She doesn't seem to have the faintest leaning towards a flirtation—wretched young 'Miss Beale and Miss Buss'* that she is—that of course would entertain and amuse her. But it isn't

* From an anti-feminist rhyme much quoted in Mary's family, about two well-known headmistresses: 'Miss Buss and Miss Beale/Cupid's darts do not feel/How different from us/Are Miss Beale and Miss Buss.'

in her yet. This, I think, considerably surprises young William, who is accustomed to see girls yielding to his spell!... Last night the men were talking about women's education etc, and they made out that women's sphere was to be men's companion etc. Ray said, when she came in to bid me goodnight, that she at last began to understand *thy* views of men. Willy was frankly selfish in his ideas of women, but he redeemed it by saying 'I'm a young goose just out of college, and I daresay I'm all wrong.' He was a good deal wrong, but he did not strike me as hopelessly so; and unfortunately he was a good deal right too. However all this is fun, and it is an excellent part of Ray's broadening out before she cloisters herself again in Newnham.

To Hannah Whitall Smith   11 May 1905   I Tatti
I found out that young people do not like to have any of their mental food, even the artistic kind, presented to them in an already digested condition. They like to do their own chewing and assimilating, even their own snatching, and the more I kept striving to provide them with peptonized sightseeing and aesthetic liver pills, the more they hated me and it!... I leave thee to imagine my feelings. Perhaps the keenest one, however, was one which it would make them perfectly furious to know, a wild keen delight in seeing them prove themselves to be real people, individuals and not mere jollifying children. They have a wider though vaguer sense of privacy than we others who, by plenty of years and practice, know exactly what we can reveal and what we want to conceal. The child is not sure; and to be poked and pried into under such conditions distresses and even outrages him or her in a very intimate way. I more or less understand this now, for with their strong young fists they have kept beating it into my hard weather-worn head: I understand it and respect it; but whether, with what they reveal to me is a very 'managing' and despotic nature, I can control my impulses enough to keep hands off, remains to be seen.

To Hannah Whitall Smith   18 May 1905   I Tatti
I do not think I HAD grasped the great principle that you can bring a horse to the trough but cannot make him drink. Ray's chances are so what I would have jumped at in my youth that I have kept thinking that they MUST be what she needs. As to any estrangement being caused between her and me, it is just the reverse, we understand each other better and better.

123

To Hannah Whitall Smith   7 June 1905   I Tatti
We did not stop to look at a single picture or work of art all the
four days. Instead we devoted ourselves to getting swims for
Ray and making her so proficient with the machine that today she
carried it on all day entirely by herself.... As for Ray she is quite
motor-mad, and Houghton has put her up to the idea of getting a
second-hand little De Dion-Bouton ... we shall see if her enthusiasm
holds out.

To Hannah Whitall Smith   11 June 1905   I Tatti
I have bought Ray a real motor cap, with the 'Eyes' sewn in, and a
false nose, and all the rest of it. She looks very funny, as thee can
imagine, but she glories in it! We put some little bags of shot in the
front of her dress to hold it down, and I got her a large long pair of
gloves, so I think her outfit is complete.

To Hannah Whitall Smith   30 June 1905   Venice
I think it is time I made a confession—that I am *quite finished* with that
wonderful young person [Willy]. He does not improve as he gets more
at ease. His egoism and native boorishness come out very un-
pleasantly. He is about the most disagreeable person to travel with I
have ever struck.

To Bernhard Berenson   26 August 1905   Friday's Hill
What thee writes about 'the world' and its values might almost have
been written by me. I have, however, come to the conclusion that my
bad dressing and lack of French really cut me off from the enjoyment
even I might have had in it. But that would never be much, even if I
were young and slender and well dressed, for it is not the sort of thing
I have ever cared for. You can't help accepting for the moment their
values but they aren't really one's own.... We are frumpy 'intellec-
tuals' and that is our world.

To Hannah Whitall Smith   20 September 1905   Savoie
B.B. thinks he really will have to put me in their [the dressmakers']
hands, for he cares so much how I dress, and finds my present style—
including my beloved Burberry suit!—too horrible. Ray will be
amused to think of *my* receiving the sort of lecture *I* gave *her*!... I keep
thinking what a pity it will be to waste so much on trying to
resuscitate the *'restes de beauté'* in a fat, middle-aged, red-faced
lady!

124

To Ray Costelloe   20 October 1905   I Tatti
Uncle Bernhard is in a very good mood, and is most interesting. What a blessing to marry a man who doesn't bore one! Bear this in mind. His greatest difficulty in writing is a thing that I notice thee manages easily—the transition*. He has just given birth to an awfully heavy one, bridging over the chasm from the great to the little painters. He brought it to me with fond parental pride, and I tore it limb from limb, to his great pain.

The only shadow on the brightness of these years was that Karin, when she was seventeen, developed serious ear trouble. She had a number of operations in a desperate attempt to preserve her hearing, but these, after many fluctuations, and despite the brilliance of her aurist, Charles Joseph Heath, were only partially successful.

To Karin Costelloe   29 November 1905   I Tatti
Dearest Karin, Grandma's letter today tears my heart dreadfully! I do not know what I ought to do! She says that thee has set thy heart on having thy operation on the seventh, and counts on getting out of the examinations by that means, and that thee will be dreadfully disappointed if I do not come home in time. I feel all this, and also I should like to get it over as soon as possible, and give thee a thoroughly good time for the rest of the holidays.

On the other hand, listen to this tale. B.B. has got his momentum on, and is in full swing of work—but at the same time terribly dependent on me. Yesterday we had tea alone together and he could not do anything but groan over the problem staring him in the face. ... 'I shall never do it, Mary' he kept on saying, and I had to encourage him by laughing at him and prophesying that when we next met at dinner it would be 'done'. Thee sees he is not quite well yet, from his nervous breakdown, and he seems to need this sort of cheerfulness. ... So thee sees I am really needed here, and I can't get away unless it is very, very important. ... Show this letter to Grandma and ask her what she thinks.

* B.B. was now at work on the fourth book on the Italian painters of the Renaissance, those of Northern Italy, to be published in 1907. Ray had written her first book, a novel called *The World at Eighteen* (1907), based on the events of her visit in 1905 and her struggles with Willy.

Diary   18 December 1905   London
Karin's operation [was]. . . . a perfectly terrible one, and unexpectedly
so. The doctor thought it would be a more or less ordinary mastoid
operation, but he found a terrible abscess and the bone frightfully
diseased.

To Bernhard Berenson   18 December 1905   London
They told me to go but I couldn't. I stayed very quiet. I was
interested, but it was more awful than I thought to see the child cut
up. However I made no trouble, and it was a kind of comfort to be
there and hear all they said. They hammered and hammered at her
poor bone, like driving tacks in a wall, and this gave her concussion.
So she did not become conscious again till half past two.

To Hannah Whitall Smith   20 January 1906   Milan
How I did hate to leave you all! It is most tantalizing to live so far
away. . . . I am slowly acquiring a philosophy to use when thee makes
thy escape, but I count every month as so much gained, and
deliciously gained, on the inevitable. I think about it a great deal, for
thee has been a thousand times more to me than most mothers are to
their children. Thee is woven into the very closest texture of my inner
life, and really I do not think an hour ever passes without my being in
some way occupied with the thought and feeling of thee. And it is
always delightful—how few children can say that of their parents!

To Hannah Whitall Smith   22 January 1906   I Tatti
I called for him [B.B.], and came in for a moment, and then the
Countess Serristori came. She was really quite wonderful, the way she
talked. In a way it was all B.B.'s training, his very ideas, in fact, but
put into French with such admirable clearness and comprehension
that they startled him. She is certainly the most brilliant woman I
know. He was delighted, and as we were going, he said to her 'I adore
you!' 'O don't say that when your wife is here!' she cried, blushing—
which is rare for her—'Mary knows it' he said—and I said 'I didn't
hear his remark' (I hadn't) 'but I hope it was something very
complimentary and affectionate.' 'You're an angel!' she said. Italians
find it *so* hard to understand a wife who isn't madly jealous. What a
people.

To Hannah Whitall Smith   12 February 1906   I Tatti
B.B. is lunching at D'Annunzio's. A half an hour ago a Conte and

Contessa Gregory were announced. She turned out to be a pushing little Englishwoman and he a naval officer. They had photos of a picture they wanted to sell, and they came not to ask B.B.'s opinion but to force him to say it was a Giorgione. I saw at a glance that it was by Romanino and I got the portfolio of photos and 'proved' it to them. They were furious, and said it was impossible to judge without seeing the picture, and that della Rovere of Venice had said it was a Giorgione, and Herbert Cook and Dr Williamson, those great luminaries, had been 'much puzzled'. 'I advise you,' I said, 'to stick by the critics who call it a Giorgione.' 'Well how *is* one to tell!' she replied. 'I can tell perfectly,' I answered, 'but I have no way of bringing my knowledge to you, unless you go through the training I have had.' She went away furious. They're all like that—it is too tiresome.

To Hannah Whitall Smith   14 February 1906   I Tatti
I fully endorse thy simile of the ways of men and earthquakes and avalanches as overwhelming and unexpected and irremediable. B.B. is now in a very earthquaking stage, that is to say he will not decide anything, not a single thing, he who used to fix his plans like adamant years beforehand. . . . But I shall undermine and perhaps have a better result to send thee pretty soon. I think it would be a good thing for him to come for awhile to London, but he seems not to want to. I think a hatred of England has got into him along with a hatred of Connoisseurship, as part of his nervous breakdown. But I do not intend to let him give in to it, although I may have to humour him for awhile. But it does make me laugh, and I fully sympathize with thy idea of men's wills as irresponsible, incalculable forces. It is the obverse side of their power, for after all it is the men who do the things that count in art and science and invention. So we must make the best of them.

To Hannah Whitall Smith   19 February 1906   I Tatti
It does put you so in the wrong to lose your temper, no matter if you were in the right to start with. If we could only get this firmly fixed in our minds, what a blessing it would be! That book on Breathing says that if you are angry, the thing to do is to fix your eyes on some distant spot, smile, take a long breath and slowly raise your arms, expelling the breath as you slowly let them fall. The fiercest anger is warranted to give way before this treatment—an argument, Karin, for the dependence of our emotions upon our physical reactions.

To Hannah Whitall Smith   27 February 1906   I Tatti
We had a good piece of news today, namely that the American dealer who bought our Lotto has resold it and is sending us a cheque for fourteen hundred pounds—making eighteen hundred in all, more than double what we paid for it. I should like to burst right out and get a motor, but the prudent B.B. says he is going to apply it to paying off our debt at Barings—for a good many years ago he borrowed £2000 from them to give his brother, and on this we pay every year £100.... B.B.'s great hope is to get together a large enough income to stop worrying over money or selling or anything of that kind, and of course he is right.

That year it had been arranged for both Karin and Ray to go out to Florence, to be further 'broadened'. Alys was asked to choose two young Englishmen to join the party, and her choices proved to be more congenial and a little more sophisticated than Willie Taylor the preceding year. They were Maynard Keynes, who had just finished at Cambridge, and Geoffrey Scott from Oxford, nephew of the renowned C.P. Scott, editor of the *Manchester Guardian*. Geoffrey was intelligent, full of aesthetic sensibility and handsome, but highly neurotic. Maynard was rather taken with Ray.

To Hannah Whitall Smith   23 March 1906   I Tatti
Alys's young man, Geoffrey Scott, came to dine tonight (Keynes was arriving at Florence later) and we all liked him, including Uncle Bernhard. He was really a success, and I am looking forward to our trip with much less trepidation. I was pleased with Ray, too, for she said a lot of very subtle interesting things. She has come out tremendously since she went to college—she often takes part in the conversation and never says anything banal. Young Scott was quite up to B.B.'s most startling paradoxes, and afterwards we were laughing over it, and saying how young people take as commonplace the things we have taken painful years to elaborate. He was really a success with us all, and I beg thee to tell Alys and thank her for sending us such a pleasant travelling companion.

To Hannah Whitall Smith   25 March 1906   I Tatti
We met Mr Keynes at the Uffizi today, and found him very nice. We all had tea together, and a discussion about Mathematics, and things went very well. We are off today.

To Hannah Whitall Smith   25 March 1906   I Tatti
We got across the bridge in Florence and *broke down*! Another motor
came and tugged us back to the garage.... We started out in a new
motor (a beauty!) went about 15 miles and then got out and ate our
lunch in the rain, seated on a pile of stones in a muddy road.

To Hannah Whitall Smith   1 April 1906   I Tatti
I *was* glad no other grown-up was along—I could not have borne more
than my own discomfort! But to them everything was fun—the scrappy
lunches under trees in a drizzle, the arrival at cold, carpetless and fireless
inns, the horrible meals, the mud that one day simply covered poor Scott,
penetrating even to his teeth and tongue, and covering his face with a
yellow slime, the punctures (we only had two), the enforced changes of
route ... everything was the occasion for laughter and merriment.

To Hannah Whitall Smith   14 April 1906   I Tatti
Thee will be amused to hear that by now the young people have quite
emancipated themselves from me.... Last night I could not get them to
bed ... and I was torn between my duties as a chaperone and my
irresistible longing to get to bed. Just then a terrible thunderstorm came
on, shaking the house, followed by swift rain. We ran out on to the
balcony. I am afraid it *was* I who then said 'What fun it would be to go out
in this rain in old clothes!' There was an instant yell of delight and each
rushed off to put on their oldest things.... This is just the experience I
wanted for Ray and Karin—nice, thoroughly intellectual boys who
rouse all their intellectual ambitions and do not lead them into any
nonsense. It is a thorough success. How different from Willy.

To Hannah Whitall Smith   Easter Monday 16 April 1906   I Tatti
Keynes was too funny, he lay curled up in a rug, all huddled together
and looking indescribably wicked. He is quite a clown in his way, and
now that he feels at home, he does the most ridiculous things. And
even the great Scott is unbending more and more.

The girls and the young men went home, but there were more
pleasures to be had that spring, when two Balliol friends of Logan's
came to stay at I Tatti, Donald Tovey and Frederic Kelly, both
musicians, whom Mary persuaded to play for her.

To Hannah Whitall Smith   24 April 1906   I Tatti
I wish they [the young people] were here now, for all this music, and

these *very* nice bandersnatches, Tovey and Kelly. Tovey, of course, *isn't* a bandersnatch—he is like a great full reservoir, and we put in our little pipes and receive more water from the reservoir than our shallow vessels can hold. To change the metaphor, we feel quite drowned sometimes.... But he is wonderful, as a mind, as a talker, and of course as a musician—wonderful!

To Ray, Karin, Scott and Keynes   30 April 1906   I Tatti
It is what is called the stroke of midnight: and as I have no one to sit up with or for, I will send you all another letter, to tell you I Tatti news. For you are still here with me, in an intangible but very real way—much realler than my present guests or even the delightful musicians who have just gone.... Of course we had constant discussions about Bach versus Beethoven—the latter of whom we find too expressive, too moving for pure Art. Kelly said something one day that put me on the track of our difficulty. He said he found both painting and sculpture terribly demoralizing—far too exciting to be safe. This had never occurred to me. Of course he didn't know how to look—and I feel pretty sure that in regard to Beethoven we don't know how to listen. We let our feelings for life get the better of our appreciation of art. It was one of those remarks that throw a light. Now they are gone, and there are two places where I cannot go without a heartache—one is the cypresses where we all used to sit, and the other is the music-room where I heard such divine things.

To Hannah Whitall Smith   24 May 1906   I Tatti
To think that poor Uncle Horace has passed away! Of course it will be an immense relief to all his family, though I daresay they will scarcely admit it even to themselves—and certainly not to anyone else. Probably also he will be a *little* missed, doesn't thee think? For he had his sweet sides; and they are sure to remember these now....

When we were driving back we saw on the hill a most fearful apparition—a round waddling mass, and a tall blaze of bright brown beside it. These queer things turned out to be Gertrude Stein and her brother, she fatter than ever (but fairly clean) and he with an enormous bright brown beard and corduroy clothes to match, made with wide trousers and fly-away jacket, like the typical Parisian 'art student'. They simply hurt one's eyes, and Emily [Dawson, a cousin] and I drove on, after shaking hands with them, in pained amazement.

To Hannah Whitall Smith   3 June 1906   Teramo
Our motor gave out twice, but it was all so beautiful we didn't mind—
I mean the 'back seat' didn't mind, for poor Albert [Henraux] was
utterly furious, and gave his poor chauffeur a most epic scolding. At
the first breakdown we had tea, and at the second we walked on and
explored the little village. On the way we invented a new saint, the
patron saint of Rubber Tyres—*Santa Cacciuccia (caoutchouc)*. Her
emblem is a wheel, like St Catherine, but of course of rubber, and she
holds a palm and a pair of goggles. She performed her first miracle
yesterday on the return journey. It was getting late, and we prayed to
her to preserve us from a third smash. Presently—bang—whizz—and
Albert stopped the motor, throwing out his arms in despair.... We
were all *sure* it was finished, and that we should have to wait an hour
and a half, for he had no fresh tyre, but would have had to mend this
one. To our stupefaction, everything was all right and we went on our
way praising our new Saint!

To Hannah Whitall Smith   6 June 1906   Abruzzi
By this time he [Placci] and Albert and the French chauffeur Leon all
firmly believe in *Santa Cacciuccia,* and not for *anything* would they omit
her litany at the stony bits of the roads. And it *is* true that since we
began to pray to her, we haven't had a single accident to the wheels,
and we've been over the *most awful* roads! I can easily understand how
people come to believe in their own inventions, for even I would be a
little uneasy if we omitted the customary prayers. *Santa Clavina* (of the
Keys) was less propitious to us today ... still we did see everything in
the end, so we think she heard our prayer *'Ora pro Portis'.* Placci is
bursting with *another* patron saint he has invented, who is so *Latin* I
can scarcely tell thee about her. But of course on a trip like this, in
such a country, the question of W.C.s is of almost first importance.
They are sometimes too horrible to use. So he prays aloud to
Sant'Aquacloacina 'Ora pro locis' (*les lieux* as they say in French) and I
must say she has heard our petition since we began to send it up.

To Hannah Whitall Smith   12 June 1906   I Tatti
B.B. has taken such a loathing to Connoisseurship, and especially to
the work for his 'Northern Italians', that I am tired of urging him to
go on and finish up just this job. It is clear as daylight that if he wants
his lists to be decent, he must go to Milan and Germany. He has been
complaining and complaining about this, and saying I forced him to
do work he loathed and considered of no importance, and I suppose I

have gradually been getting sick of it, though I did not realise it till this morning. I took him in the notes on Milan, so that we could choose out just the necessary things and stay as short a time as possible. He was rather disagreeable about it, and very cross. Finally I begged him to get on with the business and not row, or I should be tempted to burn the whole thing. 'I wish you would' he said. This seemed to me so silly that I left the room. Then I thought what was the use of urging him on, for maybe he really is too ill, and he seems to hate it so. So I came back and told him I thought he had better give it up for the present, as it evidently made him sick, and did not conduce (for me) to his agreeableness as a companion. He said 'If only the fire had burned up all the beastly thing!' So I said it was very easy and again he said he wished I would burn it all, the whole thing. So I said I would, and took the typewritten lists, and all our notes, and hid them away. I told him they were burnt, for I wanted to see if he was genuine or only silly. It appears to me to be the latter, unless he is losing his mind, for now he seems set on going to Germany by himself and trying to make out afresh his old lists. If this continues, of course I shall bring him back his notes, and I hope I shan't hear any more of these complaints.... I do feel sorry for him, for he isn't well, and I know how irritable that makes one. But, all the same, he has *got* to learn not to be cross with me about the work, for it is too disagreeable for me, and is something I don't feel called on to stand.

To Bernhard Berenson   4 August 1906   Friday's Hill
[Geoffrey was staying with Mary and her children for a long weekend.]
We made a fire under the trees and sat about it singing and reciting poetry till midnight, and then stretched ourselves out upon our earthy beds. Alas I can no longer indulge in these juvenile sports. My limbs ached intolerably, and whenever I fell asleep I woke myself with groans. So at 3 o'clock I went indoors, after taking a look at all the young people, including Geoffrey Scott, who were sleeping peacefully.

CHAPTER NINE

Portents

August 1906–March 1909

Two highly important events occurred in the course of the next two years: the Berensons bought the villa I Tatti, and B.B. began to work with the great picture dealer Joseph Duveen, who was to wield such an influence on his career.

When the lease of the villa expired, and the landlord would not renew it, B.B. and Mary had to decide whether to move—possibly to England—or to raise the money to buy the place, and after much thought and worry, they decided on the latter. They paid what was then the large sum of £6000, and had to borrow from a number of friends, including Janet Ross and their neighbour, the wealthy American banker, Henry Cannon, as the picture market was in a very depressed condition.

The first meeting between B.B. and Duveen occurred at the end of 1906. To start with B.B. dealt with him in the same way as with other dealers, but by degrees the firm—which had branches in London, Paris and New York—absorbed the greater part of B.B.'s efforts as an expert, as it had absorbed the greater part of the American market in pictures. Bernhard never liked 'Jo'—later to become Lord Duveen—though bound to him by financial advantage, but Mary had a sneaking affection for his piratical exuberance.

Meanwhile, undeterred by their penchant for young men, Mary had been much taken with Maynard Keynes and Geoffrey Scott, preferring (unlike her daughters) the helpless fragility of Geoffrey to the more independent brilliance of Maynard. She worked very hard to cherish Geoffrey, and to find suitable jobs for him, and in the process saw more of him than B.B. liked. B.B.'s rages were becoming more frequent, and the clashes between his demands and Mary's preoccupation with her family and her protégé were becoming sharper. He was developing a marked taste for the society of the fashionable ladies he met in Paris and St Moritz, and they for his.

To Bernhard Berenson   5 August 1906   Friday's Hill
[Geoffrey had told Mary that he had wished on the full moon that his love affair might not become sordid.] Of course I had to be very careful in what I said, not to frighten him, and yet not to encourage him in what will probably lead to disaster. So I took the line that such affections might well be beautiful and inspiring in youth but become dotty and disgusting if men persisted in them into middle age. He knew this, and cited several Dons and said he knew he must get out of it in time—but then, he said, it was so wonderful to adore a handsome, talented, beautiful youth, he wasn't sure that it might not be worth everything in life. I hope I talked to him wisely. I tried to... I haven't any very strong views on this matter, has thee?

To Bernhard Berenson   11 September 1906   London
This last week Ray has seen a great deal of Keynes (who is a perfect dear) and, as she isn't a bit stupid, she gathered from his talk, which is sometimes rather wild and mystical, the whole doctrine of the peculiar *culte* to which he and Scott belong—I mean the more spiritual sides of it—and I very much doubt whether, in their cases, it has gone much further. Scott, I know, is a practiser of thy theories of ideated romance. But what interested me was to see how very wide-awake Ray was, yet without a touch of Latin 'curiosity'. The case would interest the Serristori, she could hardly believe it possible.

Diary   19 September 1906   Milan
Most delightful to see Bernhard again, who is more interesting than ever. He is quite worn out with Mrs Gardner, who besides being a Sorceress is a Vampire. She preserves her marvellous youth by preying upon young men.

To Hannah Whitall Smith   20 September 1906   Milan
This morning B.B. said 'Mary, there is just one picture here in Milan that knocks all the rest into a cocked hat.' I immediately replied 'I'm sure you mean the Bellini *Pietà'—and he did*! He was delighted that I knew without a word what he meant. It *is* fun to have the same impressions, it gives them more than double value.

To Ray Costelloe   4 October 1906   I Tatti
I had a letter from Scott some time ago, elucidating his psychology for my benefit in this wise. 'I like an ideal margin between me and "facts"

in which I can advance and withdraw and move about generally without appreciably affecting a situation. Without that I feel neither safe, nor tranquil nor happy, nor able to appreciate value and enjoy what there is to enjoy.' ... B.B. is very much like that in his 'world'. I never feel a bit afraid of 'facts'. I *like* 'em; for they give more substance to the dream (it always is a dream), which to me is the most fascinating when it clings close, like a veil, to the mysterious thing that is other-than-myself.

To Bernhard Berenson   27 October 1906   London
I dined with Keynes last night, his first visitor in his bachelor's quarters near here, a nice little flat, like College rooms, with a nice dinner, well served. He feels rather desperate at being labelled* and is ready to do almost anything to escape from the impending monotony of doing the same thing every day at the same time for the next 40 years. I daresay he would get married—it is the psychological moment—if he weren't too wrapped up in his men Friendships.

To Senda Berenson   26 November 1906   London
I think he [Berenson] has lunched or dined—sometimes both—with Lady Sassoon fourteen days out of the sixteen he has been in London, the other meals he has eaten with his other adorer, Mrs Leslie, commonly said to be the mistress of the Duke of Connaught, who, by the way, is awfully jealous! This is what he has risen (or sunk) to— making Royal Personages jealous! It is very diverting—and I am glad if it makes him like to come more to England.

To Hannah Whitall Smith   19 December 1906   I Tatti
I am fighting a cold with the aid of cinnamon. But what is harder to fight is our depression over B.B.'s book [*The Northern Italian Painters of the Renaissance*] and our disgust with it. I read it aloud to him in the morning, and we both think it sounds so awful that we are discouraged and disgusted. He wants to throw it all into the fire and be done with it. He says if it is really as bad as my revolting way of reading it makes it sound, he certainly won't publish it or anything else about Italian art all the days of his life. We wrangle over it and then laugh, and then pick up the pieces, and end, by lunchtime, in collapse from ennui and fatigue and contempt. But I keep hoping it will get better as we go on.

* Keynes had just been appointed to the India Office.

135

We are still toiling over it, to make the transitions easier, and to elucidate some of the cryptic ideas. It is crammed with ideas, but they are so condensed and so clumsily stated that it is hard to follow them. We have begun now on the lists, and here all my faults of carelessness and slovenliness are boomeranging back on my own head. I am alas very inaccurate, and these lists are *despairing*. Altogether this new book is going to be the result of much anguish....

The Countess Serristori came. She was radiant and most amusing. I told her what Dora Labouchere's stepmother had said about revenge, *c'est un plat qui se mange froid*—that saying which appeared to me so *perfectly horrible*. She wasn't a bit surprised at it, she said no Italian or Spaniard or Pole could be, for nearly every one of them felt that way. Revenge and Hate, she said, were passions almost as strong and far more lasting than Love. She gave instance after instance of it, as she had herself seen it. Among others the grandfather of her best friend, a very great and influential Florentine, Conte Ricasoli. He suspected his wife of loving someone else, so he drove her to his castle near Siena—Brolio—a fortress-like castle on a dreary mountain, and there he told her she was to stay till she died, and never go out of the gate until she was carried through on her bier. He did not tell her why (though I dare say she knew) and he gave her as sole companion (and gaoler) one of his own mistresses. She lived there seventeen years before her death. That was eating your revenge cold if you like! As she went on and on with similar stories which seemed to come straight out of Stendhal's novels, I got a queer feeling of being on a frail little raft on a stormy sea, with great waves of horrible passions breaking all around me. It is hard to imagine that life is like that. Certainly, certainly *we others* are more civilized!

I went to Mrs Ross's this afternoon, leaving B.B. and Algar* asleep on separate sofas. She had that young American violinist Albert Spalding, who has been making such a stir in London and Germany, and he plays most beautifully. He is only 18, a regular boy, full of fun and folly—but he has a divine talent. They are coming here tomorrow to play Bach and other real things, for he played rather rotten emotional things at Aunt Janet's.

*Algar Thorold, English Catholic writer.

To Hannah Whitall Smith   4 January 1907   I Tatti
They played the sort of music Mrs Ross likes, modern and emotional, and as I was in for it, I abandoned myself to the mere sensuous pleasure of it, mixed with the sentimentality it evoked. It was certainly *pleasant*, and it interested me, for I believe that's the way most people listen to music. But I felt a little disgusted all the same, and when I came back, and told B.B. and Algar (who had spent the afternoon napping!), B.B. called it 'wallowing'. Algar confessed it was *his* way of listening to music, but, when pressed, admitted that he would not for an instant tolerate similar effects in literature—which is the art he takes most seriously. After all I suspect all nice people are quite seriously moral somewhere, about the things they care most for. It crops out in queer places and leaves queer gaps in some people, certainly, but it is always there. B.B. says he is an uncompromising Puritan in the Arts, and even I tend that way. When you *really* care, you can't bear to be put off with anything but the best.

Diary   8 January 1907   I Tatti
B.B. got into an awful rage and behaved like a naughty child: so I took the key and went off into the woods. It was *un jour entre les jours*, and I grew calm and happy. I think I should have been very agreeable on coming in, but it is not right for a man to be so disagreeable, and so I told him at lunch that his way of taking things made it extremely unpleasant for me to take the practical burdens off his shoulders as I try to do. I said it made me loathe that kind of work (if only he were nice about it I shouldn't mind *anything*!) at which he got furious and pushed away his plate and rushed out of the room saying 'Well, go on loathing it' like a bad boy.... There is still a glower on, and we are merely polite. I do *wish* he weren't so bad tempered.

To her Family   11 January 1907   I Tatti
When I went in to give B.B. the top of the morning today, I found him in bed not even reading, but lying there sadly meditating his life. He mysteriously said that he was at a great crisis and did not know what was going to become of him. I asked him if he would permit me to describe his crisis, and upon his signifying his assent, I said 'The truth is that THIS time you have really and truly come to the end of your mental energy. *All is over.* You will never write or think again. Your brain is already attacked with fatty degeneration and you are doomed to pass a dull, idle, unthinking existence. Of course these symptoms, in the past, have come about as regularly as the trees shed their

leaves, about once a year, but THIS time it is of course utterly different; this time it really IS all over!' He could not deny that I had hit off his mysterious complaint pretty well. I have noticed that he always feels like that a few months before he sets to work on something new. You might, with some indelicacy, call it the 'morning sickness' which precedes the birth of a new book! Are we all as unconscious as that, taking our habitual peculiarities with such gravity? Again, *je me demande*.

To Hannah Whitall Smith   16 January 1907   I Tatti
As I certainly don't want to add to thy burdens in any way, but on the contrary, to lighten them, I write at once to say thee really may lift Geoffrey Scott out of thy cart, for of course I won't force him upon you who do not like him—especially not upon Ray, who is clearly in the man-hating stage. I like him, it is the sort of mind and character that always interests me, and it interests me to see it so young, before it is grown up at all. But I see his defects and impossibilities very clearly and am not particularly hopeful about his future. Unfortunately many of the people I like are lame ducks; sometimes I think that is why I like them.

To Hannah Whitall Smith   20 January 1907   I Tatti
We have had a young architect named Cecil Pinsent, the Houghtons' 'adopted son', staying here. He seems nice, but not very exciting. Miss Blood [a neighbour] came to dinner and Hutchins Hapgood afterwards, and we talked and talked, and the boy listened in a sort of daze. At the end he said 'How educating!' but I wonder if he could have meant it.

To Hannah Whitall Smith   24 January 1907   I Tatti
Tomorrow I hope to begin regular work with B.B. again, [on *The Northern Italian Painters*] preparing our revisions. Though we rage so, it is fun. What tremendous luck it is after all to have bagged (excuse the inelegant word) a congenial life-companion. There's always a kind of point to things when I have B.B. to share them. It makes all the difference.

Diary   27 January 1907   I Tatti
Our work is really at last *en train*, and we are rushing along in a most exhilarating way. B.B. says he *loves* it when he really gets at it.

To Ray Costelloe   1 February 1907   I Tatti
I am appalled to think of thy going in for politics in a 'serious' way.

But I am sure it will bore thee to death. I don't mind its interfering with thy mathematics, but I grieve to think *what* a burden it will all be! However it is clear to me that thee is, to put it elegantly, thy own funeral.

Some years previously Hannah, who had become very crippled by arthritis, had moved from the house in Grosvenor Road to a flat, and in 1906, since both the girls were now away from home at boarding school or college most of the time, Friday's Hill was also given up, and Hannah took a riverside house with Logan, at Iffley, on the outskirts of Oxford. Soon after they had settled in, and been 'called on' by local residents, as was customary, Karin had to have another operation, and Mary returned to London to be with her.

To Hannah Whitall Smith   6 March 1907   I Tatti
So you aren't a 'County Family'—it is very sad! As to thy 'not knowing yet' whether you're Upper Middle or only Middle, I *was* amused. I do wonder which it is—it is really very important. Probably the prospects in life of Ray and Karin depend on the settlement of this delicate point.

Diary   13 March 1907   I Tatti
My going to England is a great weight on our minds—it does break things so awfully. But I feel as if I couldn't really enjoy anything after a certain time of absence from the children. It is like a thirst that little by little pushes to the front and crowds out all other (even pleasanter) experiences.

To Hannah Whitall Smith   17 March 1907   I Tatti
I am glad to be assured that I am coming home to an *Upper* Middle class family! It is well to know, and I think thee is right in considering that the Archdeacon's visiting cards settled the vexed question!

To Bernhard Berenson   1 April 1907   London
She [Karin] *must* stay in town for awhile. Of course it is terribly important for her, her life's happiness in a sense hangs on it, for deafness is such a shockingly maiming thing. But at the same time I am not unaware that these very weeks are part of *our* life also—and we haven't an endless succession of Springs to pass together. I have been thinking of this a great deal, and as thee really is my dearest dear I

shall try to arrange more and more for our existence to be less broken up by these other dear—but less dear—beings.

To Bernhard Berenson   7 April 1907   London
Blaydes had the next table ... he is now studying surgery at St Bartholomew's Hospital. He looked fat and bald and heavy, with an indescribably off-class air of swagger about him—rather offensive looking, and ... talking with a touch of fatuity. The years have not done him any good—and I did not feel as if I cared to see him again.

To Bernhard Berenson   11 April 1907   London
Jephson came and took Ray and me out to lunch today. Ray thought him insufferable. He was, rather, from the outside; but I know some very nice qualities he has, and was better able to put up with his boasting etc.

To Hannah Whitall Smith   2 June 1907   I Tatti
Poor Roger Fry is rushing over Italy in a closed automobile, the biggest, heaviest, swiftest, strongest ever built, with Pierpont Morgan, his mistress, Mrs Douglas, and a nominal chaperone, who emits a gurgle before every work of art the way a motor-horn toots before every obstacle. The prize chauffeur goes as fast as he can, of course, and executes almost impossible feats, such as running up on the platform of churches, and the courier, swollen with pride, shouts '*Avanti!*' in loud tones on every possible occasion. Morgan pretends to hate it, but really loves his royal receptions, and the crowds of dealers who line the passages in every hotel he goes to.

To Bernhard Berenson   9 August 1907   London
I got so low that I *had* to do something.... or rather *it* had to, whatever the it in us is that takes care we don't fall below a certain level. I cannot weave any myths about it, but I can understand how religious people feel when they pray '*Agnus Dei, qui tollis peccata mundi, Dona nobis pacem.*' For there is something that, at the worst, comes and lifts the human burden and soothes one into peace. I have loved the children in an unreasoning way, with an instinctive belief that no serious misfortune could befall *them*, whatever happened to the rest of the world. And the tearing out of that illusion has been terrible. But the operation has been performed, and now I must get well again ... and yesterday afternoon, going in a bus to my Bath, the change took place.... I have very little of the mystic strain in me. I come nearest to

140

it perhaps in a certain thrill I get sometimes in realizing how human life continues from one generation to another—there always being young things who are going through those enchanting phases I remember so well. The spring of life wells forth inexhaustibly—and I get a certain deep joy watching it. I wish thee felt as I do—doesn't Gladys appeal to thee in that way at all?

To Ray Costelloe   12 August 1907   London
Ray, I'm terribly discouraged about Karin's hearing. The labyrinth has now gone wrong. I cannot find 'the handle by which it may be borne', though I could bear it easily for myself. I feel as if it would be easier to die than to go on living and seeing her shut out from things and suffering from it as I fear she will. It is *too awful*. She cried all the way home in the cab, quietly to herself. I hope thee will never live to see a child of thine unhappy.

To Bernhard Berenson   2 September 1907   Harrogate
I am *awfully glad* thee has made friends with Gladys again! The adjectives thee used to describe her—'sane, balanced, judicial' nearly overcame me with amusement.... I adore Gladys and always have, without any break even when she wasn't 'judicial', and I am enchanted to think of having a visit from her... In fact the more we can attach that radiant creature to ourselves the happier I shall be. She is one of the greatest romances of my life.

Diary   26 September 1907   I Tatti
Scott has been quite ill ever since he came, unable to stir from the sofa. Dr Giglioli came up this morning, *per salutarmi*, and I persuaded Geoffrey to see him.... The doctor says it is nothing definite, but sheer nerves, of course more difficult than anything.

William Rothenstein, later to become Sir William Rothenstein, a distinguished painter and an old friend of the Pearsall Smith family, had been invited to I Tatti to paint Bernhard's portrait.

To Hannah Whitall Smith   22 October 1907   I Tatti
Rothenstein is going to take me now to see Gordon Craig*, Ellen

* Gordon Craig was the illegitimate son of the actress Ellen Terry and an influential figure in the history of stage design. He was at this time living in Settignano.

141

Terry's son, who is by way of revolutionizing the stage in a sense of which we approve.

To Hannah Whitall Smith   24 October 1907   I Tatti
I must tell you all, now, about the famous Gordon Craig. We went to see him in his house, where he lives in a sort of community of an indeterminate kind—best not to enquire too closely!—with a number of young assistants of both sexes. Regardless of such minor distinctions as male and female, they all wore bare feet and sandals and square-cut blouses.... Gordon Craig himself is a very handsome man of about 35 with long light hair. He wore very baggy trousers and a shirt unbuttoned at the neck (and considerably further down) and spoke like a prophet, with all the ladies turning up their eyes and heaving appreciative sighs. He showed us, however, some *first-rate* etchings, of great originality and beauty, rather Blake-ish things, and he gave us a little puppet show to explain his ideas on the new style he is working for. This is extremely impressive, and one could forgive him much. But his followers!

Diary   30 October 1907   I Tatti
Scott got wild over his packing this morning. I drove him down in a hailstorm and saw him off at 3. How he hated to go! And I to have him go, for besides caring extraordinarily much for him as a person, I do love having young creatures around to do things for and to make happy and spoil. But it is over—and now 'to fresh woods and pastures new'.

To her Family   7 November 1907   I Tatti
Now I must tell you about Gordon Craig who came to dinner last night, in an open cellular shirt and sandals, looking, however, very handsome and distinguished. He is really a *charmeur*, for all his wildness, and we all talked with great animation and interest. He abhors the Stage, as it is, considers it low and abominable, pandering to the worst tastes. He says the only thing is to banish actors and especially actresses from the boards, and substitute cubes of various sizes, which move by machinery and are lighted in various complicated ways. There are to be no words, nothing but light, form and movement, and all entirely impersonal and unrepresentative.... What is nice about him is that he is a clever man, in spite of his crankiness, and takes his fad intellectually, not personally, so that he will listen to anything one has to say without taking offence.

To her Family   9 November 1907   I Tatti

Well, we had quite a visitation from Gordon Craig yesterday. I brought him up from town with me. He sat on the sofa and began to tell us about a letter he had written to the Duse, urging her to give up her horrible style of acting and come over to him. As a sort of halfway house between real acting and the movement of Cubes, he proposed to allow her to 'interpret' the Song of Solomon. We asked him a great many questions about this, but could not arrive at any very clear idea of what he meant—in fact we came to the conclusion that he did not quite know himself. Apparently there is to be a stage formed of 'the Children of the Cubes', Screens, hundreds of them of all sizes, which can be opened and shut as the mood demands, giving immense vistas or narrowing down to a small opening in a wall. In front of these Screens (I use a capital letter, for he always spoke of them in a hushed voice, as of something very sacred) there will stand ten or twelve or twenty veiled and draped figures, representing the potential moods of the Song of Solomon. Madame Duse will glide in, and as she recites the poem, she will waken to life with gestures one or other of these Moods, herself putting on various masks appropriate to the sentiments. B.B. asked if these masks would be lying on a shelf or concealed under her robes, or how she would get them, but Craig waved this away as quite irrelevant. He seemed to think it would make it all more remote if she recited it in Latin, although of course it would be far better if she did not recite at all, but let the Screens and the lights do all the work.

To her Family   8 December 1907   I Tatti

You all seem agreed that we had better buy I Tatti, and so we have made an offer of 140,000 francs. This includes the two big *poderi*, worked by two families of *contadini*, and their ovens and houses and everything. Also the carpenter's house at the bottom of the field, and the little villino on the road opposite it.

To Hannah Whitall Smith   15 December 1907   I Tatti

I left off for lunch, and then came the Fattore to tell us that this place is ours!!!!!!!! Lord Westbury has accepted our offer and now there remains nothing to do but to settle terms for the oxen and cows and horses of the contadini, and to pay. The latter is the painful part, but everyone says that the place is a good investment at six thousand pounds.... When will Logan come down to help us in the planning? I don't want to do a thing about the place until I have his advice.

143

To Hannah Whitall Smith   8 January 1908   I Tatti
Both B.B. and I are very much relieved about Karin since we have
had the chance to watch her all this time. She is REALLY HAPPY—
happier by far than most people, in spite of her anxiety. It is her
nature aided by philosophy and it is a splendid thing.

Diary   9 January 1908   I Tatti
Bernhard and I aren't on quite satisfactory terms at present.
Marriage is so difficult. It seems so flat to be merely friendly and
devoted, after romance, that one accepts it with indignation and
bitterness—at least I think that is Bernhard's feeling—although he
allows and encourages himself to indulge in the most romantic
feelings towards Aline Sassoon. I must have the courage to talk it all
out with him, for it is a pity to go on with unsaid dissatisfactions and
grievances. He wants me to be more devoted than I *can* be.

Diary   26 January 1908   I Tatti
I read a letter from B.B. to Aline Sassoon (a wrong thing to do, but I
wanted so to believe him, and yet couldn't, by instinct somehow, yet I
hoped the letter would be less devoted than the last one) and he said
he had thought and dreamt of no one else while he was at Siena, that
she must never doubt him, that he was '*tuo, tuo solo*' and so on. I
cannot truthfully say I *could* write like that to anyone, because I am
really fonder of Bernhard than anyone else, and Scott, the only male
human being I feel much drawn to, is too young. The idea of love of
that sort with him is inconceivable, but still I am awfully fond of him
and do think about him a great deal.... Literature has nothing but
contempt for an old woman growing fond of boys, and one reason I do
not tell Bernhard about it is because he at once uses these hackneyed
forms upon me, and they hurt and disgust me. I could quite well make
fun of his devotion to the brainless fashionable lady—but I don't, for I
am sure to him it doesn't come under that obvious category. It is life
and sweetness to him.

Diary   26 January 1908   I Tatti
I got off an article on Giotto to the *Rassegna d'Arte*.

Diary   2 February 1908   I Tatti
There is something amiss with my attitude; I think if I had another
child, I should be quite satisfied, really. But nothing would induce
Bernhard to have one!

To Hannah Whitall Smith   18 February 1908   I Tatti
Placci was amazed today, and remained behind to say it was perfectly phenomenal to hear a practising musician talk as Albert [Spalding] did. We were speaking of the kind of air which does what a good contour does in drawing, suggests all the modelling through pure line, and Alberto was contending that the essential harmonies can be suggested by some of the great masters in a simple, unharmonized melody. Oh Young People, Grandma! I know thee has always had a cult for them. But think what it is to feel that one has handed on ideas one has reached, say at forty, to an intelligent person who isn't yet twenty—ideas that THEY can take as a starting point. What fun to watch them go on. And I think Alberto will go on in spite of his difficult milieu and the exactions of his profession, for he has real intellect.

To Bernhard Berenson   22 March 1908   Oxford
We were talking about Val*, and his utter abhorrence of the 'intellectual' and 'moral' milieu in which he finds himself, Val being merely a stupid commonplace normal boy. Alys said she felt the incongruity very much and wished she and Bertie could 'sometimes relax from their high intellectual and moral tension'. 'But we never do' she said. Ray and Karin and I, and even Mother, exchanged appalled glances.

To Bernhard Berenson   29 March 1908   Oxford
Scott will travel out with me and I said we could put him up for a few days till Cannon† was ready for him at La Doccia—which he may possibly be at once. This makes him very happy, as I Tatti is his highest ideal of bliss. He takes the goods the gods give him very simply, however, and seems to think of me as a divinely inspired fairy-godmother, or mother-in-law—or something only *too* suitable to my age! I shall be very glad to have a chance of trying to change thy impression, which, however exaggerated, caused me many hours of pain. Thee shall have nothing further to complain of, I hope, but only an intelligent young friend added to our small circle of intimates.

* Val Worthington, a cousin whose education was being paid for by Bertie Russell.
† Henry W. Cannon, the wealthy American banker who lived at La Doccia nearby. Mary had arranged a job for Geoffrey as travelling companion to one of his sons.

To Maynard Keynes   16 April 1908   I Tatti

I have been telling everybody that Scott was engaged upon a work treating of Greek Myth in Renaissance Art. There are half a dozen people who finally believe he is writing the book. I wonder if he will? I gave him a fountain pen filled with ink to take notes, but I daresay they will act the opposite way. The real way to treat youth is to urge you *not* to do that which we desire you should do!

To Hannah Whitall Smith   18 April 1908   I Tatti

I confess I was *amazed* when they said I was notorious as an adoring wife! They said that B.B. was widely envied, not only for the help he gets from me in his work, but above all for the adoring sympathy. Indeed, they hinted that I carried it to the point of making him rather ridiculous! The funny thing is that this particular form of conjugality is one I have always been most down on!! I suppose at least I make that effect, since they say so (and others I have asked since say the same)—but I declare I'm jiggered: I did think it was the *one* fault I did not have.

However, considering it calmly, I see there is some truth in it. I *do* admire and respect B.B. very much, and his conversation interests me more than any other person's, I suppose partly because we need no preliminary explanations or definitions. And I am genuinely most sincerely fond of him.... But I really feel like a blackleg to the Cause of Woman when I think of producing that conventional wifely impression upon others. It is rather awful!

To her Family   21 June 1908   I Tatti

We had a glorious swim of 'ladies only', Miss Stein [Gertrude] going in clad in nothing but her Fat. I really didn't know such enormities existed. She didn't seem to mind particularly, though. I felt quite slim and girlish in comparison.

The Berensons had decided to make another 'business' visit to the States in the autumn, accompanied this time by Ray and Karin, who were to spend a year at Bryn Mawr, the college where Mary's learned and formidable cousin Carey Thomas was President.

In Paris, during the summer, B.B. made useful further contacts with Duveen, while Mary perforce occupied herself in buying fashionable clothes for the trip, suffering agonies, as she always did, in the process. On their arrival in the States they found themselves once more absorbed into the extraordinary world of the very wealthy. They returned in March of the following year.

146

Diary   30 June 1908   Paris
Bernhard went to Duveens. They were most flattering, and if 1/10 of what they say is true, a future of affluence lies before us! They said they would never touch an Italian picture but on his advice, and would give him 10% of their profit on sales!

Diary   14 July 1908   [London?]
I have been busy all day attending to my American outfit. B.B. says this time he won't make any objection to my taking money for lectures—in fact he has already got me one for $100 in New York. So I shall pay for 3 evenings, 2 tailor and one afternoon dress I am getting.

To Ray Costelloe   15 July 1908   London
The peerless Maynard dined with me. He is *too* happy at having shaken himself free of the India Office. He hopes to get a fellowship at King's for £100, another £100 for lecturing in Economics, and his family will give him still another £100. But he will never rise to £1000 a year and a KCB. But he said that if you were going to sell yourself you would want a bigger price than that!

To Bernhard Berenson   29 September 1908   Bryn Mawr College
Ray came in after dinner to consult about her courses. Carey [Thomas] was magnificent and started her just as I should wish, banishing from her fancy forever those silly dreams of 'electrical engineering', I know not what. She said 'Ray, it's *ridiculous* to imagine you aren't going to lead a life of Culture. Of course you *are*, with all your advantages,' and went on to praise that life above all others (she is never in doubt about her own opinion) and Ray came right round.

To Hannah Whitall Smith   29 October 1908   Dorchester
Mrs Gardner came to lunch with us the other day, and was as full of lies and charm and provokingness as usual. She is trying to sell her diamonds (some of them) now to pay the fine of $152,000 demanded by the Government for that ill-advised attempt of her friend to smuggle in some of her possessions. She says it was done without consulting her—*chi lo sa?* None but myself believes her, and I'm not sure I do!

To Hannah Whitall Smith   5 November 1908   Boston
Somehow this time the people do not particularly interest me. Not that they are less cordial or hospitable, but somehow that I do feel definitely as if I belonged to a different world, geographically,

intellectually, morally. We haven't the same values, and I feel as if the mere human friendliness were just the common race denominator which one might as well experience in Tuscany as come 4000 miles to seek. I know I am wrong, but there it is.

To Hannah Whitall Smith   24 December 1908   Washington
I will send thee a line to describe our interview with the President [Theodore Roosevelt] .... he came along to us and, pinning on a most expansive smile that showed some of his back teeth, he said '*So* happy to meet you Mr Berrington—no, Mr Fischer, you needn't introduce him, the name of Berrington is an introduction in itself.'

To Hannah Whitall Smith   28 December 1908   Washington
Thee asks after my dress [a dog had been sick on it]. It is such a pretty one that I wear it on small occasions, although the two spots with the colour washed away are very visible.... I wore it last night to a small informal dinner at the house of the Keeper of the prints in the Congressional Library, Mr Parsons. I cannot think what the 'informality' was, for the hostess and the three other ladies were most gorgeously dressed and we had terrapin and all sorts of things. *I* obeyed the text of the invitation and wore my spoiled dress and adorned my feet with gumshoes which *I forgot to take off*! I discovered this after dinner when I was talking to Mr Putnam, the head Librarian. My feet felt simply boiled, and I looked about to see if I wasn't sitting over a register. Then I discovered those huge ungainly things hiding from sight my nice bronze slippers and bronze silk stockings! So I took them off then and there, and everybody laughed at me.

To Hannah Whitall Smith   15 January 1909   New York
The other night we attended a 'red' dinner—ie all the favours and ornaments and candles and cakes and fruits and ice-creams were red, and I dare say a lot of other things I didn't notice. There were about 20 people, about two million worth of diamonds and no lady except myself had on a dress that cost less than £75. My hostess said I was to have a Mr Archer Huntington on my other side (her husband being on my left) and she hoped it would be all right, he was very queer, and almost never went out except to their house, but a very interesting man etc. So a huge man in an especially large chair provided for him took his seat—we passed the time of day. Suddenly he asked 'Who is your favourite poet?' 'Milton, I think,' I replied. 'Good God! Do you

148

mean it?' 'Yes'. 'Great Scott! To think I should hear a woman say this. Is it possible you are fond of reading?' 'I am,' I said. 'Well,' he said, 'you are the first woman I ever met who is. You're sure you aren't a fraud?' 'About that, no.'

After this opening we got into a great talk. This monstrous (but very jolly) creature spluttering and gasping at almost everything I said, about as if I should hear a lap-dog talk!... After dinner he rushed up to our hostess and said 'I have never met such a wonderful woman! I can't believe it! It is like discovering Niagara!' We were hardly to be separated for the rest of the evening, and the very next day came invitations from his wife to dine etc, etc. Well, who was he? He was the *one man in America* we most wanted to meet for every reason. And we had almost given up hope, for he is rather inaccessible. He already has about a hundred million dollars and will inherit 80 million more, to mention the grossest fact first.... and but for 'Society' we should probably never have met him! So thee must admit, even thee, Grandma, that for our circumstances, fashionable dinners and so on are most useful.

To Mrs Gardner   31 January 1909   New York
The 'Ramus [a name Mrs Gardner gave B.B.] has just called out to tell me to do a thing that absolutely takes my breath away, namely to propose myself modestly as a lecturer in your divine music room, either for some charity, or just for a few of the people you might want to invite. He says I should repeat the lectures I gave at the Colony Club, which, it appears, were quite a success, and which I have been asked to repeat in a great many places. I'm not going to though, but IF it were *votre plaisir* to repeat them (with improvements) in your house, it would make me happier than anything else would. In that case, I should illustrate them as much as possible with slides from your pictures —for many of them could perfectly bring out my points. The lectures are about the four influences that started the 'New Art Criticism'— Morelli for Connoisseurship, Milanesi for History, William James for Psychology and Pater for Aesthetics—and the end is a kind of peroration on the Enjoyment of Art which nearly made 'Ramus faint, for he said I had stolen the central idea of his Great Work.

To Hannah Whitall Smith   6 February 1909   New York
We have (alas!) sold the Perugino* for £2000 (do not let this go out of

---

* The *Madonna and Child with Bird in Hand*; *see* p. 94, note.

the family), which will go towards paying off the debt on I Tatti. I will write later about how it is to be sent.

To Hannah Whitall Smith   *16 February 1909*   *New York*
We spent yesterday at Princeton with two millionaires, who were awfully nice as well. They told us that everyone in their set in N.Y. was discussing which really knew the most, Mr or *Mrs* B.B. We have been so tactful that all the ladies uphold me, the men B.B!

To Ray Costelloe   *18 February 1909*   *New York*
Mr Pierpont Morgan's secretary, Miss Belle Greene, a most wild and woolly and EXTRAORDINARY young person, wants thee and Ellie* to go to the opera with her, in her box, on Thursday March 4th.

To Mrs Gardner   *22 March 1909*   *SS* Mauretania
The end of our fantastic American adventure has been finding ourselves, all undeserving, in what is known as the 'millionaires' Corner' at a table with Mrs Potter Palmer. The voyage has passed quickly and pleasantly. As you can imagine, the 'Ramus has been flirting with the prettiest lady on board, Maxine Elliot, and with the naughtiest, Lady Cunard.

---

* Ellie Rendel, a school and college friend of Ray's and niece of Lytton Strachey, who went with Ray to Bryn Mawr. She later became doctor to Virginia Woolf and many other Bloomsbury characters.

150

CHAPTER TEN

A House Divided

April 1909–April 1911

B.B. and Mary had ordered a number of radical improvements to be made to the villa while they were in America. On their way home B.B. stopped over in Paris for discussions with Duveen, while Mary went straight back to Florence and found that nothing in the house had been done right, and that everything was in disorder.

She sacked the Italian architect and employed instead Cecil Pinsent, the young English architect whose acquaintance they had made before the trip, and persuaded Geoffrey Scott to work with him. Both the 'Artichokes', as the family called them, were almost continuously in residence and working at the villa for the next two years. Cecil's ideas, including those for a new library, were excellent, but his control of Italian workmen left much to be desired; Geoffrey had excellent taste, but his health and energy were minimal.

Mary's preoccupation with Geoffrey had meanwhile become all-consuming, while on his side B.B. had fallen passionately, though not happily, in love with Belle da Costa Greene, librarian to Pierpont Morgan, whom they had met in New York. She was a wild, unconventional, handsome and learned young woman, the one Mary had described to Ray as 'extraordinary'. These parallel emotional involvements, on top of the appalling chaos in the house (which lasted throughout the period, and which B.B. blamed entirely on Mary), rendered relations between them more and more strained.

I Tatti was quite uninhabitable, and Mary stayed first with 'Aunt Janet Ross' and then in a little villa nearby.

To Hannah Whitall Smith   4 April 1909   Poggio Gherardo [with the Rosses]
Just a line to say I have got here safely. I was met by Roberto and the cook and the *Ragionare* [Estate Manager] and the Signora Triulzi,

each one with a tale of woe. *Nothing* is done, not even the kitchen! Nor the electricity. It is too awful.

To Bernhard Berenson   13 April 1909   Villa Linda
As he [Geoffrey Scott] doesn't feel a spark of romance about me, although gratitude and affection, my excitement about him has come to an end, I almost regret to say. And I am not sure whether a mere friendship, without a touch of sex, is possible to me. He isn't my child after all.

To Bernhard Berenson   18 April 1909   Villa Linda
I am sorry thee feels sometimes as if thee wishes thee had never known me. It is when I try to take paths around to compass my ends. This is certainly a habit I have, and I have been confirmed in it by my great dread of thy falling into a rage. Quite often thy rages don't come off because thee doesn't know things. But the system is a very bad one, and I do not really like it one bit. It is a more destroying thing than rages, and I daresay may quite well make thee feel like giving up the ghost, for it is dreadful to meet mush when you want something firm to catch hold of. About a great many things I am likely to deceive thee less as I understand—and approve—thy point of view—which I apprehend fully at last—namely that one must shut the door on anything that tends to *break up* or really damage the life we have undertaken in common, with full and intelligent consent. That I really understand at last, and I shall not do anything against it for love of man or child. But I am likely to conceal from thee arrangements which seem good to me to make, and which might not seem so to thee—for the person who enters into personal relations with servants and such has to muddle along as best *they* can, and I know thee won't be consulted at every stage. Then when thee enters in with fury at some given point, thee will probably meet with deception or else a return rage that makes me ill for days and disgusts me with everything. But I should rather be open with thee, and I can just vaguely conceive how sick it makes thee when I'm not. So I shall try, and thee must help me by humour and kindness.

To her Family   18 April 1909   Villa Linda
I shall truly be in Despair. Logan and I felt like Babes-in-the-Wood today, before the things we had to settle. I am thankful he is here though—it is a great support. You wouldn't imagine how many things come up in the smallest bit of property. Why did we buy it? I

wish B.B. were here. I should propose simply taking a piece for ourselves, and letting the rest on lease, and bothering no more.

To Bernhard Berenson   *24 April 1909*   *Villa Linda*
He [Geoffrey Scott] is perhaps a little on my nerves for his limpness, but I try not to turn against him, for he can't help it. And his presence has absolutely hindered me in nothing. We have almost completely talked ourselves out, and the only inexhaustible topic is the depressing one of his future, which we have discussed *ad nauseam*. I mean to remain fond of him, instead of throwing him over in my disgusting Cyclopean way, the moment he ceases to produce an agreeable sensation in me, and I want to be kind to him *in so far as I can without interfering in thy comfort or the general things we want to do.*

To her Family   *7 May 1909*   *Villa Linda*
The avalanche has begun to move! I took B.B. to the villa this morning, and he came back in such a state of absolute depression that he not only found everything was entirely *my* fault, but he wanted to sell the place and all our possessions and go and live in hired rooms in a non-Italian town. I have never seen him so depressed and miserable and cross (not to put too fine a point upon it!). I suppose he can't help it, he has '*certi nervi*' but I began to wish he hadn't come down.

They finally managed to move back to the villa, but B.B. was desperate for Belle Greene, and even a visit from the lovely Gladys did not raise his spirits.

To her Family   *25 May 1909*   *I Tatti*
Cecil [Pinsent] ... is terribly afraid of B.B. and B.B. is gloomy and preoccupied. Cecil gasped when Gladys tweaked B.B.'s beard and called him 'Bibbins', but we all cheered up, she made us laugh, even while we were grieving over her reckless and absurd behaviour.

To Bernhard Berenson   *4 September 1909*   *Méru, France*
I know my whole personality is so curiously (and delightfully on the whole) intertwined with thine that I never have the faintest atom of real rebellion or imagination that it could be otherwise. ... But how to make this all clear to thee? I despair sometimes, and sometimes I think it so absurd that at our age we should still be going on like this, that I can't bear to say anything.

To Bernhard Berenson   *24 September 1909   I Tatti*

Bernhard, I want thee please to promise me a genuine kindness for which not only *Dio* but I will *renderti merito*, and that is if thee sees Scott not to say anything to lead him to suppose there is a 'situation' as regards him. He feels that he overstayed his welcome last spring, and is very repentant, but I do not think he has any idea of any other complication, and thee will really be doing me a kindness I shall never forget if thee leaves him in ignorance. If I have been stupid about him and disagreeable to thee (for which I am very sorry), it is all my doing, and not at all his, and our friendship is now so quiet and suitable and satisfactory, and I think such a comfort to him, that thee would make me really unhappy if thee upset this peaceful condition.

B.B. returned to Paris in a state of deep gloom, and Mary joined Karin in Switzerland, still not fully aware that his infatuation for Belle Greene was the reason for his misery, and afraid it was all due to her sins.

To Bernhard Berenson   *29 September 1909   Vevey*

Anyhow I should want to see only thee and no one else. Or is thee too preoccupied and busy? I am really almost too sad here, thinking of thy being unhappy, I should come *dans les meilleurs dispositions* to see what I can possibly do. Thy being sad really hurts me, I can't get away from it.

To Bernhard Berenson   *30 September 1909   Vevey*

I do not want to do anything except to see thee and find out what is the matter, and what thee wants me to do. It is very hard to quarrel by letter, and I am feeling so ill I cannot go on, at least I *can*, but it is very miserable. I am distressed to have thee unhappy and I am quite sure there is no real reason for it. I think even sometimes it may be a blessing to pull us both out of our reserves—for we have not been quite open with each other. I don't mean as to facts, for I have none on my conscience, but as to feelings.

To Bernhard Berenson   *2 October 1909   Vevey*

I do want us both, now we are entering upon the 'maturity of middle ages' to be nothing but frank. If we can be—*ohne Feindschaft*, as thee says, all will be well. I know thee hasn't been quite frank with me—I don't really mind, because, well, I don't know, it rather endears thee to me, bringing thee to the common level, and anyhow I like thee as thee is, without schemes for changing thee.

To Hannah Whitall Smith   *23 October 1909   I Tatti*
I found a most terrific warfare on between Roberto and all the household. He had bought a pistol and had threatened to kill Aristea, Beppa, Cecil, Ammanati and the Contadino. Cecil disabled the pistol secretly, so there was no real danger, but Roberto was like a madman—and all because I said I would keep Aristea's wages for her. I must admit there is justice in his idea that if she had any money she would at once leave him *planté là*. He is so revolting that I should quite sympathize with her, and even his children are revolting, and he encourages them to be hateful to her. However I consulted Ammanati and he said it was Italian law, and Aristea herself has offered to give up her wages to him for a quiet life, so things are settling down. But I foresee that I shan't keep Roberto very long. I have taken a thorough dislike to him.

To Mrs Berenson   1 November 1909   I Tatti
Bernhard got home from Paris last Friday, and although we are still in confusion, with dirt and noise and lots of workmen about, he is delighted to be here. He feels very well satisfied with his stay in Paris, where he had made enough money to pay for all our improvements *and* the automobile.... We have asked a French painter [René Piot] whose work we admire to paint us some frescoes in the new room, and he is so happy and excited over it that his wife says he wakes up at 3 or 4 in the morning to tell her his ideas. He feels that he is 'made' now that Bernhard has taken him up.

To her Family   21 November 1909   I Tatti
I think you must hate my letters, all full of woes, and with no fun in them. But there it is, we are having a hard grapple. I hope it is *once for all*. But it has brought to light all the latent or semi-covered differences between us, the different things we want to get out of our few remaining years. B.B. wants perfection of physical surroundings, and his taste for luxury is modelled on a style of life (and income) I have absolutely no desire to emulate. My ideas go no further than comfort, and beauty in general lines, and friendly people when one isn't at work or reading, and a little spare money to go on sprees with, such as taking people—particularly young people—on motor trips and the like. The kind of thing B.B. wants involves a sort of supervision I

155

don't want to give. I should sooner live in a cave. . . . This is by far the worst matrimonial crisis we have had, and I do not at all see the end of it. Still, I daresay we shall obey the Universal Rule 'Thou shalt muddle along somehow' and perhaps when peace and quiet comes and B.B. is able to settle down and work, he will find himself contented with humble comfort.

To her Family   1 December 1909   I Tatti
Every shadow of bitterness and indignation has faded from my spirit, and with that the difficult spiritual load has gone. All the rest is remediable, but that horrid sense of being unfairly treated is what blackens the universe. B.B. has it, and I think it is the source of the worst evils of the present situation. . . . When one steps aside one sees it all. If one only had as clear a vision of *one's own* failings!!! . . . I have made up my mind to set myself quietly and immovably against fashionableness in any form. As I think B.B.'s wishes are not quite reasonable, but the result of instincts not under the control of his intellect, I shall oppose them not [only] by arguments but also by unreason. . . . I am *convinced* that it would be a mistake to try to live as worldly people, and I shall not make the attempt . . . but in everything that touches B.B.'s own comfort I am going to be specially careful.

To William Rothenstein   16 December 1909   I Tatti
I fear we saw our last of Gordon Craig yesterday: he grew unmistakably cold and even bitter when he found that we would neither 'write him up', nor form a syndicate for supplying him with unlimited money for his experiments. We asked Placci to meet him, for if anybody could help him, it is Placci, but Craig was so vague and vaporous in response to Placci's questions, talking about 'Love and Confidence' as the only things necessary for the Reform of the Theatre, that after he had gone Placci said '*C'est un fou enfermé*'. . . . It seemed so amusing, so gay and Bohemian when we first went—and now it seems inexpressibly sordid and anxious.

To Gertrude Stein   19 December 1909   I Tatti
We have made the hills echo with discussions of your book [*Three Lives*], but I daresay it would bore you to hear them—some people are bound to take one view, and others another, and with your insight I daresay you can readily group the people and their views together! B.B. joins me in congratulations and thanks, and in best Xmas greetings.

To Ray Costelloe   26 December 1909   I Tatti
Uncle Bernhard is quieting down like a lamb, and I think now all will
go well. It is odd, but I feel fonder of him than ever, in spite of all his
horribility—for he has been *horrible*! I feel if I can endure him after all
this, it means that I truly do love him—and after all it is a queer thing
being fond of a person. I really don't believe he could put me off
any more than thee or Karin could! So our woes have had one nice
result.

To her Family   8 January 1910   I Tatti
Today I have been grappling with Cecil, who just slides through one's
fingers like an eel. He never *finishes* anything, and B.B. is getting crazy
with these months of temporary makeshifts.

To Bernhard Berenson   6 February 1910   Oxford
Dearest, dearest Bernhard, I am most awfully sorry thee had a
second's uneasiness and distrust. I want never to give thee *that* kind
again—there are plenty of others inevitable to our two characters, but
that surely is superfluous. But I entirely understand thy not trusting
me, and I beg thee always to say out at once if thee thinks I'm not
running straight. I told thee all there was to tell about Scott, and did
not mention him again because I did not see him again.... I have
never felt so tender and truly loving towards thee, Bernhard, and I
wouldn't for anything cause thee anxiety or trouble.

To Mrs Berenson   13 February 1910   I Tatti
Ray has come with a notebook and a stylographic pen to take
shorthand notes of the next time Bernhard gets into a rage, to send to
my mother, who can't really believe that such an 'angelic man' (for
she admires and loves him beyond words) ever can turn into the old
fiend I describe! They think I malign him, but fortunately for my
reputation for veracity he did get furious with Lucy [Perkins, their
secretary] at the station yesterday and said such fierce things to her
that Ray's hair fairly stood on end. She is now upstairs writing an
account of it.

To Hannah Whitall Smith   7 March 1910   I Tatti
I really cannot think God is like thee, for isn't it expressly told us
'Whom the Lord loveth he chastiseth' and that cannot be said to be
thy practice!! No, alas, he seems to me much more like the 'mysterious
and unscrupulous Providence' of the old Negro. But seriously, I take

thy argument to be that the whole must be greater than the parts, and that if the little part which is thee rises to such heights of love as *thee* feels towards thy children and grandchildren, the Creator of thee must feel that and much more. It isn't an argument, but I can well believe it is an *insight*, and that thee doesn't believe it, but thee *knows* it. After Karin's second operation, as I sat by her bed, holding her hand, not sure whether she wouldn't drift away from touch and sight, I seemed to *know*, by love, that I should never lose her. Only, alas, my mind won't agree that this is any proof of an objective fact.

To Ray Costelloe   19 March 1910   I Tatti
I dreamt a most savage dream last night, of somehow having thee and Karin shut up in a room upstairs in the house in Filbert Street that Grandma and Grandpa used to live in. I hadn't seen you for ages, there was some barrier, and I was going round the dressmakers and galleries and dinners, keeping away from the idea of you. But as I was having a dress tried on, it got too much for me, and I snatched off my clothes and rushed naked (I regret to say) through the streets, burst open the door, flung a sponge I was carrying at the head of the butler (our new one) who tried to stop me, bounded up the stairs 3 at a time, and entered upon you, who were busily playing 'Demon'. 'Why Mother!' you cried in horror at my wild appearance, and I woke up saying 'When the maternal passion is unsatisfied a woman is quite crazy.'

To her Family   21 March 1910   I Tatti
Do the Liberals really expect a victory? I told B.B. it would be *un très beau geste* if he would give Bertie £1500 to stand for Parliament, but I regret to say his lack of sympathy with Liberalism amounts to a positive disinclination to assist in its triumph. To me, I fear it would appeal in a more personal way. I should like Alys and Bertie to have what they want. This betrays little public spirit, and must be set down to the Italian climate....

Just after lunch they came to tell Cecil that the water pipes had broken in Grazzini's house at the bottom of our place, and he went down to see to it. He came back full of laughter, for it seems the water had stopped running some days ago. Grazzini first tried with a wire, and then applied his lips, which after severe suction induced two half decomposed lizards to come forth. I can understand *one* lizard, but why did he suck out a second?

To her Family   9 April 1910   I Tatti
When we got home, B.B. found a letter that made him perfectly furious. One of the big Paris dealers had sent him an enormous photograph and two thousand francs, asking him to write on the back of the photograph the *opinion he had already expressed* when he saw the picture in their shop, that it was a portrait by Moroni. As B.B. had never seen the picture, and as in any case it could never be said it was a Moroni, for it wasn't, he at once returned the money and told them they were under some delusion. The picture is better than a Moroni, but not by anyone we know by name. Last night came a letter partly bullying, partly cringing, saying that the dealer, his son and his nephew all distinctly remembered B.B.'s pronouncing the picture a Moroni, and that on this guarantee, they had sold it to Sir William Van Horne who now required B.B.'s written guarantee, that they wouldn't for anything have had such a mistake happen with one of their important clients, that they would pay B.B. 15,000 (fr) and more for getting them out of the business, and so on, that they wanted to present him with various objets d'art and *traiter des grosses affaires* in the future and so on—evidently an attempt at intimidation and bribery at the same time. To which B.B. replied that he had certainly never seen the picture, that if he had he could never have called it a Moroni, that their letter seemed a very strange one to him, and that if such a misunderstanding ever happened again he would be afraid ever to go to their shop, that he could accept no presents from them and so on. It is rather disgusting to have one's nose rubbed in such cheating. I hope Van Horne will return the picture on their hands.

To her Family   28 April 1910   Rome
He [B.B.] has just torn up a cheque for two hundred pounds! It came from a dealer who was grateful to him for selling his picture, but B.B. says he cannot take presents (except in the way of strict business) from dealers. I daresay he is right, but I hated to see it go!

To her Family   22 May 1910   I Tatti
I enclose B.B.'s cheque for £200. He says it is really satanic of him to lend it for such a purpose, for he hates the idea of Bertie wasting his fine intellectual powers on politics! Also he is a Tory, and has a fearful dread of all this Liberal-socialistic legislation. *Et voilà pour lui!* But all the same he is delighted to send the money, and he sends his love to thee and his thanks for thy letter. He *is* nice, in spite of his 'rages'.

159

To her Family   24 May 1910   I Tatti
Dr Giglioli said that B.B. was certainly getting worse and that he needed a thorough psychical treatment of some kind. We went together to his room and tried to talk to him, and B.B. repeated ... that there was no one he could trust to carry out his wishes, that he hated this house and all Italy, that life was hell, and he was going away never to see it or us again. Dr Giglioli says it seems to him very serious and I am indeed troubled and anxious. It is a kind of obsession, an *idée fixe*, which is gradually taking entire possession of him. And yet we are *all* working for him in every way, doing our best.... It is not certain that I am the best person to go with him [on a suggested cure] as so much of his irritation is directed against me.

To Mrs Gardner   5 June 1910   I Tatti
Gladys is in Paris 'on her own'; but it is mysterious how extravagant she can afford to be.... When she comes to Florence, she wears only one old dress, no gloves, torn slippers, no underclothes but stockings, and is incredibly dirty, scarcely combing her hair and living without a maid in a little room with a dozen dogs and laughing and happy all the time. She is the despair of her friends.*

To her Family   17 June 1910   I Tatti
Miss Stein came, fat beyond the limits of imagination, and brought an awful Jewess, dressed in a window-curtain, with her hair completely hiding her forehead and even her eyebrows. She was called Toklas.... It was a 'nawful' party, but they all stayed till midnight.

To Bernhard Berenson   21 August 1910   Oxford
I was really quite charmed by Miss Greene [Belle Greene was on a visit to Europe], and wish this might be the beginning of a permanent relation, such as our middle-aged bourgeois, romantic souls sigh for. Men are supposed to like Episodes, but I do not think thee is that kind, and I hope thee will make this into something lasting and agreeable. I shall certainly help thee, both for thee, and *per conto mio*, for I love her youth, her *élan*. I find her remarkably attractive, too.

One thing, dear, I want to say in thy ear. Don't boast to her, either of thy moral or intellectual qualities. She will enjoy them more finding

* Gladys Deacon remained single until she was forty, and then married the Duke of Marlborough. She died in 1977.

160

them out. I have played the serpent's part in encouraging thee to talk too much about thy virtues and excellencies. It seemed balanced by thy attacks of humility, but I think it is a mistake with other people, and I saw she had noticed it. For example, if the conversation *is* unusually good *chez nous* (which I am by no means sure of) let her discover it when she comes, *und so weiter*, especially about thy own differences from and superiorities to the rest of mankind. Excuse this marital word: but I want thee to appear at thy best and I know how young people laugh at our middle-aged self-complacency.

To her Family   7 September 1910   Munich
I have just got back from the [Moslem] Exhibition, dead tired, but *so* interested and pleased that I really can't express half. *All* my sort of foolish prejudice against Oriental Art has gone—I begin to understand its fascination. I have no more 'grudges', and I have *thoroughly enjoyed* these days! It is perhaps the biggest sort of experience open to one at my age, this plunging deep into the heart of a new art, a new way of seeing the world, a new standard of values. Not that one art is essentially different from another, but one kind gives a different emphasis, and now I do understand the charm of this particular emphasis on colour and decoration apart from, even in contrast to, representation. It has been a real 'unbuttoning', Grandma, like some of thy sudden 'openings', and I am rejoicing over it.

To her Family   19 September 1910   I Tatti
I am sorry I haven't written today, but B.B.'s arrival turned everything topsy turvy. Strange little man! Why are we all so terrified of him? The mere rumour of his coming sets us all from the meanest scullion to Piot-the-frescoes in unwonted activity, clearing away things likely to offend his lordly eye and smartening up things. Agostino [the new butler] shaved off his moustaches which he had grown in honour of his marriage.... He arrived, I regret to say, in a rage, and I hardly dared to bring him up fearing he would massacre Cecil.... M Piot was positively trembling with excitement when B.B. entered the library, and Geoffrey went wandering about all day feeling, he said, exactly as if twins were being born in the house. B.B. liked the frescoes, he liked the new corridor, he was on the whole pleased with everything. And now he has gone and we are all relaxed.

To Bernhard Berenson   20 September 1910   I Tatti
Dearest Bernhard, I am trying to go over the whole tale of our life

161

together in the light of the things we said yesterday. We used to quarrel dreadfully even before I fell in love with Obrist and it was generally (not always) because I either concealed things from thee or misrepresented them. Of course this was worse each time I fell in love because thee would not believe that that *need* not alter a really sincere devoted already existing relation. I only knew it myself after one or two experiments, but I believed it by nature. It was not possible to be open with thee, when thee disbelieved in it root and branch, and had no sympathy with what nevertheless seemed real to me, was real though not permanent. So I have fallen into the way of not telling thee a good many things that I feel would rouse thy scorn or wrath in opposition. Yet thee is so sensitive that thee has felt a secretiveness there, all the more annoying and baffling because it was so incomplete, because it alternated with sincerity! Poor Bernhard, it has been thy cross, such a heavy one. I am trying to see it from thy point of view....

I am rather terrified, my dear, to discover the extent and depth of thy present feeling [Belle Greene, had gone to Venice with the Berensons]. I fear it is not all for thy happiness. Yet I suppose thee would not wish it otherwise. I am only afraid for you both when she has to go.

To her Family   26 September 1910   Venice
B.B. has of late complained bitterly that I 'managed' him and even deceived him, and I said it was quite true, I did. I explained why (not for the first time, either!) because he was unreasonable and furious and difficult and also because his nerves got upset and he felt ill, so that to save myself bother and him strain I did often try to keep things from him. He refused to believe that was the reason, and said I did it to annoy because my deeds were evil and my heart black. So I said I would tell him everything in the future, even the things he hates to hear, and we left it at that.

To Hannah Whitall Smith   1 October 1910   Venice
He [Scott] is, as thee says, a 'milk-coddling sort of person' (wonderful phrase), but he is extraordinarily entertaining and really good, and as soon as he and Cecil make a little money (which they are in a fair way of doing), he will be all right.

To her Family   3 November 1910   I Tatti
About the frescoes—they are really more horrible than words can

162

paint. Cecil says that in mechanically reducing [enlarging?] them, millimetre by millimetre to the required scale, they lost at each change something of their grace and ease ... and indeed the result shows it, for the figures are wooden and distorted—horrible beyond words. I do not speak of the colour, for he says that will change as the walls dry, but still none of us believe that it will ever get cool or pleasant. I cannot imagine a more complete fiasco. I wonder how B.B. will get out of it.

To her Family   9 November 1910   I Tatti
At the gate stood a huge crowd of people, Aristea, very voluble in their midst, who explained to me that at last they had found the cause of the awful smell that had pervaded the house for the last month, coming in whiffs from the library. This had been severally put down to the smell of the frescoes, to the smell of Piot and his workmen who slept in the library, to the boiling of his glues, to dead rats and cats in the floor—to I know not what. This morning it was discovered that the little room under the library where the furnace is, all the whitewashers and all the *zoccoli* [painted wainscots] varnishers had used as a W.C. and general refuse ground, burying their filth when they left under a mound of shallow earth. They had excavated down to the rock to get a place, and that rock is now so impregnated with the filth that it has to be blasted and then coated with whitewash. The men who were excavating were coming out nearly fainting, and Aristea drew me to a choice place just inside the gate where I got a blast that nearly knocked me down.

To her Family   10 November 1910   I Tatti
The unbroken list of misfortunes can be taken up at any point and continued backwards and forwards, I fear indefinitely. I think we must be what poor Beppa firmly believes herself to be—'*stregata*'— that is, tormented by witchcraft. She thinks Roberto has taken one of her hairs and put it in a frog's mouth, and thus filled her with evil spirits (the 'thus' doesn't sound very logical to us, but it satisfies her!) and when she has rumblings in the stomach (which might happen to anyone even unacquainted with Roberto) she says these are the hungry spirits crying out for food. They have a cricket in the kitchen and when its 'Kri-Kri' is heard she thinks it is a spirit after her. I daresay Roberto has *stregato* the whole household, how else can our fortunes be explained?

To her Family   13 November 1910   I Tatti
B.B. arrived last night in a fairly peaceful frame of mind, very enthusiastic about all we have done in the house, and disposed to like everything. He took a horrified peep at the frescoes, but decided to adopt the pose of not having seen them, and silence towards poor Piot, which *I* think is much more cruel than telling him right out. Whether they will be covered with whitewashed canvas, or plainly whitewashed, or whether they will be cut out of the wall and given to Piot or to the French Institute here, is to be decided later on. Keep them he agrees we cannot.

In spite of Piot's assurances the colour of the frescoes has remained an undimmed combination of tomato and ultramarine. After much toing and froing, they were covered with whitewashed canvas, and remained covered until there was a Franco-Italian exhibition in Florence in the 1970s, when the organisers negotiated their resuscitation with the Director of the Harvard Center for Italian Renaissance Studies which is now based in the villa. At the time of writing (1982) they are still uncovered.

To her Family   15 November 1910   I Tatti
I will tell you the Fireplace Woe. I already explained how our continual smell of soot came from two chimneys in one. The day before he [B.B.] came, we had that put right, but the man sent down such lots of soot, even through the closed flue, that the hearth was all stained. So I had the mason in to clean it. His boots ruined the pavement, so the varnisher had to come and give retouches. Then the fire was carelessly lighted with the damper closed, and the first puff of smoke that came out stained the grey whitewash round the opening. So I got the whitewasher to do *that* over, and in spite of spreading of many cloths and newspapers, he contrived to stain the hearth again, so the stone-mason had to come back, and I assure you it was finished only one hour before B.B.'s train got in!

To her Family   18 November 1910   I Tatti
I am evidently not the person to take care of him, as, at the sight of me, all his grievances and worries come up. I am seriously thinking of coming to England at once. If I find myself getting bothered by him, I will, because it is silly for me to break down as well. . . . So you may see me very soon, for certainly I thought him very trying yesterday, and it tired me out. Alas, Ray, I tried to get thy new motor out of him: in

some moods he would have given it to thee ... but I cannot take it for thee out of my joint account with Uncle Bernhard here without his approval, though *I* approve very much. He said 'I won't help her to get a motor for those beastly Liberal elections.'

To her Family   21 November 1910   I Tatti
B.B. is lying and quaking over the Piot business—he feels he is so much in the wrong to have expressed the confidence he so often did in Piot, and also to have declared himself satisfied with the sketch. Somehow he was thinking of other things, and was possessed of an almost lunatic optimism. I tell him if he likes he can put it *all* on me, that I cannot have my house upset for another two years.... By the way did I tell you that Beppa is quite well since burning a sheet of Roberto's handwriting by the light of the full moon, and burying it at the cross-roads? She seems a new person. I have advised her to take the precaution of repeating the ceremony *every* full moon. But she knows I do not believe in it, I *couldn't* quite go so far as letting her think I thought it all true.

To her Family   2 December 1910   I Tatti
I find his crossness—never a day, scarcely a meal without something unpleasant and inharmonious, depresses me more than it should. I understand readily how I can get on his nerves, for I am untidy where he is scrupulously neat, inexact where he is punctiliously exact, lacking in judgement, where he would have a plan, and so on. But by this time he really should know me. I know his defect of patience is only a fault like my untidyness, but it is a dreadfully anti-social fault, so ugly, really, that I don't know how to make satisfactory terms with it, and the outlook upon years of petty strife bores me. I cannot think of a real remedy either.... If I am too good-natured and affectionate, then he doesn't realize he is in the wrong. If I get cross, then the situation is really most distasteful to me. Most of the meals are taken up with grumblings about the food and I quite hate to go down to them sometimes. Well, we all have our trials. A mean man, an unsympathetic man, a boring man (above all!) would be much worse.

To her Family   29 December 1910   I Tatti
I do not dare to tell B.B. [that Cecil's stupidity had resulted in some of the cypresses blowing down] for it would be the very last straw—I am sure he would never see Cecil again.... I cannot help though, taking a

lot of blame to ourselves, for giving so young and inexperienced and cocksure a man such a free hand. It is like the frescoes, which I regard as *our* failure, quite as much as—even *more* than Piot's.

To Bernhard Berenson   22 February 1911   Oxford
I am sure thee feels generous and kindly towards me, but it is not love at all. I cannot tell thee how many times I have kissed thee and thee has *instinctively* turned away or put out my hand to thee and thee has not seen it, or, having seen it, disliked the idea and so paid no attention.... I have Mother and the children and Geoffrey to be fond of and care for in ways that express affection and augment it pleasantly, so I am not complaining about loneliness or my lot. But of course the inner core of our companionship is gone, and I have to manage the best I can. My limitations are many—it is doubtless true, as thee sometimes says, that I never made thee really happy; so I am being punished for it. I cannot say the same of thee. Thee has for long spaces been the cause of very great, the greatest happiness to me.

To Bernhard Berenson   1 March 1911   Oxford
I think if thee had told me everything when thee first came I would have tried to help thee bear it. Later it was more difficult for a good many rages had come between us.... As to *choosing between* Belle and me, it is ridiculous. Thee will never, by me at least, be put in such a position.... I like her myself, as a brave, generous, genuine creature.

To Alys Russell   13 April 1911   I Tatti
Thy letter puts a question one *should* ask oneself from time to time—what am I really working for? To answer it honestly I could only tell thee that at this present moment I am only scrabbling around. It is the *Sturm und Drang* of expiring middle age. On the other side is Old Age, and I want that to be peaceful and full of love and also of impersonal interests. I also hope to provide the right conditions for B.B.'s (I hope) best work. But at this moment it is more scrabble than anything else, alas.

To her Family   26 April 1911   I Tatti
I have always been hoping B.B.'s spirit would change, but now I think I must recognize his irritability with me as one of the fixed symptoms of his physical condition. He would certainly control it if he *could*, for the doctor and Agnes [Steffenberg, the masseuse] have both told him

166

that it was bad for me, and indeed he can see it is. But how hard to learn that another person is different from one's self! With him it passes in a few minutes, and he *feels better* for it, if it hasn't been a real Rage, but with me the slightest ruffling of my temper makes me ill for a long time, sometimes for days. I should rather do almost anything than get angry with a person I care about.

CHAPTER ELEVEN

Family Affairs

May 1911–July 1912

At the end of April 1911 Hannah had a stroke: it was quite unexpected, though she was seventy-nine years old, and delighted with the idea of death. Mary was sent for, but her mother died before she arrived.

That spring Bertie Russell fell in love with Lady Ottoline Morrell, the wife of Logan's greatest friend, Philip Morrell. Despite the nine years of agony when she and Bertie had continued to live together although Bertie had ceased loving her, Alys still hoped that he would turn to her again, and was unwilling to divorce him. Lady Ottoline refused to leave her husband and child and the affair eventually died. Bertie, however, did not return to Alys, and she set up house with Logan.

Karin, who had been tutored in Philosophy for her Cambridge exams by Russell, secured a First Class, with Distinction, becoming the first woman to get a Distinction in that subject at Cambridge. That same year Ray fell in love with Oliver Strachey, brother of Lytton Strachey, who had just returned from India, where he had been a Regional Traffic Manager on the Railways, and married him almost at once. A year later she had a daughter, Barbara—Mary's first grandchild.

Back in Italy Geoffrey Scott had now begun to fall in love right and left, and Mary, half jealous and half vicariously thrilled, listened as he poured out his agonies over his various loves. Bernhard, too, was still suffering over Belle Greene.

To Karin Costelloe   5 May 1911   Oxford
We are just starting to take Grandma's dear body to be burnt. How glad she would be to know it, and what jokes she would make about her 'old cocoon'. Her last letter to me came today. She said she was *rejoicing* in the idea of paralysis—she could not believe the good news of death, but she wanted me to feel as if the other, which she had

always dreaded, had lost its terrors. She thought of us at the last, not of herself. Oh if we could only believe she is now having half the joy she so confidently expected.

To Bernhard Berenson   5 May 1911   Oxford
Dear mother's ashes were brought back last night, and we thought how she would have laughed with joy to see us putting them in the corner of the cupboard where she kept her inexhaustible supply of stationery. Yesterday, to be Irish, would have been the happiest day of her life.

To Bernhard Berenson   6 May 1911   Oxford
Ray has, during this quiet year living with her grandma, 'found herself', as she feels, so that we all rely on her and have a sense of restfulness and trust and wisdom from her that is a surprise and delight to us all. She tells me she thinks she may marry Oliver Strachey.... They seem to understand each other, though they have apparently not spoken of love, and Ray means to go on with her work.*

To Bernhard Berenson   11 May 1911   Oxford
I am more concerned for Alys than for any of us. She is really in the midst of a serious nervous breakdown, caused, Emily [Dawson, a cousin of Mary's] and Ray tell me, by the fact that Bertie can no longer conceal the positive dislike he has for her. They think he tries very hard, but he is a queer nervous man, and it comes out in every detail. Also his friends treat her as a rank Outsider, and this makes things harder still. She practically told this to me, saying that it was her getting on Bertie's nerves that had broken her down. So she has no one to turn to, not even children, only Logan and me and her nieces, and the friends she has, who all feel she keeps them at arm's length. But in spite of this, she has been *splendid* all this time, so helpful and careful, so ready to do everything necessary. She has put Logan's house in order for him, has answered most of the letters and written to the necessary people, and she seems composed and cheerful. But she tells me she is really *desperate* ...

To Alys Russell   13 May 1911   Cambridge
This is my first, as it is thine, journey away from home without

* Ray dropped her earlier plan to be an electrical engineer and divided her energies between women's suffrage and writing.

169

Mother to write to. We feel exactly the same about it, I am sure, so I needn't say anything. But it is a *great comfort* to me to have thee to write to, and I feel as if she would be glad to have us keep up the family habits of intimacy.

To Bernhard Berenson   15 May 1911   Oxford
Oliver [Strachey] will stay until Wednesday I think, perhaps longer. I cannot think he would have come unless he had 'intentions'—but Karin and I are not *sure* that he is in love with her. What Karin thinks (he has flirted with her quite a lot) is that he wants to marry, but after 5 years in India is bewildered by the niceness of English girls and cannot decide among them. Probably Ray, with her direct methods, may bring him down with her little arrow. Her behaviour is 'simple as snow-flakes' and fills Karin with amazement to watch it. There is of course nothing unladylike about it, it is just a calm assumption that he cares.

To Alys Russell   24 May 1911   I Tatti
I really do not mind what seems his greatest folly [Belle Greene] for there is always something big and fine when a person of character and feeling falls in love—the generosity of the impulse (he who is very selfish about his own things is giving some of his loveliest pictures etc to her)—the *élan vital*, if nothing else, are compensation, but it is a dreadful blackness and bitterness of spirit that hangs around him, almost as bad as around poor Father, with his grudges ... He ought to realize that success *has* to provoke hatred, but he takes it as if it were deliberately plotted. And he greatly exaggerates. A new feature is appearing in this (which Dr Giglioli says is almost 'persecution mania') and that is that he begins to say that no one who is friends with these particular people can be his friends. This is too silly and very despairing for my poor eggs that remain in his basket, for Roger Fry is one of those people ... the *very* worst is that I feel scarcely the moral courage to bear it without contamination. I could never share it, but it breaks my courage towards life and destroys my serenity. Last night I wept bitterly—which is so different from sadly—for hours and hours. ... One feels so alone now. I can write to thee for I think thee can understand it all.

To her Family   15 June 1911   I Tatti
It is too dreadful—it seems almost worse as time goes on—not having Mother as our bond of reunion. One is so desolate cast adrift. I really

170

could not live here if I didn't feel that England was somehow 'really' Home.

To Bertrand Russell   17 June 1911   I Tatti
I have just received a telegram telling me of Karin's success in her Tripos, and I cannot help writing to express my gratitude for your overwhelming share in bringing this about. I feel most sincerely grateful. I cannot but hope further work of the same nature may be temptingly put in her way, for she seems to have a capacity to do it well, and it might 'make a man of her' so to speak.... I won't say anything about the decision you and Alys have come to, except to send you my love and sympathy in all you have certainly suffered over it, and to assure you of B.B.'s and my continued friendliness and good wishes.

That summer Bessie Berenson came out to stay, and promptly started a flirtation with the handsome Geoffrey.

To Bernhard Berenson   28 June 1911   Foligno
What she [Bessie] has enjoyed has been ... flirting. She and Scott were in each other's arms, literally all one day.... I did not speak to her, as she gets hurt so easily, but I did to him, and he said he was very much embarrassed by it, although it was not unpleasant, but he was so afraid of hurting her feelings.

To Bernhard Berenson   9 July 1911   Oxford
I feel such a passion of pity for thee I can hardly bear it. Unfortunately the pure pity gets spoiled, in spite of my deepest wish, by something more superficial and I find it so extremely hard to keep genuine and profound about it that I am often tempted to give up trying, and to go back to the conventional attitudes thee always took to my 'affairs'. Perhaps this would have been pragmatically better from the beginning, as *real sympathy* is an achievement for gods, not for mortals, or let us say for mothers, not for wives. However I have started in that path, and I do not think it would improve things now if I turned back. But I assure thee the variations between intense sympathy and amused contempt this affair of thine has caused me to pass through have been most agitating....

Bessie hasn't the faintest inkling of it, and Geoffrey only the faintest, but I was awfully 'hurt' (which is a decent way of saying jealous) when on the Abruzzi trip I found that Geoffrey turned

171

entirely to Bessie for sympathy in his enjoyment of what I had so looked forward to enjoying with him.... Demands are *never* fully satisfied, but love that finds its reward in just loving is perfect. How far away from that I am! But a spark of it is there, even towards thee, Bernhard.

To Bessie Berenson   14 July 1911   Oxford
The effect, or one effect, of my frankness about B.G. [Belle Greene] has been two letters repeating all the flattering things about her people say to him, how all and sundry admire her character, or her person. Strange that he shouldn't know perfectly well that people make a point of saying these things to him, particularly dealers who want to stand in with him!

To Bessie Berenson   21 July 1911   Oxford
I'm terrified of the rage B.B. will be in. I wish I weren't going to see him for a year. It makes me quite ill to think of what he will say, especially about my letting the boys [Cecil and Geoffrey] take it [the car] to Siena. I find he is frighteningly jealous of my interest in them and of everything I do for them. He says he must have my entire and complete attention and devotion, and that every sign of interest I display in their work or lives alienates him and fills him with resentment. I daresay I shall have to give them up for peace, although he spends at least 2 hours a day writing to Miss Greene, and manages to be so little engaging towards me that I do not think he has a right to these exaggerated claims.

To Bessie Berenson   5 August 1911   Oxford
B.B. is taken up with the idea that no one ever 'convinced' him of their devotion except B.G. (!!!) and is always spying out for instances of my having put him in second place, often indeed imagining them. He says if he had life to live over again he would try to marry a woman who had no other thought or interest but Himself. Bessie, how can men be such monstrous fools? I am sure wives would be only too glad to merge their existences in their husbands' *if they could*, but human nature isn't made so, and alas men are not so thrillingly absorbing as all that, except in that fatal period of being in love.

To Bernhard Berenson   17 August 1911   Oxford
Alys's situation is much worse, and she seems to grow sadder and sadder as the days go by. She says she hasn't the *faintest* hope of ever

172

hearing Bertie's voice again, and yet she cares for nothing else but news of him, his plans, his work, his health.

To Alys Russell   16 September 1911   I Tatti
This time Cecil has really kept his promises. The new little library is a *dream*—Logan would love it—the frescoes are gone—the house is as clean and dainty as a jewel.... I have decided to write to thee as if thee were Gram, and thee must take an interest in *everything*, all our woes and joys. I shall half think I am writing to her, somehow, so thee and Logan must simulate an interest if you do not feel it.

To Alys Russell and Logan Pearsall Smith   7 October 1911   I Tatti
Karin has taken to sitting up again, and she certainly resents my interference a good deal. She *cannot* see how unkind it is, for it seems so unreasonable of me not to go to sleep. But I can't do it, while she remains up, partly because I am somewhat worried for fear she may take to playing some prank or other, and partly because she sleeps over me, and if I were asleep would wake me by walking over my head. This trouble has now been to the fore ever since I have had young people staying here. You know the habits of the Artichokes [architects]. Willy was just as bad, and Val even worse, and so on—and I wish I could give up the struggle and let them go their own way. The only one it seriously hurt is Geoffrey, and anyhow they are all lazy and idle and can sleep till 10 or 11 in the morning. *I* can't, unfortunately, for everything goes wrong if I am not ready by 8 to give the day's orders and attend to things. So I *have* to have my massage at 7.15. I confess to getting very 'hairy' sometimes, when the youngsters who are getting everything from me, and scrupling not to take full advantage of it, get so carried away that they will not consider me at all ... I confess it is a trial to have young people here, and the enjoyment of their youthfulness is heavily paid for.

To Alys Russell and Logan Pearsall Smith   17 October 1911
It is what Grandma would call a poor prospect for Ray; but somehow I feel as if she would manage. They *had* to get married, of course [or they could not have lived together openly], but she said the other day it was a pity, and I half think if it were to do again I should be tempted to offer the Villino and seclusion without the formality of the Registry Office. It is very hard to know. But I simply

173

cannot think she will continue to be happy with Oliver—even with Oliver well!*

To Alys Russell   20 October 1911   I Tatti
I really don't see *how* one can get the victory over some things without religion. Lacking that help, there is only Time, and I daresay thee is wise to begin a monotonous and uneventful life, partly for rest and partly for the kind of dust it sprinkles over things. The surroundings seem favourable, and some day, I hope thee will wake up and find that resignation has stolen in upon thee. I can almost see myself in pretty much the same case, if B.B.'s irritability increased and I felt myself unable to cope with his exactions. The whole fabric of life would crash down, and I do not feel at all sure I should have energy enough to build up anything afterwards. But the *possibility* of this happening gives me the keenest sort of sympathy with thy present situation.

To her Family   16 November 1911   I Tatti
This morning has been so given over to miscellanies that I felt like a scalloped oyster. First came the lace-mender who bored me to death trying to sell me things I didn't want. Before she went, Bessie's French teacher called to pay her *devoirs* (and ask for work), and who clashed with a man who had a bronze to sell, who overlapped a dealer with a real Fra Angelico. At the same time two photographers were working here, one a plain one, another a colour-photographer: a man was studying B.B.'s Persian Manuscripts, and some rascals of the fiercest description were trying to sell me a lame horse. At the same time, some bulbs, a lot of sweet peas and some roses arrived, and a stone-mason to ask me about some steps, and a man with frames for pictures. I wished them all and myself at Jericho.

To Ray Strachey and Karin Costelloe   20 November 1911   I Tatti
That blackleg Geoffrey tells me that our quiet polite secretary† is amazed and horrified at the troops of self-assertive middle-aged females who surge through the house—he alludes to them all by their surnames—Wharton, Crawshay, Strong, Priestley, Blood and so on. He did not know there *were* such people, and is firmly convinced that

* Oliver had returned from India in poor health.
† Their secretary was now Lance Cherry, an Englishman who was killed in the War in 1915.

174

it is B.B.'s peculiar taste that has sought them out like rare needles in a haystack. In vain does Scott assure him that the world is full of them, he cannot grasp the idea. *Ces dames* all find him 'a nice courteous young man' and think no more of it. Does thee remember, Ray, Willy's bewilderment at the same class of person? 'Poisonous' I think they were, or to-be-poisoned. *I* think they are very nice, myself—and by God, I'd better, seeing I am one of them!

To Bessie Berenson   23 November 1911   I Tatti
I wrote to you that B.B. cabled [to Belle Greene, from whom he had not heard for four months] did I not? It was on Saturday, and on Tuesday morning he came into my room fairly *worn out* and suicidal from having got no answer. I said it was *sure* to come, and indeed in half an hour it did. 'Have been so blue and miserable and so very very tired, had no heart to write, but am writing Mauretania today. Never question my absolute love.'

You would be *amazed* to see the difference this has made to him.... He has begun again writing those endless letters. So it has all begun over once more. I cannot but think it a misfortune. He says he would go to America in a second if she wanted him to—but she evidently doesn't. He asked me to write and invite her here for a 'Rest Cure', which I did: but I should be very much surprised if she came. I am afraid it will take him *years* to get over it.

To her Family   2 December 1911   I Tatti
We went to call on Lady Sybil Cutting* who lives in the Villa Medici at Fiesole. She is interesting and pleasant, and she has a dear little girl named Iris.

To Alys Russell   16 December 1911   I Tatti
I suddenly woke up in the night with a 'conviction' that her [Hannah's] personality was not gone. I found myself believing in the 'future life'—irrationally, of course, but instinctively and vitally. It seems to help everything a *lot*, and is therefore pragmatically true.

To her Family   12 January 1912   I Tatti
Lady Sybil and her friend came to call yesterday, and stayed for hours

* Lady Sybil Cutting, daughter of an Irish peer, Lord Desart, and widow of a wealthy American, William Bayard Cutting Jr.

as we found we all liked each other very much. I shall be glad if B.B. finds someone in Florence whom he really cares to see, especially now that Placci, since the beginning of the war*, won't come near us, and the Serristori is so taken up with a dull female friend of hers as to have become a rare and not over satisfactory visitor.

To Alys Russell   13 January 1912   I Tatti
B.B. seems to be engaged in vast operations—telegrams, express letters—fearfully exciting things. I find I get *too* excited, so I don't try to know all the stages of his affairs. But he seems to be making money, and he has generously offered to give Rachel and Senda houses to live in, in Cambridge and Northampton—a very nice way of spending his money, I think. I hope he will give Ray and Oliver a house, too.

To Karin Costelloe   26 January 1912   I Tatti
Cecil and Scott have been making up their accounts for the year— receipts £470, expenditure about £760! And really very little to show for it. Scott is in despair. He is certainly very economical but Cecil is wildly spendthrift and entirely unregulated—as thee can imagine. You cannot make him run on the rails of common sense.

To Alys Russell   12 March 1912   I Tatti
What a quiet creature Ray is in the house! One would never know she was here. She fills up her time reading and writing, the old clam! But she is a great dear. All will be changed when Karin buzzes in. It is funny about her, what a whirlwind she carries with her. Ray says the bother she gave them travelling, with her money and her trunks etc etc was beyond description... But then she is so vivid and jolly you end by forgiving her....

There is scarcely a day but people or letters come saying it is impossible to sell Italian things without his [B.B.'s] 'certificate', and the business he has in hand now is of a very big nature. Yesterday a young man appeared with a letter from his uncle in Paris asking him (at *whatever* price) to get B.B.'s certificate for his Donatello, his Desiderio, his Mantegna, his Bellini and his Perugino. I interviewed the man, and confounded him by saying I was sure B.B. would not give it without seeing the things, and 'Buono Dio!' in a tone of despair was all he could think of to say as he departed. Such an idea had never

* Italy's invasion of Tripoli.

176

entered their minds as that a certificate could not be bought. It is the same country that produced the 'Vet' who offered me a certificate for the cow's health for a franc, but said it would cost 10 francs if he examined the cow!

B.B.'s contract with Duveen Brothers and the growing closeness of their association involved the Berensons in many meetings and much correspondence with the firm. As in his dealings with Mrs Gardner, Mary was a constant source of helpful advice in this field. She would frequently draft difficult letters and B.B. was happy to leave her to act on her own judgment when he was unavailable, even when large sums of money were involved.

To Louis Duveen*   *15 March 1912   I Tatti (Draft)*
Acting on my husband's instructions I went to Volpi's to see about the Jerome by Botticelli.... The Secretary said that Count F.F. had refused to consider anything less than 200,000 francs paid in full to him. This price does not include the export duty, but the Secretary said that as the picture was very small, and had not yet attracted the attention of the Italian Government, he would simply put it in his bag and take the train de luxe to Paris or London and deliver it there. I declined to consider this, and said nothing would be connived at, but they must arrange everything themselves. He said he was sure Volpi would be content with 'the merest trifle' (ie 10,000 Frcs), as the picture was not his and they were doing it for the Count in a friendly way in return for other services. But this probably means that they will get more out of it. These people tell lies, you can only guess at probabilities. The probability seems to me that you *could* get it for 200,000, and that you *certainly* could have it in your hands in a week for that price plus 5 or 10 thousand francs more.

To Alys Russell   *19 March 1912   I Tatti*
This week with B.B. away has been very agitating for me, for I've had to carry on his business. I've just had a wire buying a small Botticelli for £8400 (sterling) and I can only *hope* that I have been *guided* to give the right advice about it.

To Alys Russell   *22 March 1912   I Tatti*
Thy last extracts from Grandma's letters were very wonderful. That

* One of Joseph Duveen's seven brothers, then running the London branch of the firm.

about the loneliness of the world was really wonderfully felt*. She didn't know *how* lonely it could be, though, for she always had that idea of God. I do not at all know where to look for real satisfying companionship. The only thing I can think of is to love people—but one's heart is disappointingly meagre and hard, at least mine is. And they only want a little of our love, just what is useful. I find it rather ghastly, if one stops to think. But there is no way of getting God back again that I can see.

Karin came out to Florence in the spring of 1912, and Geoffrey at once fell in love with her, more seriously than he had with Bessie the previous year. Mary was guardedly enthusiastic, but Karin took fright at Geoffrey's intensity and fled to Munich.

To Karin Costelloe   15 April 1912   I Tatti
Le brave vieux [Geoffrey] is really *so* nice. He honestly means thee to *get the most* out of his devotion, and he feels that the sensuous element may be there only to break down reserves and add joy and *élan*, but for thy sake doesn't want it to be an end in itself. I believe you can pull it off, dangerous as it is. I had a moment of utter funk, just as I had over thy being a drunkard (!!!), but I am now restored to confidence and will most sympathetically and loyally see you through. If anyone ever could succeed, it is you two.

To Karin Costelloe   17 April 1912   I Tatti
I am so anxious for thee to do nothing in this *joli mois de mai* that is coming, to compromise thy future. Anybody would fall in love with anybody in May—here—and it is not hard to take it seriously when you are in that condition. *Pourtant, ce n'est pas temps de te marier*, if one looks out ahead at the long stretch of years to come. I married first just from impulse, and it turned out badly simply because our temperaments did not agree and we did not like the same sort of life.

* At this time Alys was sending Mary extracts from their mother's letters of 1891. The extract referred to was probably the following, from a letter from Hannah Whitall Smith to Mary Costelloe, 16 August 1891: 'I believe it *is* good for thee to be alone for awhile. . . . I do trust thee utterly to God Who is the Heavenly Father, and Who loves thee even more than I do or could. It *does* comfort me, for I know it means a tremendous reality. . . . God is often hidden from our sight even when he is most really present (if there can be any "most" in such a thing). . . . I am *sure* He is round about thee and leading thee, and will bring all out right sometime.'

Thy father wanted bustle and activity, he was ambitious and loved people and power and influence, and I wanted a quiet life, out of the world, with one's real adventures in books and art.... Of course if thee decided to carry out thy original plan and spend May in Cambridge the immediate danger would be averted; but really that would be very hard, I am sure, and I could scarcely face Geoffrey's disappointment.

To Karin Costelloe   19 April 1912   I Tatti
Cecil spoke to me about it the other day, and said he was very anxious about the time when Geoffrey's eyes were opened to see that he wasn't doing his share of the work. Which is true. Cecil works very hard, and Geoffrey practically doesn't work at all: and I think it is really becoming serious as regards Cecil. Therefore if thee could come back and get *ton pauvre chien* into better training, it would certainly be a blessing—for what *would* he do if Cecil suddenly turned and said 'Look here, you don't do your share and I see you *won't*, so we had better part.' I am so afraid this might happen.... So if thee decided to come soon, it might be a good thing. Of course thee can imagine how *I* should love to have thee! The sooner the better. But there is one thing I must beg of thee to do for my sake (I don't often ask thee to make that a reason for action), and that is just to make a rule not to sit up after midnight. For me, I cannot stand the strain. I can't get to sleep, and my days (for *I* have to wake early) are weary and nervous in consequence. For Geoffrey, he becomes a dreadful wreck, as thee knows, and when his nerves go to pieces, everything is difficult for him. Therefore if thee won't promise me this and stick to it, I should really rather thee didn't come.... Thee must appreciate that I want to give you every reasonable (and almost every *un*reasonable) opportunity for working out your relation to each other. But it isn't fair to ask me to sacrifice my health to a scheme of which my judgment disapproves.

To Bernhard Berenson   26 April 1912   I Tatti
She [Karin] adored Obrist with whom she spent about four hours on Monday. Her account makes me quite long to see him again. Age has not withered his whimsicalities. What a pity I wasn't really nice and open about all that. These young people seem so far superior to me, so much more acquainted with themselves, so much freer from deceit-producing taboos, so much wiser ... I wonder what thee would have done if I had come frankly to thee about Obrist? I really do not know. Even thee then understood so little.

179

To her Family   3 June 1912   I Tatti
Ray's birthday is upon us, and it is awful that I have not thought of it
in time, for I mean to give her a present of gratitude for existing, and
also for being in the process of giving me some one else to love, whom
I suspect I shall love more than I have ever loved anyone yet. It is a
queer thing, I must say, to feel that you have oceans of love ready for a
being that does not yet exist, whose character may turn out to be
entirely unsympathetic and whose sex even you don't know! Sometimes I think I must be making it up, because I have known so much
of the love of a Grandmother—if this is so, blessed be the power of
'Pretend'. For I anticipate perhaps the greatest pleasures of my life
from loving these young ones. DO have twins, Ray.

To Grace Worthington   5 June 1912   I Tatti
Karin's visit was a mingled cup for me, because it ended in Geoffrey's
falling dreadfully in love with her, and I could not feel that she really
played *quite* fair. Perhaps this is too much, for the circumstances were
peculiar, with me to watch over things, but I am left with a sad feeling
that she lacks delicacy and consideration in her mad rush for
excitement and 'fun'. This of course is no news to any of us who have
lived with her; but I foolishly thought that getting to know well and
intimately such a person as Geoffrey would somehow educate her a bit
in human relations. But I am afraid it has had the opposite effect: and
for him it has been a disaster. Showing how foolish all one's plans and
predictions are!!

To Bernhard Berenson   6 July 1912   Ford Place Sussex
I think I could have told thee beforehand (if thee had asked me) that
every woman who lives for society (and many others!) craves always the
excitement of sex in any man she is attracted to. How should any of them
be up to *thy* normal friendship, who don't read or think or work? I believe
the same people *at a crisis* would be tender and considerate and helpful—
(when pain and anguish wring the brow, so to speak). For *that* is enough
excitement in itself. But to think that *Talk, Thought, Philosophizing,
Chatting on Literary Subjects* etc etc excites people who care for none of these
things, is absurd. I think Mrs Wharton and Mme de Cosse and the
Countess Serristori and (possibly) Mme de Loches, are exceptions. . . .
How few men care about *us* unless we are sexually interested in them.
Remember that. Thy agreeable friendships have that generally as a
foundation, and that makes them pleasant to thee. Of course if thee
doesn't play up, they are disappointed!

180

To Mrs Berenson   *18 July 1912*   *Ford Place, Sussex*

Ray's little daughter ... was born yesterday morning at 3 o'clock....
She was quite conscious but felt no pain at all.... We telegraphed to
'Grandpa Berenson' (that is Bernhard) and one of his friends writes
me—'B.B. is profoundly happy about it. He has your telegraph in his
pocket and reads it perpetually'!

CHAPTER TWELVE

Interlude

August 1912–July 1914

Mary was contracting the habit, then fashionable among the rich, of attending a Cure every summer, and usually sampled a different one each year.

B.B. was now working so closely with Duveen Brothers that he was offered the first of a series of remunerative—though not publicized—contracts as their adviser on Italian Art. Its terms bound him to give them first refusal of 'First Class' Italian pictures of which he had knowledge. The financial arrangements were complicated, but basically he was to receive 25 per cent of the net profits on the sale of every picture on which he advised.

Bernhard and Duveen remained in close, but generally uneasy, contact from this time until 1937, when the association was severed. B.B. was as suspicious of 'Jo' as he was of art expert colleagues, while Duveen was a master of delaying tactics, particularly in paying out cash. There were frequent clashes and recriminations, and when such contests were in progress B.B. often left it to Mary to write, or to meet Duveen, though he always preserved a close eye on proceedings.

Mary, though fascinated at the idea of a grandchild, was not much taken with Ray and Oliver's 'Bloomsbury' friends, and deplored Ray's genuine interest in politics and the Suffrage movement. Karin's taste for philosophy and psychology were more congenial to her, in spite of Karin's more difficult character.

Geoffrey's star, meanwhile, was still in the ascendant, and Belle's had begun a slow decline. Edith Wharton, despite their adverse first impression, had become a close friend, and Count Keyserling, a young Austrian philosopher, came to stay and aroused somewhat variegated reactions.

To Bernhard Berenson   18 August 1912   Aix-les-Bains
I am *dreadfully fat*, Bernhard, and I am working over it, and mean to

go on. But they don't hold out much hope, unless I exhaust myself by ten miles' climbing a day for the rest of my life. For my peculiar fat is healthy and tenacious. The most I can expect from the treatment here, including vigorous massage, diet and semi-starvation, iodine and iodine soap, aperients and mild exercise (which is really all I *can* take) is that I may perhaps lose—four pounds! And I need to lose 40. It is like Alice and the White Queen who had to run for their lives in order to stand still. For if I *don't* I will become colossally fat!

To Bernhard Berenson   19 August 1912   Aix-les-Bains
It is no use for me to go to Paris without someone to help me about clothes. I can no more clothe myself nicely than thee could paint a picture. I haven't the faintest idea how I look, or what suits me, or where to go, and if I go alone to a good place, they see through me at once, and treat me accordingly. But Elsie [de Wolfe]* whose taste is really perfect, is a very busy woman, as busy at her play in Paris as at her profession in New York, and I cannot feel it would be right to ask her. Furthermore I am very fat (the scales showed that I had *gained* 3 pounds in spite of everything!!!) and Elsie is used to a slim figure in herself, and the poor result I should produce *at the best* could not appeal to her. If she helped it would be for the pure gold of friendship, and I am sure it would give her a lot of trouble. And I do hate to ask people to take trouble over a matter I ought to settle for myself but just *can't*.

To Bernhard Berenson   26 August 1912   Aix-les-Bains
What is thee going to do about Belle? . . . I should think if any life at all is to remain in your friendship, you would have to meet. But I am afraid, from observing thee and seeing the misery it has brought thee, that my view is that thee will be happier to let it die. This is a very hard thing to say to certain feelings: but sometimes outsiders can really judge more sanely. And she is so unsatisfactory to thee, and must always be so, by her character and habits and associations, that I feel sure thee will lead a happier life if thee can be delivered from that preoccupation.

To her Family   11 October 1912   St Raphael
Mrs Wharton is really very nice, so easy to get on with. Indeed she is

* A fashionable interior-designer friend.

more *our* sort than most people—more than any Latin person could *possibly* be. Our past is the same as hers, a tempered New Englandism, and she has never quite got over the Henry Jamesy sense of contrast. She and I had a very interesting talk about Growing Old. She says it is the most interesting thing that ever happened to her. I wish I could say the same. She said she wasted her youth trying to be beautiful, but now that she has given up all hope she feels freer. She *is* heavy-handed, but when you like her it becomes rather endearing. I think she is a very good friend to her friends.

To Ray Strachey   6 November 1912   I Tatti
Ray, my beloved child, I want to give thee a Christmas present, and I should *like* it to be a fur coat for Oliver, because I can imagine nothing more important for the happiness of us all than to keep him well. And for a person who suffers from cold, as he *must* do after all those years in India, a fur coat is next door to necessary. Therefore get it at once, not as a dole, but as a Xmas present, which in one form or another I should naturally be giving thee.

To her Family   11 November 1912   I Tatti
These daily letters are more than I can possibly ever tell you. I should feel really desolate without them—but they keep the imagination filled.

To her Family   21 November 1912   I Tatti
I am sending Gertrude Stein's latest amazing (and horrid) pro-duction* along with Bertie's article. When you have hated it enough, send it to Grace to keep. *We have another* sent by herself to B.B. What can he say? And many people take it seriously as a new and worthwhile 'departure'. It isn't even funny, only horrible. I should like to see Logan's face when he opens it.

To her Family   25 November 1912   I Tatti
It is very funny, my own desires have come to an end, or else they are so more than satisfied that I think they are over. I want neither dress nor fine linen nor *oggetti* nor elegance nor a motor nor servants nor a library—nor any of the things I fuss over all day long. I only want to give *you* all these things—which is silly, as I daresay you don't want them any more than I do!

* *Portrait of Mabel Dodge at the Villa Curonia*, privately printed (1911).

To Mrs Berenson   *23 December 1912   I Tatti*
I had three days at Edith Wharton's in Paris, which I enjoyed, although I feel very sorry for her, as her husband has what is called *folie circulaire*, periods of excitement when he does reckless things and spends money madly, followed by long periods of melancholy and hypochondria. Yet he isn't quite mad enough to be shut up. I had an Uncle that way, but while *his* manias limited themselves to bringing negroes home to dine, buying paper flowers, trying to introduce horse-meat into the English kitchen and erecting monuments to Swiss reformers, Mr Wharton's mania leads him to buy houses and motors for music-hall actresses, to engage huge suites in hotels and get drunk and break all the furniture, and to circulate horrible tales about his wife.

To her Family   *30 December 1912   I Tatti*
Something in Eugénie Strong seems to force her into an animated and absorbing *tête-à-tête* with B.B. *whenever* we have guests. It is one of the most awkward and embarrassing things conceivable and I really don't see how she can do it. This is the fourth time it has happened ... On she thumps straight through the meal, completely absorbing B.B. so that he never addresses a word to his neighbour on the other hand, and I heard 'Dr Ashby'—'The School'—'Prenestine Fragments' —'The Herzian Library'—'The Museo at the Villa Giulia'— etc. I have never known a person so confined—I mean a person who mingled in general society. But I like it except on these dread occasions. Who could have thought she would turn out so tactless and so heavy-handed? It makes me wonder with dread what I am like. How can I find out?? *Do* tell me if you have any hints to give me on this point.

To Senda Berenson Abbott [Senda had married Herbert Abbott in August 1911]   2 January 1913   I Tatti
B.B. has been less well than ever since Carlsbad,* but very much more tranquil in his nerves, so that everything has been calm and peaceful and harmonious, and even, when he is a *little* better, gay. Only, as he said to me this morning, 'It's an *awful* thing to be in love with a person three thousand miles away'. and as B.G. is by no means constant or considerate in what she *does* write, she makes it no easier

---

* Mary had for once managed to persuade Bernhard to attend a cure, though a different one from the one she went to.

185

for him. Last winter her four months' silence drove him to despair. The same game has begun again, but he says he cannot get into such a state *twice*, and he is taking it more calmly. I almost wish we weren't going back next autumn—much as I want to see you all, for I fear it will only flare up again and bring more wretchedness. And yet, it is perfectly true, Senda dear, that *if it made him happy*, I could rejoice in it. For what with ill-health, and nerves, I think he doesn't have half the good time he deserves. But it has been chiefly misery and worse nervousness.

To her Family   10 January 1913   I Tatti
I am inclined rather to go to one of those thorough German cures, where they keep you hopping all day with their treatment. Then again I feel like trying Dr Steinmann's treatment, which consists of having the juice of ants injected into you three times a year, *e basta*. It sounds the easiest, I must say. I don't think B.B. will ever go to a Cure again. Many people say they only do good to leathery robust people, of the kind I am, really—I am certainly going to try again.

To her Family   12 January 1913   I Tatti
Our excitement yesterday was the visit of the Duveens, who came about some important business. Think what a life they lead! Ernest, the youngest partner, went from Paris to London on Monday. On Tuesday night to Edinburgh. Back to London on Wednesday night, crossed to Paris Thursday, started for Florence Friday and starts back to Paris today, Sunday. Not all the riches of the Orient would tempt me to lead such a life. And he doesn't sleep on trains! They brought with them a funny, fat little Cockney, whose name was so funny I could not bring myself to pronounce it—Toozer. They all dined here, and we talked politely on various topics for the first half hour—and then I broached the selling of pictures, and a loud sigh of satisfaction went up to the ceiling, and we settled in to a thoroughly congenial topic. They have an immense satisfaction as a Firm in the first-rate 'goods they have handled' since they began to take B.B.'s advice. It ain't bad, considering they've had two Titians, a Giorgione, a Donatello, a Crivelli (what a jewel!), two Bellinis, various Tintorettos, a Perugino, a Pinturicchio, a Fra Filippo, a Botticelli, a Filippino and I can't tell how many others. I *loved* hearing them boast, for each one means some fun for us all—motor-trips, house-furnishings, B.B.'s *oggetti*, opera-boxes (!) and so on.

186

To her Family   28 January 1913   I Tatti
I think I broke off about Cecil at an interesting point. I will explain to you how he lives. He has strange periods of purposeless activity, when he will sit up all night to get a new sort of clip fastened onto his old piles of letters, or a new kind of cut in the papers that mask their photographs, or some such futility. These fits overtake him just when his clients' affairs have reached *le moment psychologique* when he can either finish things on time and get the details to suit them, or when, by delaying, he throws everything behindhand, scamps the details, rushes through the work at double pace and extra pay, gives his clients the idea of disorder and inattention, enrages and despairs them, and undoes or rather negatives in their minds all the really good work he has done up to this point. This is just the moment when his partner is or could be very valuable, for Geoffrey foresees everything that people will feel, he understands the psychological effect that will be produced. And he does not fail to tell Cecil, and *sometimes* it does good. But Cecil is a human eel-monkey and slips out of his grasp and chatters in a tree, so to speak.

To her Family   8 February 1913   I Tatti
I wish thee would find time, Logan, to tell me of thy impressions of Miss Stein. It makes me see red even to think of her, I am sorry to say; though as a matter of fact every time I actually am with her I like her. But she and her brother have been such a weight on me for *years*, ever since that awful summer at Friday's Hill, so persistent, so insoluble, so—well, dirty, so horrible in their ideas—(as for instance that the disgustingly silly book by Weiniger on 'Sex and Character' was 'the greatest and most important book that had been written for 50 years') that I cannot endure the thought of them—*pas même l'odeur—surtout pas l'odeur!* But they hardly come at all now, for I'm sure they hold us in horror too, so I ought to be able to calm down.

To her Family   9 February 1913   I Tatti
We are in the last stages of the new rooms [extensions to the library]—what a deal of bother the boys have with them. The workmen have been fabulously incompetent, and every possible thing has gone wrong. But I don't recount the 'Woes' for Geoffrey bears the brunt of them, and B.B. knows nothing, and I very little and humorously. How different from the days when Cecil ... muddled everything and B.B. cursed and I wrung my hands.

To Ray Strachey   28 March 1913   I Tatti
'Uncle Henry' Duveen* has been writing and telegraphing B.B. to go to him in Monte Carlo, but B.B. has steadily refused to leave his quiet and his work. Consequently Mahomet has come to the Mountain, and he turned up this morning. He is dining here tonight. His head is full of vast 'Deals', but who knows how many of them will come off?

To her Family   29 March 1913   I Tatti
'Uncle Henry' came to tea yesterday and stayed on to dinner. The time flew as when Scheherezade recounted tales to the king—he is a wonderful genial old rogue—the best salesman in the world, B.B. says—and he, as it were, unbuttoned himself, and told us dramatically long tales of contests with various American millionaires. We roared with laughter. He is quite wild to get more Italian pictures. His one epithet is *'cachet'*. He found we had 10 or 12 things with so much *'cachet'* that he would undertake to sell them for sums varying from 5 to 10 thousand pounds each! That Aubusson carpet, which Logan got us to buy for £16 he would pay £400 for!! One's head reels before these figures.

To her Family   26 April 1913   I Tatti
Placci has come round to the quarrelling period and was simply full of teasing and boring little *digs* of all sorts. Finally he said to B.B. 'Our friendship is at an end. We have nothing in common'. 'If 20 years of affection counts for nothing with you in comparison to a difference of opinion over the Balkans, then there really isn't much to go on' B.B. replied. The great thing will be to keep out of his way, till his mood changes.

To her Family   29 April 1913   I Tatti
A dealer is with B.B. He has brought a *real Botticelli*!! And a portrait of Giuliano dei Medici!!!† It is almost too exciting to be true. He brought it yesterday, and B.B. and I couldn't believe our eyes. We spent hours

---

* Henry Duveen was Joseph Duveen's uncle and an active member of the firm.
† This portrait of Giuliano dei Medici was bought by Otto Kahn in 1914 and is now in the Crespi collection in Milan, where it is listed as a Botticelli. There are a number of other versions of the portrait (in Washington, Bergamo and Berlin), and most experts now accept that the one in the Washington National Gallery of Art, with a quail, is the original.

looking at it and studying all the photos in connection with it. The man did not expect it to be called anything but 'Amico di Sandro'*, but it is very fine, and it grows on one, and with wonder and surprise we have come to the conclusion that it is by Botticelli himself. Imagine the joy of the dealer! I am sure he would give B.B. two or three thousand pounds at once. *I* couldn't resist it, but B.B. made up his mind once for all to be perfectly correct in all his dealings and as he is going to recommend someone to buy the picture, he won't take more than the agreed percentage. Of course his pronouncing it a Botticelli makes the percentage a greater sum: but *I* couldn't resist the cash down, I know. It is well I'm not in the trade. I should soon be kicked out of it I fear. But the thought of what I could do with a so to speak irresponsible couple of thousand pounds makes me quite faint. Don't let's think of it.

To her Family   1 May 1913   I Tatti
Friendship is a very difficult art! But there are some people with whom it is particularly difficult. I need hardly say that I allude to the Michael Fields. Poor Field is off and on about her dying (it is a *dreadful* way to go)†, and I can well believe that Michael is almost out of her mind—especially as she is such an idiot as to refuse to have a nurse to help her, even with the surgical part. It is really frightful. But now they want to move to Hampstead, and they expect me to come home to move them. I simply can't ... it is more than I feel called on to do, for it is too upsetting to B.B. and all my plans. But it is horrible to know that they will receive from it a mortal wound, and will never regard me again as anything but a traitor.

To Geoffrey Scott   12 May 1913   I Tatti
My conscience does prick me a little, remembering that I really encouraged B.B. in the affair partly for my own reasons.... I thought it would make up to him for the unhappiness of all the building upset and for not finding me very satisfactory (which I wasn't) but I also thought it would leave me much freer, which it did, as you remember. So I am honestly and truly responsible for its gravity, I cannot pretend I am not. B.B. never brings this up against me, but I know it is so, and it makes me feel that I ought not to make it

* A painter 'invented' at one stage by B.B. to account for a number of 'Botticelli School' paintings he believed to have common characteristics.
† Edith Cooper had cancer. She died in 1913 and Katherine Bradley the following year, also of cancer.

hard for him by absolutely changing my policy now that I have won my point.

How *sweet* Barbara must have been! I do so long to see her and cut up some foolish antics to bring a smile to her jolly little face. The swing has come, and I'm torn between the longing for her to have it as soon as possible and the wish to have her associate the fun of it with me. I'm tempted to be selfish, for I must get an innings somehow!

To her Family   *6 June 1913*   *[Venice ?]*
We've had a splendid trip this year ... also very good food. I'm having a bust before the Cure—as I really must have something *to* cure.

To her Family   *16 June 1913*   *Munich*
We have just come back from lunching at the Obrists'. He asked me to go and look at a fountain of his, which we did. It made us quite uncomfortable, for it seemed to be composed of three *derrières* (*fonctionnantes, col rispetto parlando*!!) jumbled up with flying buttresses and Gothic ornaments and dull geometrical figures. Of course he is too clever not to discover that we didn't like it, and this made him unduly sad. He is not the self-confident Obrist *dei tempi passati*. Long years of non-success and neglect have damped him a bit. He gave me rather a sad feeling.

To Bernhard Berenson   *30 June 1913*   *Ford Place, Sussex*
As to our talk, it is asses-milk-cum-water to the talk of the Bloomsbury set.... Ray thinks it is much better than the old-fashioned hypocrisy. Are thy Paris friends as open as all this? Roger [Fry] is a prime leader in these revels. Ray said, quite simply, 'Of course he and Vanessa Bell are in love with each other.' 'What does Clive think?' I asked. 'O he doesn't mind, for he is in love with Mrs MacCarthy.' 'And what view does Desmond MacCarthy take of it?' 'He doesn't like it, for he's not in love with anyone.'

To Bernhard Berenson   *2 July 1913*   *Hampstead*
And now I must tell thee some more of the 'Gloomsbury' doings. At Ray's party Duncan Grant, disguised as a woman, was suddenly seized with labour pains—doctors and midwives were summoned, and amid horrid groans he gave birth to a pillow.... Ray sat on my

bed with her sweet serious face and candid eyes, telling me all this, and saying of course it couldn't be done unless all the people were 'perfectly nice'. 'But the young men are all Sods' I said. 'Yes, that's what makes it all so nice,' she answered. 'It's *so* much better than when the young unmarried men of a set frequented prostitutes.'—! Well, as Alys says, *we* didn't solve the problem in *our* day. It is now for them to try. But how awful, Bernhard—horripilent, as thee says.

To Mrs Berenson   20 July 1913   Ford Place, Sussex
Yesterday she [Ray] and Alys and Grace and I marched in the Suffrage Pilgrimage for a couple of hours. These pilgrimages, from all over England, are converging upon London at the end of the week, where there is to be a monster meeting in Hyde Park, with women (including most of my family and Ray's family-in-law) speaking from 24 platforms. Generally speaking the Pilgrims are very well treated as they pass along with their banners and music. People offer them refreshments and sometimes pelt them with flowers—but once or twice also with rotten eggs and cabbages.

To Geoffrey Scott   28 August 1913   Brides-les-Bains
B.B. has telegraphed a cordial approval—so now hurrah for the Rhône and Provence.... My darling old 'Me First', that is really the way I like you to be with me, it shows such confidence in my affection. You are like a baby sometimes, and I love it like that, when you just ask or demand and don't think of anything but what you want. Of course I shouldn't like you to be always like that—but there's a long score against *my* graspingness and selfishness I have to work off! And so often you are tact and sympathy and helpfulness such as I have never known from anybody, dear.

To Geoffrey Scott   1 October 1913   Paris
Things are very hard sometimes, and this is one of my hardest trials, not to know always how you are, *intérieurement*. It is only half living, Geoffrey dear. If you want something to count on all your days, my deep affection is there.

To her Family   8 October 1913   I Tatti
Well, the latest from the Count's [Keyserling] den upstairs is that he has upset his inkpot which, apparently, he keeps on his pillow, all over the bed, ruining a pair of my nicest new sheets, two pillowcases,

191

2 blankets and the carpet and valance to the bed. *He*, of course, makes no apology. I daresay he hardly notices it. I have given orders to put *servants'* sheets and blankets and bed-cover on his bed, and pieces of matting wherever he is likely to *sporcare* and to take away all the dainty things from the toilet table. It is too horrible. Also the house is gradually filling with flies, for he said he is suffocated by our window wires, when I asked him to keep them closed, and he sits with windows and doors open and the flies simply pour in and B.B. is nearly wild with them, for they attack him, and it is for his sake, chiefly, that we have put wire-nettings at every window. Well, well. *Per contra*, he was really *very* agreeable and entertaining last evening, and we sat chatting till eleven o'clock. He is certainly unusually thoughtful and observant and keen, but I cannot say he seems to me great in any way. B.B. says he writes extremely well, and thinks he may make a name in literature rather than thought.

To Geoffrey Scott   20 October 1913   I Tatti
Dearest Geoffrey ... Would it be a better plan to meet her [Karin] or is that too painful still? Karin would fit in with anything you decided. ... I fear this is the kind of letter that will make you dread the sight of my handwriting, as I call up so many worries one after the other. Do excuse me, and please love me, Geoffrey. I need it to live at all. I know you do, and it is at the very centre of my life—this enduring friendship we are gradually building up. But I know I make it very hard sometimes.

To her Family   25 October 1913   I Tatti
B.B. is beginning to indulge in very gloomy prognostications about his further continuance of business with the Duveens. They are continually at him to make him say pictures are different from what he thinks, and are very cross with him for not giving way and 'just letting us have your authority for calling this a Cossa instead of school of Jura' or 'allowing us to take it you will approve us calling this by the master's hand, as it is so close' etc etc. They sent up an emissary the other day to say a certain picture here had been pronounced an early Titian by Dr Sirěn, Dr Bode and Dr Gronau, and why couldn't B.B. agree—and although he didn't, he thinks they have bought the picture all the same, and that it is the beginning of the end. The Duveens are notoriously fickle, and they have found B.B. very unyielding, so I should not be surprised if he were right. If he is, it may mean a great necessity for us to draw in our horns, for we have

been living not on income, but on incoming capital ... If it were not for the various people I love to give money to, I should not be at all sorry to be poor again. I am *never* comfortable in my mind about being rich and extravagant.

In the winter of 1913–1914 the Berensons paid yet another visit to the States, though Mary had been far from enthusiastic at leaving Geoffrey to his own devices and secretly reluctant to allow Bernhard within reach of Belle Greene again.

To Geoffrey Scott   15 December 1913   Boston
I must tell you that my mind is really at rest about Belle Greene. I have talked more with her, and I am sure B.B. is right, that beneath her vulgarity, behind her horrid habits as a letter writer—a kind of loquacious aphasia—and aside from her unsympathetic amusements, there is a nice creature there, a 'good sort' who knows how to be a friend, and who is lovable. I cannot resist the impression. And I am perfectly sure there will be no more follies. The circumstances that upset B.B. so terribly were quite exceptional and cannot occur again. It really seems to me the most natural and the sanest thing is to *let* his unkillable affection for her run a simple unchecked course, guarding as much as possible against the annoyance of scandal. That is where I really *can* help. As you know, my whole object in the thing has been his happiness out of it, and the consequent freedom I should get for myself, a freedom I have always more or less taken, but not always with the feeling that it was *fair*, and certainly with many material hindrances, which by not hindering him will grow less and less. That is my selfish point in it, and you know why. But the consideration of his real happiness is honestly the chief one, and (rightly or wrongly) I believe it lies in continuing his friendship for Belle, and gradually humanizing (i.e. de-sexing) it. This nature will attend to, and *her* nature, too, for she isn't passionate, and I fancy her sexual life is only by the way. I also feel he will have some other outlet (perhaps worse) if he can't have this one. And that, when I have you (and also Barbara) to love, it is only fair for him to have something.... I will quote you what Belle wrote of me (I am sure not for my eye, though as a matter of fact B.B. shows me all her letters) ... 'She is so big that she makes me feel uncomfortably like a weasel. I have all sorts of new feelings in her presence—the most persistent (and the most horrid) one is that if I met her much more and she could let me know her— that I might be *more true* to her than I would to you!'

193

To her Family   4 January 1914   Boston

B.B. has started Mrs Gardner buying Italian pictures again in spite of her avowed poverty. She says she will do anything we like if we'll only remain here. But oh! I should rather live on two hundred a year *over there*.

To her Family   10 January 1914   Montreal

B.B. said to her [Mrs Gardner] the last day that although he had found her fascinating and wonderful before, he had never loved her until this time, for she had never been lovable. She wept at this, and said it was true, and perhaps she would have gone to her grave with her hard heart and selfish character if it had not been for a Japanese mystic named Okakura, who was attached to the Boston Museum as expert. He was the first person, she said, who showed her how hateful she was, and from him she learnt her first lesson of seeking to love instead of to be loved. She admitted that many of her bad habits remained, but said that the core of herself was quite different, and she wanted to get rid of old evils. It was really touching. She is truly one of the most astonishing personalities we have ever known, and at last we really care for her as a human being.

To her Family   18 January 1914   New York

She [an American friend] gave me Tagore to read, and I confess it seemed like fervid higher commonplaces. I mean why should one *read* such things? Life and experience make you know them, if you have any capacity for spiritual growth, and if you haven't, or aren't yet ready, it is all what the children used to call 'jaw'. I felt as if he could pour it out endlessly and that is such a discouraging feeling....

The 'little mother' came over from Boston to see her adored son, who hadn't a word to say to her unless I whispered suggestions in his ear. It is tragic. All the same I intend to have her and 'Abie' [B.B's brother] for a month next winter,* because her whole inner imaginative life is just Bernhard, and I want her to see the house and pictures, to dream about forever after.... I shall have the visit strictly limited, so that I shan't get crazy, for there is something in that family, all except B.B., that really drives me wild. I wonder if they know it? I don't *think* so, for they smother me in sweet praises—but still I suspect real things are felt, and I get so wild with ennui and exasperation with

* The visit was overtaken by the War. Neither B.B.'s parents nor his brother ever visited him at I Tatti.

them, one and all, that *le monde se noircit devant mes yeux*. It is awful of me.

To Geoffrey Scott 27 January 1914 New York
I could not leave B.B. to prosecute this campaign alone. For here, more than anywhere else in the world, I am useful to him. People take me up as much as they do him, for women have a different position over here, and 'count' for a lot more in a society which is run almost exclusively *by* women. They seem to trust me, and I am a guarantee of his trustworthiness. So that for what this is worth—and it is our worldly all—I am doing my share to earn our daily bread, and I should be missed practically at once.

To her Family 4 February 1914 New York
I think things are working out all right. He [B.B.] has already made plenty of money which will come in during the next 4 or 5 years (people pay slowly) and quite make up for the trouble of such a trip.

Forgetting her own protests as a girl, when her letters from school had been circulated, Mary had taken not only to writing family circular letters herself, but also to circulating the replies. Both Ray and Karin protested violently against this habit, and as a result Mary had to rely, to a large extent, on Alys for news of Ray and Barbara, though Karin was a good correspondent most of the time.

To her Family 16 April 1914 I Tatti
It is no use my trying to leave off the drink habit. I'm a confirmed family letter writer!! There are a lot of things I want you all ... to know, and oh how *little* letter-writing time I have. So we'll leave it this way, that I continue, but vow to answer at once every personal letter I get, and you know how I *love* getting them. But ten days have passed, and I've had nothing from Karin, and only one letter from Ray—that one absolutely delightful. I really couldn't live on such meagre—no I won't say meagre, but infrequent fare, I who for so many years had the joy of a daily letter telling me all about you. So I am fearfully grateful to thee, Aunty Loo, for writing to me every day. I don't expect it of you others, not even of Uncle Logan! But do write when you can. I shall answer at once, and often, I daresay, write on my own account in between. But the habit of feeling you all with me in the semi(?) absurd life I lead is too strong to be eradicated at my age.

To Alys Russell   16 April 1914   I Tatti
He [B.B.] is never a nuisance, for he is so keen always on his own things, and really I can't get him long enough. But what I do get is really astonishingly delightful. His character has certainly changed. I am awfully glad for him, for his rages used to poison him, and awfully glad for myself, because for several years he was so difficult that I really didn't see how I could go on. Now it is all pleasant, and he is even trying not to let his Italy (a peculiar black and horrible peninsula inhabited by villains) get on his nerves.

To her Family   21 April 1914   I Tatti
B.B.'s Virgin Martyr face so worked upon me that I ordered 2 dresses yesterday and 6 blouses and 4 white skirts, and bought 2 hats. It made me feel quite sick to find myself at the old business again, smirking around in front of a mirror and turning my head sideways, to see if things were 'becoming'.

To Alys, Logan, Grace & Emily [Dawson]   25 April 1914   I Tatti
Fate has decreed against Family letters, and I shan't write more *than I can help.* It is like the drug habit, I know I shall fall from time to time, but in a general way I see I must check the facile flowing of my pen, and write to individuals. Karin, I must say, pays up, the letters are splendid and full of interesting details. Ray, I am afraid, will scratch a hasty and impersonal note once in 10 days, and of course Oliver will not write at all. *Pazienza.*

To Alys Russell   30 April 1914   I Tatti
This is all private to thee, so I can tell thee I've had a charming letter from Oliver, telling me about Karin's book* etc. He is a lovable darling person. I shall get extremely fond of him.

To Alys Russell   22 May 1914   I Tatti
I think thee and Grace were quite right in suppressing my Family Letter wail. It was just *not* the thing to do, and the worst of it is *I knew it when I wrote it.* But my pen has a life of its own (as thee may have noticed ere now). Karin is an angel about writing—her letters are frequent and intimate and detailed. Ray has shut up into the Strachey shell.

* Karin had written a thesis on Bergson's philosophy. It was later expanded and published under the title *The Misuse of Mind* (1922).

To Alys Russell   29 May 1914   I Tatti
Ray, I judge, has a sort of general 'ump at present—probably coming
from the 'interesting condition' she is in. Karin writes advising us all
to leave her alone for awhile, and above all *not to ask her any questions*
about anything, even Barbara, and not to expect any letters. She is
evidently in a queer state. I suspect she is trying to do too much along
with her pregnancy. So don't telephone her for news to give me. I
must get on without it. I am writing to her absolving her freely from
news. I must just put up with it till she comes out of what Karin calls
her Strachey tomb. She has always been queer. The more we leave her
alone at present the better, I think. She isn't a bit like us.

To Alys Russell   19 June 1914   I Tatti
I fear the impending quarrel with Michael [Field] is not to be staved
off. She and Field kept intimate journals and put down everything
B.B. said and did. And these, though they contain his intimate youth
and all his confidences to them (for he thought they were real friends
instead of literary monsters) they are going to hand over to Sturge
Moore*, although, as Michael says, 'I recognize that S.M. is an enemy of
yours'. B.B. is furious at being treated as manuscript for a minor
minimist poet. He wrote Michael a cursing letter, and won't even read
her silly answer, since she hasn't changed her mind. She considers
that Sturge Moore 'has a very delicate appreciation of Michael Field's
work'—hence all their human relations are to be sacrificed.

To Bernhard Berenson   8 July 1914   Schinznach-les-Bains
It was rather more exciting to try to read Karin's Thesis last night. It
was worse than a dentist! I had *awful* difficulty in grasping what it was
all up to, and finally persuaded her to re-arrange it and in part re-
write it, for what Bergson meant, what he had a right to mean, what
people thought he meant, his mistakes, their mistakes, etc etc, were all
jumbled together. In the end I faintly understood (but I've forgotten)
whether quantitive or qualitative muliplicity was homo- or hetero-
geneous. This morning walking over the bridge Karin confessed it was
mere dialectic logic (most of it) and as such extremely frivolous. She is
very open-minded, and her psychological studies are teaching her to
keep close to fact.

* T. Sturge Moore, brother of G.E. Moore the philosopher, was a poet and
wood engraver. He edited *Works and Days* from the journals of Michael Field.

To Geoffrey Scott   23 July 1914   Neufchâteau

I am sorry you should think the state of being 'in love' so lasting. It has been my experience that once I knew that there was either impossibility or more still fundamental intellectual or character incompatibility, the 'love' gradually died of itself. For in our kind of person there's no such thing as watertight compartments. I feel hopeful you will find this your case (but probably more slowly) even if 'something else' doesn't immediately turn up.

CHAPTER THIRTEEN

Hostilities

August 1914–November 1917

The outbreak of war found the Berensons in England. They were at first unable to leave, and were much alarmed, as they had many debts in Italy, their bank accounts were frozen, and the sources of their income threatened to vanish overnight. Things did not, however, prove to be as damaging as they had feared. Italy declared herself neutral, they managed to get back to I Tatti in November, and in the following spring Italy came in on the Allied side.

In September 1914 Karin became engaged to Adrian Stephen, Virginia Woolf's brother, and they were married a few weeks later. As the war progressed, Adrian and Karin became pacifists, and a quarrel developed between them and the more bellicose Berensons. Their involvement in 1915 in various anti-war societies and Adrian's registration as a Conscientious Objector led to Mary's regarding Karin as 'out of the family for the time being', while B.B. would not hear her name mentioned, and in 1916 Mary had great difficulty in preventing him from stopping Karin's allowance. Matters were smoothed over after the war, but Bernard—he had now dropped the Germanic H from his first name—with his usual rancour, never really forgave or forgot, though he remained financially generous.

Ray and Oliver, on the other hand, were much approved of, as they were both working for the war effort, Ray in helping to organize women into war work and Oliver (who was over fighting age) in the Code and Cypher Department of the War Office.

To Senda Berenson Abbott   18 August 1914   Ford Place, Sussex
Naturally B.B.'s business is at an end for years. The superfluous goes first, and if anything in the world is superfluous, it is Italian pictures. We shall be cut down to about 1/10 of what we have been spending. We've dismissed secretary and valet and the chauffeur is volunteer-

ing; we've stopped building and buying and cut down wherever we can. It will be a tight squeeze, B.B. says.

To Bessie Berenson   *20 September 1914*   *Ford Place, Sussex*
Karin has just told me that she is engaged! She brought down three days ago a young man (30) named Adrian Stephen, son of the writer Leslie Stephen, and a nephew of Thackeray's daughter, a very nice fellow and a lawyer.* They settled things up yesterday. We all saw how it was going, and on the whole it is a nice match, although I'm not very enthusiastic. He is very clever but not likely to amount to much, I fear, as he is lazy and feckless. However she may improve him. He has some money I am glad to say.

To Mrs Berenson   *22 September 1914*   *Ford Place, Sussex*
Curiously enough, the Stephens and the Stracheys, the two families Ray and Karin are marrying into, were chosen by Galton as noted instances of 'Hereditary Genius', there being a striking number of able and distinguished people from father to son and grandson in both lines. I do not myself believe that either Oliver Strachey, Ray's husband, or Adrian Stephen, Karin's fiancé, will amount to much more than clever, cultivated, pleasant companions, but their stock is good, and their children will have a fair chance.

To Mrs Berenson   *11 October 1914*   *Ford Place, Sussex*
We are still here, and still waiting, utterly unable, owing to lack of money, to make any plans.... If we could pay our debts in Italy, we should return there, and Bernhard would try to get work. If we can't do this—we don't know what to do.

To Senda Berenson Abbott   *18 November 1914*   *Paris*
I have found a really very nice maid, who is also an excellent valet for B.B. and satisfies all his fastidious requirements. Odd to be thinking of such things in the middle of the most terrific upheaval and ruin the world has ever known! But it is a positive *relief* to do so....

B.B. in the end decided not to go to America. I am not sure that the last weight that tipped the scales was not a rather romantic friendship that has grown up between him and our neighbour in the Villa

* Adrian Stephen was the younger brother of Virginia Woolf and Vanessa Bell. Their father, Sir Leslie Stephen, had married Thackeray's daughter as his first wife. Adrian, Vanessa and Virginia were, in fact, the children of his second wife, Julia Jackson.

Medici, Lady Sybil Cutting. You can imagine I encourage that all I can! It began to cast B.G. into the background, and Sybil is *such* an improvement on that horrible creature! She is really an awfully nice person who can have nothing but a good influence on anyone who gets to know her.

To her Family   27 December 1914   I Tatti
During the long period of not writing, his [B.B.'s] style has grown frightfully rocky, and Geoffrey and I have been in despair trying to make it intelligible and readable. He begins his sentences fairly well, but then slips into conditions and hangs on modifying clauses, and adds hints and innuendos till the result is more like a tapeworm than anything else. We were quite worn out by luncheon, and since then I've been typing.

Geoffrey had for some years been falling in love with almost every attractive woman he met, and was feverishly anxious to find a wife 'to look after him'. Mary was sympathetic, but determined that he should marry someone congenial to her, so that she might continue to hold his friendship.

One young woman whom they had met just before the war fulfilled all her requirements, and when Geoffrey seemed attracted to her she did her best to encourage the affair. Nicky (Elizabetta) Mariano, half-Neapolitan and half-Baltic aristocrat, a cousin of Count Keyserling, was all Slav to look at, and entirely charming. She eluded Mary's grasp, however, and went to stay with her sister and brother-in-law in the Baltic Provinces, where she was caught, first by the war and then by the Revolution, and reappeared in Florence only when the war was over.

Diary   21 January 1915   I Tatti
Days of heavenly do-nothing. I mean nothing involving others, but just the work I like to do in this library, with no one to bother me. I love such days, though I love them more when Geoffrey's sitting opposite to me, also at work.... If it weren't for the War I should be happy.

Diary   19 February 1915   I Tatti
Geoffrey and I had a gloomy walk, especially as, at lunch, B.B. was in such a rage with Cecil he wouldn't hear of any terms we might make about at least finishing the library. Geoffrey was upheld, though, by

201

having had a really charming letter from 'Nicky' Mariani [Mariano] who is in Russia. He is half in love with her already. Well, I have Barbara and envy no one.

Diary   22 February 1915   I Tatti
A 'submerged personality' took possession of me, and I raged and said things that I should never have said had I been 'myself'. It was a very strange experience, and as I was self-conscious through it all, it has taught me a *lot*. But it really did get hold of me. It kept me awake at night simply furious and disgusted. B.B. was quite frightened, and became as meek as a lamb. It all started with my finding him kissing Naima [the masseuse] and feeling disgust, which was silly, as I know it is the only thing one can do with that wild goose of a young female. This, however, brought up all my 'grievances' from Belle Greene to Sybil, and I said the nastiest and most devilish things about them all and about B.B. The worst of it was, I enjoyed it.

To Alys Russell   15 March 1915   I Tatti
I haven't had a word from Karin yet, so don't send this on to her. I must find some way of waking her up to the duty of at least acknowledging a present of ten pounds! I am sure Adrian's influence on her is very anti-family and 'Bloomsbury', but she must learn that those habits will not do with civilized people.

To Alys Russell   26 March 1915   I Tatti
Ray is certainly queer with her hatred of speaking of Barbara and her excessive reserve and spirit of criticism. But I do not know how to change her. I am thankful beyond words that she has a husband who seems to understand her and make her happy. It is a real miracle. With me she is a sweet hedgehog. It is like walking on eggs.

To Grace Worthington   Easter Sunday [4 April] 1915   I Tatti
I have found it frightfully hard to write letters this year, but that is no excuse. It is no use speaking of the war, and yet it is hard to turn one's mind to anything else.... It is all grisly and ghastly and I fear it will last for years ... Karin and Adrian, I regret to say, are deep in the 'Union of Democratic Control'* which seems to me a foolish and a

* The Union of Democratic Control was not explicitly pacifist, but was in favour of a larger role for Parliament in peace terms etc. It had a number of distinguished members, some Pacifist some not, including Norman Angell and Bertrand Russell.

very mischievous organization. I judge chiefly by the praise it gets in the fiendish German papers. . . . B.B. goes to see Lady Sybil Cutting every afternoon and dines with her about twice a week, so I daresay *he* is getting through this awful time fairly well!

To Alys Russell   14 April 1915   I Tatti
How silly it all is. I suppose it is human—but I shall some day explode with ennui. Living in the country it is so difficult what with sending for people etc and cross arrangements, with a telephone that works like the devil. I shall just give up kindness and decency. . . . All this 'seeing people'—what is the sense of it?

To her Family   24 May 1915   I Tatti
I find that even worse than the gouty headaches are the gouty *tempers* that overtake me. It is truly horrible to get 'mad' as often as I do now. I suppose everyone is nervous with this war; and it seems to me as if all the people I live with really go out of their way to be provoking!! But I know it isn't that, but my own gouty state.

Diary   26 May 1915   [Perugia?]
Went to Fossombrone and were shut up as German spies, until the commanding officer got too hungry to wait any longer for his *collazione*. Strange sensation to be gazed at by myriads of hard, unfriendly eyes. The people are quite off their heads with excitement and would have *loved* to lynch us.

To her Family   13 June 1915   Fiuggi
He [B.B.] is awfully keen about the war, and, as you can imagine, generous to a point about the Red X and all the national and local charities. But he has never been one '*de payer de sa personne*' and the War hasn't changed him.

Mary managed to get back to her family in England in the summer of 1915 and again in January 1916 for the birth of her second grandchild, Karin's daughter Ann. Travel was becoming more and more difficult, and B.B. more and more opposed to her leaving him, but in spite of these obstacles she returned in November 1916 for the birth of Ray's second child, Christopher. The following year restrictions on travel had become even more troublesome and her efforts to bring Alys and Barbara out to Italy failed, though she did manage to get back once again in November.

203

Plans for another trip to America finally fell through, much to Mary's relief. Belle Greene's influence was at last beginning to fade, as B.B. turned to Lady Sybil Cutting, his neighbour at the Villa Medici in Fiesole. Before long, however, Mary came to find her scarcely more tolerable than her predecessor.

Edith Wharton was now engaged in war work in Paris, and Mary was able to discuss Sybil with her there on her way through to England.

To Geoffrey Scott   29 July 1915   Ford Place, Sussex
I never told you that we had a heart-to-heart over Sybil the last evening. We feel exactly the same about her, though I try harder than she does to like her, and I know that her illness isn't hysterical exhibitionism, which is Edith's unshakeable view. Edith said she made a dead set at PL [Percy Lubbock]* who fled terrified. She also talked a lot and very naively about B.B., from which Edith drew the most polyandrous inferences. As I felt in my bones that E would be 'off' B.B. if the real state of things was revealed to her, I said there was a little something (to deny this would have been too palpably untrue) but that PL seemed to divide her heart, and that she and B.B. didn't see a very great deal of each other.

To Grace Worthington   3 August 1915   Ford Place, Sussex
Besides my strong desire to see Alys and Logan, the youngsters and Barbara, I was about fed up with Lady Sybil, whose unceasing flow of chatter is more than I can bear. She was always on hand, and I was glad for her to be, for she's an immense improvement on Miss B.G.: but her talk is more than I can bear. She's a very nice person really, but as Logan said, like a mermaid hid behind a cataract (of words), whose shape you can scarcely discern....

When I reached Ray's I found Oliver working at top speed, and Ray quite as busy as Mrs Wharton, though in a different way. She is Parliamentary Secretary for the N.U.W.S.S. [National Union of Women's Suffrage Societies], and 'watches' all the Bills, getting Questions asked in the House and Amendments moved. She says *all* the Bills contain clauses unfair to women, and her work is to remove or modify them. She is also working to get women into the higher branches of the Civil Service and into the posts left vacant by the male Factory Inspectors who've gone off to the War. To her surprise some

* Percy Lubbock, who became Lady Sybil's third husband.

amendments she scribbled in pencil on the margin of a Bill were instantly turned into Law! The Bill proposed to give pensions of £1 a week or more to all the widows of soldiers and sailors killed in fighting. As these will mount up to hundreds of thousands of young women, it would mean a colossal charge on the nation—a danger as well, with so many young women able to live in idleness. Ray suggested commuting the pension to £20 down, plus training in some profession by which the pensioner might reasonably be supposed to support herself. This was so *obviously* an improvement that the proposer of the Bill embodied it in the Bill at once.

The 'Labour Exchange' has proved itself incompetent, and Ray's Committee are working with the War Office to provide women for hay-making and hay-inspecting, and for working in munition and air-craft factories, and all sorts of other things. I consider she is doing *very* useful work, and Oliver too, and this is my excuse for having given them what they most desired on earth, a little car to run about in!

To Bernhard Berenson   6 August 1915   Ford Place, Sussex
I find that I feel the greatest *élan* of instinctive love for Barbara *when she is naughtiest*, screaming 'I want, I want' and beating me with her little fists. It is such a vigorous assertion of her separate personality that it vivifies all mine, in so far as I have a share in her.

To Bernhard Berenson   8 August 1915   Ford Place, Sussex
How curious about Belle. We who belong to the civilized class of humanity which does write letters (and other things) simply cannot understand what state of mind lies behind the habits of those who 'don't write letters'. It seems to me rude and horrible to a degree, selfish and inhuman, and I daresay I shall continue to think so till I die, whether it's Belle.... or Geoffrey even, or Adrian and his set. One has to swallow it in a kind of way, but it is revolting to me.

To Bernhard Berenson   11 August 1915   Ford Place, Sussex
This summer I have begun to realize the incessant necessary small services that make *our* lives what they are. I watch Barbara's delightful nurse a great deal, and see her washing and mending and tidying up and cleaning and then *beginning it all over again*—the whole of a human being's time just to keep one child good and clean and her clothes and surroundings dainty. I look on amazed, as at a sort of miracle, to think that all our lives mean *this*, all along, one way or another. Are we ants or bees to support the existence of this ceaseless

small toiling, over and over again? I cannot explain to thee how it makes me feel—almost as if civilization were a leaky raft kept crazily afloat *à force de minutes soins*, never ending, using up the time and strength of our fellow-creatures baling out the leaking-in water.... The horrid upheaval of the war has upheaved *such* a lot of my prejudices. It is almost painful what one comes to think. There isn't time left to adjust even one's mental habits to it, not to speak of one's physical habits. Most learning is pleasant and exhilarating, but to have one's eyes opened after 50 to elementary things is distinctly painful!

To Bernhard Berenson   26 August 1915   Bath
The prospect of the future, unless I do something radical, is black. Mother's spirits never deserted her, in spite of stiffness but then she never had a headache in her life: and I must say when the gout goes to your head your joy in life is up. Every night since January I have lain awake wishing, or at least thinking I wished to die. Fortunately moving about in the day one feels less gloomy. I daresay lots of people go through life with these black periods never very far away.

To Grace Worthington   25 October 1915   I Tatti
I am very much distressed at Karin and Adrian having gone in for that inept 'Union of Democratic Control'. It is loathed and despised about as much as would be a band of people who retired to a safe place from a burning house and proceeded to print half-instructed pamphlets on how to keep houses from catching fire, instead of lending a hand with the water-buckets.

Diary   3 November 1915   I Tatti
B.B. and I had a violent discussion about money, and I spent the rest of the day trying to see just how it all stands. I am inclined to feel that everything is always my fault.

To her Family   7 November 1915   I Tatti
I cannot think there is any real danger of bankruptcy. During the last 7 years we have bought this place and one adjoining *podere*: built extensively and made a garden, furnished the house and added to the library and collected pictures and *oggetti* worth about £50,000 (sterling) as well as invested a good deal.

Diary   27 December 1915   I Tatti
I am well over 50 and I don't know yet *how to live* in any sense,

physically, as to my body, or materially, as to the use of wealth, or socially as to the kind and amount of companionship I want, or morally—as to anything at all!—or emotionally, as to what to care for and how much.

Diary   18 January 1916   I Tatti
Quarrelled with Geoffrey over the never settled question of punctuality. I daresay I am too fussy, and I must try to be more easy-going, for fussiness defeats the end for which punctuality exists—i.e. to grease the machinery of life.

B.B. was still trying to get to America again for a business trip, but the obstacles were too great, and the trip was finally postponed until after the war.

To Senda Berenson Abbott   5 March 1916   I Tatti
I have a very great distaste to coming over again and being put in the position in which I found myself in New York last time: and it is only too likely to be repeated. But Bernhard says his visit is far less useful without me, for a lot of reasons, so I shall compromise by ignoring the existence of a certain person and refusing to have anything to do with her. But I assure you it makes me *hate* coming, and I would get out of it if I could. But life is so expensive and we have so many responsibilities that I don't see my way for a question of pride (I have no principles) to not helping to earn our luxuries.

To Alys Russell   9 April 1916   I Tatti
I enclose K's letter (which do not allude to in talking to her). I feel her really gone out of the Family for the present, although this is without prejudice for future developments. And of course one is interested and kind, although extraordinarily (for the moment) detached. The UDC has opened an abyss, which I feel Adrian working day and night to widen. Truth to tell, she has a large dose of Costelloe in her, while Ray is *ours*, and dear Oliver cements the union.

To Alys Russell   12 April 1916   I Tatti
I got Horne* to make his Will yesterday, and to make provision for his

* Herbert Horne, English art historian and collector. He was an old friend of the Berensons, but he and B.B. had quarrelled on professional grounds, and had remained alienated for many years.

207

faithful servant. He has left Beatrice [his sister] *and his brother* all his English property, and his Palace and works of art here to the State for a Museum. He cannot live more than a few days. It wrings my heart to go and sit with him, but I have to do it. His mind is softening and he clings to me. I've known him for 31 years.

To Logan Pearsall Smith   14 April 1916   I Tatti
Poor Horne died last night, after a reconciliation scene with B.B....
We were the last people he saw, and he said B.B.'s friendliness had given him a few moments of great happiness and peace. His mind may have been weakening, I daresay it was, for all this was so unlike him. But I am glad it happened.

To the Family   17 April 1916   I Tatti
The funeral was rather awful, the assistance being chiefly Sods (excuse the word) and dealers, with B.B. and Loeser (they might be called dealers), myself and one or two Museum officials of grubby aspect. He was buried near his mother in the Protestant Cemetery. Herbert Trench* went with us, and hardly had the earth been sprinkled on him, than Trench said to me 'I wrote a great Poem yesterday, 40 lines, a real inspiration. I'll send you a copy', while Loeser was saying 'The next time I marry, it shall be a Deaf Mute.' So everybody's life resumed its only very slightly ruffled flow. I believe the only people who minded at all were Santina, his servant, and me. And Santina was so pleased with her annuity that she wasn't really sorry, *au fond*, especially as it was more than Horne had paid her. Probably I am his only mourner—and God knows I don't mourn *much*: yet I do feel it.

To her Family   23 April 1916   I Tatti
I believe I enjoy those mountain walks more than anything else I do here. Within a half-hour's motor radius we have an incredible number of footpaths and little roads over the hills, each one revealing wide views of incredible beauty as well as intimate little valleys and rush-bordered streams and quiet high pasture land. If we take our tea, and have the car to set us down at one point and meet us at another 4 or 5 miles off, it is really incredible what glorious excursions we can take. ... B.B. hasn't made much of them this spring, because Sybil has been in bed nearly all the time since I got home, and she makes a point of his going to see her every afternoon. Yesterday he got out of it by a

* Herbert Trench, Irish poet of a mystical kind.

208

headache, but all the same he was just gleefully starting with us, when up drove the car, with Sybil nearly fainting inside. It has come to be a real burden; but she says she is so awfully lonely, and is certainly so ill, that he would feel a brute not to go and see her. How hard it is for people not to be exacting! I thank Gram every day of my life that she put such a horror of it into me that (except in utter unconsciousness) I *couldn't* make claims for companionship on anyone!

To Alys Russell   26 April 1916   I Tatti
Sybil ... is perfectly sick of having officers,* and most people here think their drunken and riotous ways have caused such a scandal in Florence as to increase decidedly the anti-English feeling that is growing up. Sybil is now as boring about their misdeeds and her consequent sufferings and desire to get rid of them, as she used to be about all their characters, individuality, *her* 'noble purpose' in having them, and her joy in 'doing her bit!' Alys, she is a cursed bore.

To Alys Russell and Logan Pearsall Smith   27 April 1916   I Tatti
When Horne died, I wrote to Roger [Fry] and said it was such a pity to wait till death to make up with one's friends, and suggested he and B.B. should try to get on friendlier terms. I enclose his answer, which please destroy. At the same time he wrote a note to B.B., who has never ceased being fond of him. . . . I have written to him again full of hope, but pointing out one or two of the probable thorns in B.B.'s character which may still prick him, in the hope that, if he realizes that I know the difficulties, they will be lessened in our future intercourse.

To Roger Fry   27 April 1916   I Tatti (Copy)
My dear Roger, B.B. was very much touched by your letter, and answered it the same day. He asked me to read his answer which I did. Every word of it seemed to me genuine. It is quite true that when Trevy or someone told him that Horne had put you against him he said it was the unkindest thing Horne could have done, and that he would never go near him again. Nor did he, until the end, when Horne asked for him. He has always had that amount of real fondness for you that made you a necessary part of his imaginative life so that when things didn't go well, he couldn't shake off the thought of you.

* Lady Sybil Cutting had taken in a number of convalescent Australian officers as a form of war work.

By this time I think I really do know the ins and outs of B.B.'s character. At the bottom of everything is a curious lonely wish to be loved. It acts just the wrong way, often, making him very suspicious of *not* being loved, of raising antagonism and the rest. A person who had all the affection they could do with anyhow, wouldn't care, but would sail along gaily and perhaps in the end with more affection. I keep explaining this to him and have had some success. I almost always laugh at his suspicions, and he is certainly not half so over-sensitive as he was.... However there are several thorns in his nature. One of these is a great recklessness of statement about things where he doesn't feel responsible (combined with utter unscrupulousness if it comes to argument) while at the same time holding himself and everybody else to strict account on subjects he really does know (or thinks he knows) about. This puts off people in both ways—they rage at his reckless statements made vehemently and fiercely, and they are furious at being suddenly taken up for some lightly expressed opinion on subjects where he *is* conscientious.... In vain do I labour to show him that he is as bad on other matters as he considers some connoisseurs to be on Italian art. All his bristles stand up at once when that sacred soil is lightly trodden on.... Another thing which imposes on ladies and drives men to the lights of murder is his occasional manner of seeming to think himself omniscient. To us who know him his manner is merely funny, because he is so winningly ready at other times to confess and even point out his follies. But in renewing friendly relations with him there is the chance that he may sometimes drive you wild in that way. He's something of a spoilt child conversationally and that is inevitable out here where we all know each other's talk by heart and B.B. is our only hope.... I have been in all his business things with him and my ineradicable old Quaker standards of fairness and honesty have not been outraged. On the contrary he has been scrupulous and also very generous. I cannot understand how the opposite ideas have grown up. However this is not the point. I am perfectly thankful you are ready to try again and I am full of hope about it. I have just thought it wise to warn you of the difficulties.

To Ray Strachey   *29 May 1916*   *Naples*

I can imagine that Barbara is the scourge of her school! I wish thee could go and see her at it, and tell me just what happened. They do well to tie her hands together. I don't believe the Montessori system is made for characters like Barbara's and Aunt Carey's!!

To Alys Russell   5 June 1916   Rome
Adrian's position [he had come up before a Tribunal as a Conscientious Objector] seems logical, but nothing more. I am sure Karin
invented it—it's worthy of the philosophical mind, which works
clearly and finely on given premises but has no sense at all in choosing
its premises. I shouldn't think there was a Tribunal in existence which
would have the patience to listen to all that rigmarole, when the only
thing that matters is whether people are willing to help their country
in the way that country demands *or not*. I don't know what to do to
keep from having a vast 'complex' of impatience against Adrian
implant itself in my system. All this silly business has really disgusted me, and I feel I am doing him some injustice but yet can't
help it.

To Alys Russell   17 June 1916   I Tatti
I am so bored, Alys, by most of the people I see. What is one to do?
It's like a boil which is reaching a head.

To Alys Russell   25 June 1916   I Tatti
I cannot understand such a clear thinker as Bertie writing such a
foolish article as the one on liberty of conscience. But he evidently
doesn't weigh the premises on which his arguments are built up. For
example, that Fear is the only cause of war; when we all know that
greed of conquest is generally the cause in the attacking party. Was
Germany impelled to the war of 1870 by *Fear*, or Italy in the Tripoli
war? It is too absurd. The article creeps with nonsense of this kind. I
see he has ranged himself with the anti-vaccinationists! And at the
end comes his greatest cropper in assuming that the greatest men of
every age are great because of their conflict with the old-established
ideas, the sub-inference being that the 'maxims of the past' must be
wrong when confronted with the 'nascent wisdom of the present'. The
reverse is generally true. I hate to see a person of Bertie's mind
making such a fool of himself.

To Alys Russell   28 June 1916   I Tatti
He [B.B.] absolutely needs me here, though I cannot say he makes it
pleasant. He takes my corrections—and my goodness how awfully he
writes!—with such fury and rage (though he generally ends by
accepting them—in fact always) that I get quite disgusted. Three
days running I have got up and left the room, uttering something very
stinging as I departed. It is a new 'system', but I'm not sure it works

211

any better than the old one of patience. It's all such nonsense. I swot away correcting his slipshod sentences and tightening up his argument, and he treats me like a pickpocket! Even so I am necessary at this juncture, otherwise his books would be far more awful than they are.

To Alys Russell   6 July 1916   I Tatti
I blame us all for the muddle [in the Building accounts], B.B. quite as much as anyone. Of course had I been a careful person, I should have followed things month by month: but that I just CAN'T do, it isn't in my nature. I'd rather live in a cave. The elegance and grandeur of this house is B.B.'s wish, though also mine (to give work to the architects) and I care so little for it that I can't put my mind to it. B.B. knew that—good heavens if after all these years he expects me to be an accurate accountant he is an idiot. But he didn't expect it, that's the truth. He *let it slide*, as I did, as Cecil did. Only Geoffrey unavailingly wrung his hands from time to time and predicted the end of the world. B.B. blames me now, but it cannot be anything but a rhetorical and wordy escape from his own annoyance.

To Alys Russell   7 July 1916   I Tatti
Geoffrey thinks of marrying an awfully nice Russo-Italian girl (cousin of the Keyserlings) [Nicky Mariano]. He met her before the war, and without 'falling in love' he knew at once that she was the wife for him. Curiously B.B. said so at once, in fact we all felt it, even Cecil. She is furthermore a person who would absolutely fit into our little circle like a ball in a round hole; and this is more important than thee can imagine in a small intimate band like ours. I don't know her well, but she is adored by her friends and their opinion is unanimous that she is very unselfish and accommodating, that she makes friends with older women, who tend to treat her like a daughter, that she is sweet-tempered and gay and social, yet loves books and music and art, is never bored etc etc. She is much inclined to like me, and I feel it important to gain her personal friendship before she is up in arms against me as Geoffrey's friend (not that she necessarily would be) ... I think if she were treated with tact she might adopt me as semi-family. She will tend to be grateful to me if I give them a good time (always supposing her heart inclines to Geoffrey) and am warm and cordial to her (as indeed I feel) quite independently of him. I am *quite certain* I can live up to my part, because I sincerely *want* him married

and, so to speak, settled with his 'natural protector'.* There's not a thing of which she could be jealous, except a friendship longer than hers. But, *au fond de mon âme*, I am more than ready to take a back seat in regard to him.... I have such a warm welcome for her, without one *arrière-pensée* of regret for giving Geoffrey to her. AU CONTRAIRE. And truth will out, she is sure to know how I feel.

Diary   15 July 1916   I Tatti
G [Geoffrey] and I walked home, but it wasn't very pleasant, as I had to complain of his being so selfish about my family affections. I don't want him to be like B.B. and always put difficulties in my way about going home and generally show his dislike of my fondness for my own family. It has always made things somewhat difficult, and I cannot have Geoffrey going the same way. It is selfish of them—they want me to be exclusively devoted to them. It only makes friction, for I cannot yield there—it is too vital to me.

To Alys Russell   16 July 1916   I Tatti
Geoffrey's only source of income is as B.B's secretary and so he has to be dependent here, and it wouldn't be fair (he thinks) to ask the girl to marry him without letting her know that. She might well resent the necessary subordination into which B.B. puts anyone who wants to have an easy life with him.... He would rather she knew it first, rather than have it sprung upon her as his fiancée or wife when we return from America. However after what thee and Logan say ... I shall not alter my comings and goings so as to foment the match, but shall slip away and let 'nature take its course' independently while preparing a tactful welcome for her when the times comes.

To Alys Russell   22 July 1916   I Tatti
By the way, since thee said that love affairs were my crazy spot, I have looked into the matter, and I find *it is true* ... thanks for the hint.

Diary   7 September 1916   I Tatti
I went down to the Consul's and found that there are many difficulties in the way of travel. After an awful struggle we decided not to go to America, but to remain here till the end of the war. I don't see how I can bear not to go to England. It is *awful* for me. But I am

---

* Hannah used to say that every man who married had found his 'natural protector'.

tremendously relieved about America. To go and amuse ourselves with fashionable life there in war-time would have been intolerable.

Diary   18 September 1916   I Tatti
Perfectly miserable. *I cannot bear* not to go home. How *can* B.B. try to prevent me. It is sheer selfishness and lack of consideration for the best feelings I have.* It is really too awful. But he threatens me with all sorts of awful consequences if I go, such as his staying in America, getting to hate I Tatti, never trusting me again, etc etc. And as he is clearly the main business of my life, on which my happiness really depends, I *must* give in ... But why in hell does he want me to stay when it makes me utterly miserable and besides makes me almost hate him and rage secretly against him all the time?

Diary   4 October 1916   I Tatti
Fearful day of indecision about going home. B.B. is so against it, so afraid somehow, of being left alone, and so far from well, that I gave in and said I would not go, if he felt he really *couldn't* spare me. But there must be something he doesn't say, some complex about having to give up B.G., and wanting me to give up as much, or *something* I don't understand, to account for the violence of his expression.

Diary   5 October 1916   I Tatti
The mystery was explained by a telegram for him which was brought to me—from B.G. saying that since he couldn't come to London she would come and stay with him for 2 weeks in Paris. He had given up London—not for me, but because he couldn't stand her friends there, and her flirtations with them—and he felt bored and depressed and so couldn't spare me, not even for a most sacred duty of mine and one I cared about *awfully*. Another cause for me to love that vulgar young person! However her coming decided him to go to Paris, so I am graciously allowed to go too.

After an anxious journey, Mary reached London at the beginning of November, in time for the birth of Ray's son, Christopher, on 16th.

To Isabella Gardner   7 January 1917   Paris
B.B. has asked me to write to you about THE picture,† which I saw
* Ray was pregnant, and Mary wished to be there for the birth.
† This was Bellini's *The Feast of the Gods*, now in the National Gallery of Art, Washington. Mrs Gardner did not buy it.

over and over again when I was in London. I honestly think it is the most fascinating, the grandest and the most mysterious picture I have ever seen.... The poetry of Bellini's picture is so profound that you feel you could never exhaust or even entirely understand it; for the interpretation of the theme has an unexpectedness and originality that makes you realize it is the result of the brooding and dreaming of a great mind.... There is something in the picture deeper and more haunting than the beauty that meets the eyes. The painting has in it the thrill that certain voices have when they sing airs that we know, but, over and beyond, the melody *here* is in a new mode, with intervals and cadence of poetry that no written literature prepares us for. One looks and looks and looks, and all the time new things strike one's attention—I never knew anything so inexhaustible. It seems to me the greatest Creation of Italian painting.... I simply can't let myself think of it at Fenway Court, because it would be such a glorious thing that even to write the words (without daring to hope them) makes me feel quite faint with hoping.

To Bernard Berenson   2 July 1917   Salsomaggiore
I know the ghastly complex that makes the whole subject [the house] next to intolerable, and causes thee to fly into rages that leave thee looking haggard and worn and old (and rack my heart with regret and sorrow, for I hate to see thee look ill) and I think there has been more than enough reason for thee for the forming of such complexes, both against Cecil and me for our recklessness. The only thing that seems to me unfair is that thee allows thy quite justified general bitterness to prejudice thee violently in every individual case, so that the discovery of the truth seems quite useless. I am making in my *for intérieur* a real effort to try to stick to the facts about the things I say (I am awfully distressed to find how hopelessly I exaggerate, misrepresent and even lie). It is hard for me, but such an attempt should be easy for thee, but I don't see thee make it in any case where old 'complexes' come up.

To Bernard Berenson   9 July 1917   Salsomaggiore
I *was* anxious to get jobs for Cecil, and I am sure this made me overlook lots of things that should have warned me. And as I know he did some things for us that no one else available could have done, I, even my own self, glazed over the failures, though God knows they reduced me often to tears and desperation. NO, certainly I know I went ahead under full steam to get them work, but I did not ever think I was doing what would not turn out to be an advantage to thee.

215

To Alys Russell   14 July 1917   Salsomaggiore
I also asked her [Ray] to let B [Barbara] come out with thee for a long visit ... in view of B.B.'s longing for me to stay and his genuine pleasure in the thought of a visit from thee *and from Barbara* (he says he is beginning to feel hopeful and sentimental and grandfatherly towards her generation at last!) and in view of what is my *honest* belief, namely that if he were thrown much with Barbara now, before she reaches the shy, impenetrable age, his heart would relent about founding his hateful (and useless) Institootion*, and he would think of her and her like as his natural heirs—in view of that, and my health which always gets wretched in England—perhaps he will say yes. What does thee think?

To Alys Russell   28 July 1917   Castiglioncello
Ray says thee may bring B if thee can. What heaven!! We old girls will have a delightful time. I shall get a Kindergarten or Montessori trained nurse. But the question is *can you get permission?* I think the way to put it is thy needing the climate and change after thy operation [for cancer of the breast] (people are always sympathetic about cancer and realize the gravity) and B's going to live with her grandmother— say if necessary to save her parents the expense, as their income is reduced by the war. Probably thee can get someone to help thee, too. Ah Alys, *do* do it if thee can! I cannot possibly put into words how much I want you both.... I have already had the most blissful hours planning your rooms, B's dancing lessons ... etc etc. Oh *do* come if it's in any way possible.

To Alys Russell   3 August 1917   I Tatti
Thee cannot possibly imagine my disappointment about thy not coming. There's no use writing about it.... Italians, however, are less scrupulous than English, and I dare say Giglioli would fork out a certificate of my needing thy care—if thee would use it. There is a certain psychological justification for it, in his mind at least, for he is always trying to make me out a very nervous patient on the verge of a breakdown because of the strain of my life (as he considers it) away from my children and with a person of so uncertain a temper as B.B.; but maybe he won't, and maybe it wouldn't work at the other end. I am prepared for the worst.

* B.B. intended to leave the Villa and the Library to Harvard as a post-graduate Institute for the study of Italian Renaissance Art.

To Alys Russell   10 September 1917   I Tatti
I'll have a time yet persuading B.B. to go [to Paris] for he is set
against it, but the D's [Duveen's] agent, who has come down to see
him, has just told me that he thinks it very important for B.B. to be
there, as the D firm is reconstituting itself on a new basis.

To Bernard Berenson   26 October 1917   London
Ray has been seeing a lot of Lord Robert Cecil* over the hitch in the
Representation Bill†. She says they are really devoted to each other,
and that is much for Ray to say. If I have any trouble about getting
back, she is quite sure he will see me through, but like most English
people, she doesn't like to use her personal graft.

To Bernard Berenson   6 November 1917   London
Keynes said that he found Washington very oriental—Wilson like an
invisible Sultan spending most of his time in the harem, and all the
others talking endlessly and slowly and never getting to business.
Even Lord Northcliffe said to him, 'It is positively oriental'. He thinks
the Americans are absolutely ruthless and Wilson about the most
complete despot the world has ever seen. A thing that never got into
the papers here was the following. The IWW‡ (Independent Workers
of the World) is a very powerful and large body. They have somewhat
muddly pacifistic tendencies. One day the Chiefs of Police all over
America received a direct order from the President to seize and
imprison leaders of that organization, in each town, without trial. And
it was done, and no one protested.

To Bernard Berenson   16 November 1917   London
Of course thee must be eaten up with misery about Italy§. For Europe
to destroy it is like a man murdering his beautiful and adored
mistress. It's sheerly crazy to fight the war *there*. I'm dreadfully afraid

* Lord Robert Cecil, Under Secretary for Foreign Affairs and deeply
concerned to promote the League of Nations.
† The Act, passed in 1918, finally gave women the vote, though only at the
age of thirty.
‡ The I.W.W. (Industrial Workers of the World) was a radical organization
of unskilled labourers, held to be impeding the war effort by strikes and
sabotage. A large number of its leaders were arrested by Federal Agents and
charged with conspiracy and other crimes. Those arrested were eventually
tried (some after long periods in custody) and many were convicted.
§ Italy had suffered a severe defeat at the battle of Caporetto in October
1917.

that no effective resistance will be made till the Adige is reached—Vicenza, Verona, Padua—all those dear towns, and oh Bernard all the Campanili in the plain—and Conegliano, Colalto—all the places we know so well, Castelfranco, Villa Enco, Asolo and Villa Maser . . . the memory of each stabs me like the thought (almost) of a dead child.

CHAPTER FOURTEEN

Catastrophe

December 1917–November 1920

In the spring of 1917 America entered the war. In September of that year B.B. had to go to Paris on business, and decided to stay on there when, with the help of Edith Wharton, he obtained work as an interpreter with the US Army Intelligence. Only nominally an interpreter, he was really employed to sound out opinion among Allied leaders. He established himself in a friend's apartment, revelling in the feeling—induced by the high political level of many of his contacts—that he was influential in important concerns, and delighting, as always, in the elegant social life of Paris.

After another visit to England, Mary hurried back to I Tatti in November, fearing that it would be requisitioned for refugees by the Italians after their recent defeat at Caporetto. Soon after her arrival she was faced with the sudden shock of learning that Geoffrey Scott was on the point of proposing marriage to Lady Sybil. At first she tried to display tolerance, but despair gradually overcame her, and she became more and more frantic.

To Bernard Berenson   10 December 1917   I Tatti
Geoffrey went to see her [Sybil] ... and I think he will finish his visit there. I urge him to, for a present friend is better than an absent one; and I am absent. He must make the best of Sybil, and now that thee isn't here they are evidently more drawn together. I welcome it, not for caring less for him, but more—he needs a female ear, as she needs a male, and thy ear and mine being withdrawn what a blessing they enjoy each other's!

To Bernard Berenson   12 December 1917   I Tatti
During these days Algar and I have been consulted by Geoffrey as to whether to propose to Sybil. We both encouraged him, for reasons thee can supply without my writing. He did so last night. Naturally

there's been a lot of spooning (for Sybil is given to that) and it made Geoffrey think she meant more than she apparently did. For her first reaction was sheer funk; ... Geoffrey's task was to convince her he cared, once that done she would 'consider' ... the announceable decision will probably not be made till some time during Sybil's January visit to Rome.... I am very glad, for I think Geoffrey will be very considerate and gentle and reliable, and will be fond and affectionate and appreciate her character. Even the love part may turn out better than might be expected. And of course it's a splendid cadre for him, and she is so definite in her standards that he will be immensely braced up. He has always found her a perfect brick, and her peculiarities never made him as nervous as they made me.... *Dentro di me* I feel a natural movement of disgust that *both* my men should have been snatched away by that chatterbox: but I think I have shown no sign of this to Geoffrey.... I daresay it will cause some amused reflections on the impersonality of her affections—it has been clearly a 'man' she wanted, and one will 'do' as well as another.

To Bernard Berenson   20 December 1917   I Tatti
I have a strong instinct that the kind of intimacy I had with Geoffrey cannot continue, and it is best to make the change at once before we get on each other's nerves trying to keep life in dead bones. The fact is he knows quite well I don't like Sybil, and I daresay I never shall, after all these years of trying, and of course that will at once cause a big *gêne* between us of a kind that has never existed, and which I think will end by destroying our intimacy (it must) and unless discreetly handled, with plenty of absence, our friendship.

To Geoffrey Scott   26 December 1917   I Tatti
I must tell you frankly that the whole consensus of worldly wise people is against an older woman who tries to keep on any sort of intimate friendship with a young man she has been devoted to when he marries. That situation is *archi-connu*; and it is said *never to work* ... The old human situation is essentially the same, really: aggravated by finding it so hard to like your wife. Geoffrey, *can* we deal with it wisely? Considering that I never have dealt with any human situation wisely, and you, too, are liable to error!!

To her Family   2 January 1918   I Tatti
You can't think how seriously ill I've been—or perhaps you can, from the cessation of my in normal circumstances incessant letters! It was

of course crazy of me to take that journey with the kind of cough I had, and I realize now that at my age there's no chance of not paying for our imprudence! Instead I nearly got pneumonia. I hoped to slip through without being caught, and it seemed important to come at once, lest the unoccupied house should be taken for refugees.... So many people expect a Social Revolution here *modo russo* (some even desiring it!!) that I do not feel at all sure of ever seeing this place again.... In my spirit I am saying goodbye to everything, and I find I care less than I should have thought possible. What *does* one care for then? We've put 10 of our best years into making this house and collecting the things and why don't I really mind leaving it? I cannot understand.

To Bernard Berenson   5 January 1918   I Tatti
Thy New Year's letter came today.... Its message for me touched me very much and would touch me more if I could bring myself to believe thee really meant it. But thee has a very misleading pen for ladies, and who knows that I do not come in under that deceitful technique.... A real sting for me lurks in every single nice thing thee says to me, knowing how thee has got into the habit of using love's vocabulary to all and sundry. I have done it myself God knows, in my day, but that seems a long time ago, and my beguiling old partner is *still* going on with it!

To Bernard Berenson   7 January 1918   I Tatti
My own attitude is coming right, though not to *her*. I really detest her as I hardly ever have any woman. I got an overdose of her and tried so hard to like her. But from the first it was hopelessly against the grain, and now it is a chronic complex...

Our two express trains are running fast in opposite directions aren't they? But the nice thing is that we each reserve a compartment for the other, hoping to meet at a junction and get into the same train.

To Bernard Berenson   12 January 1918   I Tatti
If we don't know now how truly fond we are of each other we are great fools. And we do know it! The minimum of affection cannot I think ever grow less, it subsists through all our mutually sharp criticism, our follies, our weaknesses, our mistakes, and therefore there's nothing that can upset it. And as the years improve our characters—I feel they will!—the affection will increase, for that kind of real love corresponds with exactitude to the interplay of character. I confess

that having got rid of Sybil is a great help to me—and I dare say thee will say the same about my getting my penguin, Geoffrey, off my feet—although I do not think thee loathed him as I always have Sybil. Everyone in Florence will think the new arrangement remarkably astute on thy part. How many hundreds of times I have had to parry the cat-like attempts of my acquaintances to find out how I felt about the situation Sybil created for me!

To Geoffrey Scott   *19 January 1918*   *I Tatti*
Geoffrey dear, I am trying very hard to understand what is the matter with me, I don't know myself in the grip of this strange passion. I can see it is perhaps the expiation of all that was perilous and wrong in the way I loved you but how is a wretched human being to love other than they *can*? When I say I 'let myself get too fond of you in certain ways', the inner machinery gives a whirr and a buzz, and shakes off the one who says this, as if it were a fly on a wheel. The thing was somehow given—it came. I tried to make something nice of it, but at a touch all the evil is there again, and has me body and mind. The worst is in the so-called mind. There seem to be at least two latent persons all jarred into life by this intimate crisis. The Mary of everyday, the usual top-dog Mary, you and I can live with well enough, even delightfully. She is the one who loves you deeply and—as far as can go with deep love—unselfishly. That is what you call the 'real' Mary, your anchor. But two fierce demons have come and torn up that anchor. The first is biological sex—like 'Nature red in tooth and claw'—and it leads me to deeds I regret and feel remorse for, it blinds my judgment, blunts my kindness, destroys my delicacy and consideration, and works as much active havoc as it can. I know when I have it—just as you knew by your heavy pulses, that you were in love—by a dreadful inner trembling that hardly ever leaves me.... But dearest this isn't the worst creature whom the storm has uprooted from slimy primeval depths. Perhaps the most destructive, havoc-making one, yes, but in such storms there is still a vital principle, acting *à rebours*, it is true, but intensely, fearfully alive. No! the one still underneath is the one I dread most, the calm, tired, indifferent, cynical, so-called 'common-sense' which makes everything seem like *Talk*. I suppose this is the *Accidie* I heard the priest at San Martino warning the little children against!! This is my, our, worst enemy; and unfortunately Sybil has the key to unlock the cell where it is generally shut up.... I know no active and effective way of dealing with what seems to turn life into a desert where nothing matters particularly.

222

To Geoffrey Scott   [no date, no place, unsent?]
When I woke up, it was with the thought of seeing you: when I dressed (very badly) it was with the same thought, even when I did my hair or brushed my teeth (homely details) it was 'for you' in its own way. Everything that happened had value because it was to be told to you—or hidden from you if disagreeable. When I ordered things to eat it was because you were to eat them—but I needn't go on—Everything was with direct vital reference to you. Suddenly all these things are the province of someone I very much disliked, long, long before there was any idea of your giving your life to her. She dresses for you, she orders what you eat, she arranges her hair for you—Everything—for you say she truly loves you. The repercussion in me is that I *loathe* every act of daily life. They aren't only meaningless, they are, each one, horribly distasteful. If I could grow mangy fur, like a sick bear, and go and live in a filthy cave, I honestly think I should like it better.

To Bernard Berenson   22 January 1918   I Tatti
The thought that thee gave this withered chattering child the best of three years of thy life, and that Geoffrey is planning to give his entire life to her—casts over my spirit for life's social banqueting the same kind of feeling that seasickness induces in one for physical banqueting.

She rejoined B.B. in Paris in February, only to find that he had started another passionate love affair, this time with a highly intelligent and spirited Frenchwoman, Baroness Gabrielle La Caze, an art collector and traveller. His uninhibited description of his feelings for her drove Mary to real despair, and she first tried to throw herself out of the window* and then succumbed to a succession of acutely painful, if arguably psychosomatic, illnesses. B.B. too became almost desperate, and he and Mary clearly inflamed each other. In late April it was agreed that Ray should come over to Paris to fetch her mother, who was to stay in England until she was calmer.

To Alys Russell   15 April 1918   Paris
I am not *in pain*, I think I can't be with that blessed drug [Argyrol, against cystitis] but I am fairly uncomfortable. However to tell the truth, I really welcome that, because a so much worse thing hung over me—neurasthenia—and this teasing preoccupation drives it away. I

* B.B. prevented her (described by Ray to her daughter).

needn't say a word to thee about neurasthenia—thee knows too well its devilishness! You can't think pleasant thoughts, any more than you could chew your food with a mouthful of ragingly inflamed teeth. It's like a violent toothache of the mind and heart. It always lies in wait for me now.

To Bernard Berenson   30 April 1918   Le Havre
I mean to cultivate with all that is left of my shattered will, and only this, affection, understanding, devotion and the pleasures of discourse ... Don't mind this temporary separation, which I am convinced was necessary for me to get where thee wants me and I want to be.

To Bernard Berenson   3 May 1918   London
I am so glad not to be with thee—strange when I love thee so!—but today is the blackest and most desperate of all the days I ever had, and thee would hate to see me suffering, even knowing it would pass by.... I shall feel glad (if there is a nerve left to feel glad about anything except my *complete trust* in thee) when I hear thee has written to Geoffrey at the British Embassy to tell him I have been really ill and not myself and that thee is sure I shall wish him happiness when I return to even that faulty and miserable human being that used to be Mary.

To Bernard Berenson   21 May 1918   Nursing home, Chobham
Eliza [her maid] is the only one to help me, for poor Alys came to see me yesterday when I was suffering, lost her temper and went away in tears. It upset me too, fearfully, and I even don't want to see her again. She is, Ray thinks, just on the verge of a nervous breakdown herself, poor thing. Eliza *had* one, but it is a little better from two weeks in bed.

To Bernard Berenson   8 June 1918   Nursing home, Chobham
I do not forget the early days when you loved me, nor all our years of companionship and shared work and enjoyment of beautiful things. The other is like a horrible black pit into which I fall the moment I try to go to sleep, and even Medinal ... gives me very little help, for my dreams are so vivid and unpleasant that I start awake very quickly and miserably.... I feel that if I only knew you were in England and away from her [Mme La Caze] I could be tranquil, but that may be an illusion. As for Geoffrey, he has vanished like a pleasant dream that turned into a nightmare from which one awakens.

The Piot frescoes in the Big Library at I Tatti

B.B. and Geoffrey Scott in the garden at I Tatti, 1915

A corridor and (*below left*) the New Library at I Tatti

The villa I Tatti

Belle da Costa Greene,
c. 1912

Sybil Cutting in about 1907 with her
daughter Iris (later the Marchesa Origo)

Mary and B.B. in Egypt, 1922

Nicky Mariano and Mary, Egypt, 1922

Nicky and Mary, I Tatti, 1929

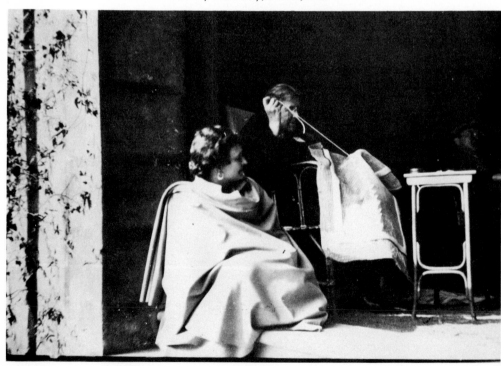

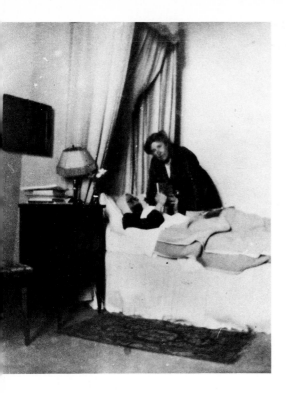

Mary and B.B. at I Tatti,
c. 1920

Mary with Barbara Strachey (on her
lap) and her cousin Ursula Strachey,
I Tatti, 1919

Bob Trevelyan, 1950

Eugénie Sellers Strong

Edith Wharton in about 1930

Kenneth Clark, 1926

Nicky Mariano, B.B., Carlo Placci and Walter Lippmann, Consuma, 1937

B.B. in Greece, 1923

Logan Pearsall Smith, Mary and
Desmond MacCarthy, Consuma, 1932

Barbara and Christopher Strachey on the shute at
Fernhurst, 1928

Judith and Ann Stephen with
Christopher Strachey, Fernhurst, 1921

Judith Stephen and her pig 'Celestino' at I Tatti,
1925

Mary, Ray Strachey and Roger,
Fernhurst, 1937

To Bernard Berenson   8 June 1918   Nursing home, Chobham
I fear I cannot possibly make even the least step towards getting well, although I shall try hard for every reason. In fact I am much worse, as to the bladder trouble, judging by pain, every day.... I foresee that we shall be separated for years unless you come now.... But I see that this is not to be, and I am fair enough to understand that a holiday in the Pyrenees, in the company of the woman you love and who loves you, would probably be better for your health and nerves.

To Bernard Berenson   11 June 1918   Nursing Home, Chobham
Dearest Bernard. I can't, I just can't bear it if you go off to spend July with Mme La Caze. I have fought and fought all day, and tried to feel old and take on the passive spectator attitude of old age, but I can't do it, Bernard! I know it will kill me. It's devil's work to feel like this, but if you go off with her I shall kill myself and have it over.

Bernard did finally come to London on June 20th—summoned by Mary's doctor—and spent some time with her in London and by the sea at Littlehampton, with the grandchildren. He returned to Paris at the end of September, after leaving her at Chilling, with Alys.

To Bernard Berenson   9 October 1918   Chilling
I won't be nasty about the children, but will tell thee that Ann [Karin's daughter] climbed up in her mother's lap and asked insinuatingly 'Have you got whiskers?' and Barbara explained to her governess that she *tried* to be good, but 'viciousness keeps looking out of one eye'.

To Bernard Berenson   1 November 1918   Chilling
I am amused at thy dubbing me thy expert in children, but it made me sad to think thee would never enjoy the real thing.... When thee is thinking of me, please remember that the life I chose with thee precluded me from whatever small gift I had for that expertise, and has been to me like the damming up of a part of me that cannot help existing, worse luck.... It is the non-functioning of an instinct, just as thee has to be in love and wouldn't stand it if I should try to cut thee off from one of thy affairs.

To Bernard Berenson   4 November 1918   Chilling
I think I now understand Alys. She has never got over her nervous breakdown [in 1902] she has only repressed most of the symptoms,

which makes it all the worse, when it does break out. And it can't help doing so every day in lots of little ways, so that one's attitude to her is half admiration for her stoicism and the other half dislike and antagonism. I hope I shan't be left like that, but I understand well how it might be. . . . I see it all so clearly in poor Alys, whose behaviour is angelic, but who freezes one's blood with hidden antagonism.

To Bernard Berenson   15 November 1918   Chilling
Please put prejudice aside, and ask thyself *how thee would feel about our common life* if I had said to thee that all I cared to take from this world to the next was the remembrance of thy eyes at a sexual climax, of Blaydes' or of some X with whom I was at the time engaged in creating these priceless memories. All *our* memories together jettisoned, all but one, and that only *one in a series* (and such a series!!) . . . thee tells me that if there is to be a continuance of memory all thee will care to take over is the memory of my young eyes, of Miss Greene's and of Mme La Caze's. It revealed to me a Bernard I did not know, who certainly is not my imagined and loved husband of all these years. It destroyed my universe.

To Bernard Berenson   17 November 1918   Chilling
O please help me, dearest Bernard, to get back to where I was before I split to pieces on that rock. My timbers, it is true, were wrenched by Geoffrey's marriage, which showed him to put his essential values on things I cared nothing for, but I could really have weathered that if I had not had to know that thee was off in another universe where I could not for an instant go—and that *that* was the most important (most worth remembering) fact in thy inner life.

By November 1918 the war was at last over. A fourth grandchild, Karin's younger daughter, Judith, had been born, and Mary began to recover, though it was not until the following year that she felt well enough to return to I Tatti.

To Bernard Berenson   18 November 1918   Chilling
I am not at all sure our wisest plan would not be to go back to I Tatti. Thee is not really happy in Paris as a sort of hanger-on—it is not a role thee likes playing. . . . I feel it would be much more dignified to go home. . . . Public affairs are not thy *métier*, but art is, and thee had better go back to that. . . . I thought 'thy adventure' was turning out so much to thy liking that there was no room for me—I mean not only

226

the one thing, but the whole round of social life in Paris. But if it is not so ... then we must be together and I will come whenever thee says.

To Bernard Berenson   26 November 1918   Chilling
I would be an idiot ... if I did not know that my attitude towards Geoffrey has made this crisis more acute. Since he married Sybil I have absolutely put him out of my heart and even of my thoughts, but of course the process has left a gash, and the nervous shock produced by such a violent surgical operation had predisposed me to take an unhappy view of everything, and naturally of the thing that counts most, my relation to thee. Geoffrey's lack of faith of course found enough to reinforce it when I arrived in Paris. But I do not believe that even what happened there would have destroyed me if it had not been reinforced by memories of the way thee created for thyself an imaginary world with Belle Greene, which thee told her again and again was the *only one* thee cared to live in imaginatively and the only one of all thy memories thee wished to preserve. ... I suffered terribly over all that (and do still): it seemed incredible that thee should throw over all the memories of our youth that we share. However I had a deep and, as I foolishly believed, satisfactory friendship to fall back upon, and I must confess Geoffrey talked a lot of sense to me about thy character and ways when he saw me so desperate. In this case I have no one, and *that* friendship is ended in a way that shows me to myself to have been an absolute Fool. ... I understand thy calling it a 'sexual crisis' but I think that is too crudely Freudian.

To Bernard Berenson   19 December 1918   London
I understand now one of the things I simply couldn't understand before, namely what it is that makes people *ask* for affection. I still think that is not the way to *get* it, but the exact opposite; but I understand the agonies of loneliness and desolation, the feeling of being deserted and shunned, that make one weak enough or desperate enough to cry out for some sign that it is not as bad as it seems! In making appeals to thee, I don't for a minute suppose they can possibly endear me to thee—probably just the reverse. They are merely frantic cries for opiates against pain. And thee kindly gives them to me, with that gentleness one uses towards a sick person.

To Bernard Berenson   13 January 1919   Hampstead
If only we could be friendly without all this appalling criticism—just like tired and silly children. I do not think you understand much, you

227

know, though the brilliance of your mind supplies you with ready and searing labels. I am not able to bear up against your scathing comments any more. If you care at all, please do not destroy me with them. Just be gentle and kind, and let me see you soon—I am so *awfully* unhappy.

To Bernard Berenson   17 January 1919   Hampstead
I want to be gentle and unselfish and tolerant, and yet I find myself impelled to be the opposite. I see what is to be aimed at, but the power to reach the necessary frame of mind is not there, only confused and hurrying wretchedness.

In April Mary returned briefly to Italy, where she renewed her plans to sweep Nicky Mariano into her net—despite Geoffrey's defection—before setting off with Bernard on a sightseeing trip to Spain and spending the summer in England again.

To Bernard Berenson   4 April 1919   I Tatti
I am bored with most of the things I have to do—or rather the people I seem to have to see. It is hard to strike them off the list for they all want, or pretend to want to see me again and yet again. . . . I called on Mme Giuliani to get news of Nicky Mariani [Mariano] who just escaped, by the skin of her teeth, falling into the hands of the Bolsheviks who burnt down her brother-in-law's castle and imprisoned him. . . . Nicky is in Switzerland with Byba Giuliani, but they are expected here in a day or two. I want to see her, as I have my eye on her for a secretary-housekeeper. That is if she must earn money.

To Mrs Berenson   16 July 1919   San Sebastian
We have had three most wonderful but very strenuous weeks seeing the most enchanting country you can imagine, and the most interesting towns. . . . What he [B.B.] would like to do now is to go to bed for 2 weeks, and spend the rest of the summer here in this charmed seaside place. Alas, I can't do that either. I have already considerably upset the plans of my 3 families in England by staying so long . . . and I don't like to cause further trouble. Besides I do long one summer to see my youngsters playing in the sea! I have been, one way or another, cheated out of it for four years, and it is something I do care for most awfully. . . . Bernard thinks he won't come to England, and indeed I shall be only 5 weeks there at the most, for I *must* go to a Cure in September, as I am by no means well yet.

To Bernard Berenson   27 July 1919   Chilling
I have had a heavenly morning on the little beach with the naked children.... Of course there's only ONE grandchild, the first, who excites in one the full rapture of surprise and hope and effort. The others lag behind, and are only the same thing again; more or less.

To Bernard Berenson   30 July 1919   Chilling
There is no line between fact and fancy in their minds [the children's], only now and then a scratch or bump breaks in upon their dreams and causes *real* yells. Fury and quarrels are part of the day-long dream, and can be calmed by charms, but pain is different. Perhaps we should never come out of our dreams at all, any of us, if it weren't for physical pain. Mental pain is only part of the lifelong dream. It is all very, very strange.

To Bernard Berenson   14 August 1919   Chilling
Geoffrey returns to London alone next week, and he begs me to give him a couple of days 'without complications or ties'. He thinks he can re-establish the friendship. I know he can't, but he begs me so hard that I may go up on Thursday.... I don't want to drag on a maimed and hypocritical relation. But he is so near a breakdown and smash over the whole business that if I am better I may be able to do enough to help him over the crisis.

To Bernard Berenson   22 August 1919   London
He [Geoffrey] has taken that poisonous and morbid hatred of Sybil out of my mind. He says he cannot imagine a more selfless and considerate and nobler creature than she has shown herself to him. Although she would have married almost anybody, its having been just him has unloosed *all she had to give*, for his benefit. I cannot hate her, I daresay I can't even go on disliking her very much, now that he has made me realize all that is fine, and alas all that is pathetic about her.... He says she is *terribly afraid* of us all, she cannot understand a thing about it.

To Bernard Berenson   8 September 1919   Chilling
There is one very unfortunate thing that neurasthenia leaves as a legacy—the unforgettable sensation of *just how one is*, whether cheerful or gloomy, well or ill, fresh or tired. As I look back I see that I did not notice half as much, or pay half as much attention to my states as I do now, I just lived along most of the time. I now understand that thee is

always acutely conscious of these things in thyself. It is a bore, isn't it? Only thy eyes pull thee out of it, I think. With me, I do forget myself hearing the children laugh. I suppose that is why I like them so.

Mary's recovery was hastened by two events. The first was her success in persuading Nicky to come and work at I Tatti as librarian, though she had had no previous experience and wondered at Mary's insistence. The other was the arrival on the scene of a new and fascinatingly picaresque figure, Carl Hamilton, a young American who had made a fortune out of copra and who now enlisted Mary's aid in buying pictures. Mary took Nicky off on a motor tour with him, and adopted his cause with a precipitate partisanship that brought trouble for B.B. with Duveen.

To Bernard Berenson   22 September 1919   I Tatti
There's something exhilarating, infectious and semi-intoxicating about this American Bacchus, with his Franciscan love of all human beings ... and his enjoyment of Italy.... Those laughing, languid eyes, and that keen, quick-witted brain and determined-to-succeed-in-whatever-he-undertakes character, are a curious combination. His simplicity and shrewdness amaze me.... The whole of civilized civilization, of European culture, is as far away from him as the life of Mars, so of course one has to suppress a lot of one's current talk. But there is something so real that the lack of the other is touching rather than ludicrous or offensive—and in the end *doesn't matter*.... It is the strangest experience possible, with this somewhat unpleasant ballast of Money. I almost wish he were a poor artist whom we could help instead of being the future source of untold wealth!

To Bernard Berenson   27 September 1919   Bologna
He [Carl Hamilton] has left a most lovable impression, but all the same it is an intellectual paradise to be alone with Nicky, who is so completely *unsereiner**!! She is a great dear. I feel very bad about Geoffrey, who I think might have had this delicious companion. She is the most congenial woman I have come across in years, perhaps ever. And such a lady!

To Carl Hamilton   9 February 1920   I Tatti
B.B. says to say that Sir J [Joseph Duveen] sent him a long indignant

* *Unsereiner*: one of ours, the Berenson name for 'people of their sort'.

230

cable about your 'Feast' [of the Gods], implying that B.B. had offered it to you and was thus disloyal to the custom of honour which provides that you shan't scoop in as clients of your own, buyers who have been introduced to you by a dealer. The scruple is, it happens, about as effective, in nearly all cases, as the Hague Convention about usages in war; still B.B., as you know, feels it is a binding one—even though it was not J.D. who made you acquainted. I confess it makes me a little uncomfortable, for it certainly was I who told you about the picture. To tell the truth, I had half an idea that the Duveens were 'in it', for I knew that they had been nibbling at it for a very long time, and that B.B. had strongly urged them to buy it, or take shares. But I confess the business part of things does not stick in my head, and I mentioned that great work *sans arrière pensée*, just wanting you to have one of the grandest things ever painted. B.B. said to me afterwards that I had been most indiscreet, but he truthfully wrote to J.D. that he had not in any way urged you to buy it. Well, there it is. He will have to face the fact that you do not belong to him. As to this Perugino, B.B.'s greatest quarrel with them for years has been that he reserves the right to advise any friend of his, whether one of his clients or not, if his opinion is asked. They would like to muzzle B.B. for their own benefit, not realizing how silly, even from their own point of view, that would be. A mere Duveen automaton would soon cease to carry weight.

In spite of her occasional over-enthusiasm, her interest in the work renewed her energy, and she finally started to undertake, as before, some of B.B.'s trickier business correspondence.

To Mr [Walter] Dowdeswell   25 February 1920   I Tatti [copy]
My husband, who is not very well, asks me to write to you for him. He wants me to say that if Mr L.D. [Langton Douglas] said that he (B.B.) wanted Italy for himself, it was a way of putting the matter that misrepresented what he had written.... The expression 'wanting Italy to himself' is very misleading. He would be only *too* delighted if you were able to do all the bargaining, all the seeing the dealers, and all the part he does not care for, and I may say, gets no profit from. He is naturally pleased to be recognized as the ultimate authority on authorship, quality and genuineness, but if it could be managed that he confined his activities to pronouncing on these points I assure you he would be delighted. But as things are it does not seem to be to the interests of the firm to have an agent of theirs in Italy raising the prices and at the same time diminishing his power of bargaining and

his authority on the question of what things are worth. The natives of this land are very subtle, and it has taken him years to learn how to deal with them.

Carl Hamilton wrote that he had had his Perugino cleaned, and that it was now almost unrecognizable.

To Carl Hamilton   10 March 1920   I Tatti
Your account of the Perugino gave us a good laugh, not at, but *with* you. One of the not very well understood things in connoisseurship—but I think you partly understand and partly feel it—is that a picture can be terribly repainted and yet preserve the character of its author. Repainters of course sometimes deliberately disfigure a picture, but not *all over*. The composition generally remains, the general masses of light and shadow are adhered to, and some characteristic movement or fall of drapery is preserved. And there was certainly enough in your Tondo, repainted though it was, to enable one to see Perugino in the photograph. It will be great sport to get the photo of the cleaned picture! Now about paying B.B. for his advice—you mustn't.... He continually gives his opinion to his friends without dreaming of personal gain. In your case it is like that, but more so, and you must feel free to ask him his opinion whenever you like, just as he will feel free to ask you, in case he needs to, your opinion about investments...

To Edward Fowles*   1 April 1920   I Tatti [copy]
In going over the X list† you so kindly sent, we are very much struck with the fact that it contains nothing except what has been recently purchased with your own cognizance; and no purchase made elsewhere on my husband's recommendation or verbal counsel... It is only by chance and through outsiders that we sometimes come to hear that they have passed into the possession of the Firm. There must be a complete record of all these things? As I said yesterday, I understand that it might be easy to overlook them in the excitement of such stirring business as occupies Sir J, but still I think that in fairness this point should be attended to in a more thorough manner.

* Edward Fowles directed the Paris branch of Duveens from 1917 to 1938. By 1958 he was sole owner of the firm.
† Commonly referred to as the X Book, the ledger in which the Duveen firm listed purchases and sales in which B.B. was involved.

To Mrs Berenson   8 May 1920   I Tatti
We have had Maynard Keynes and Logan staying with us for some
time. Of course everybody in Florence wanted to crowd up and get a
glimpse of Keynes, who is emphatically the Man of the Moment,
having had such an enormous influence on the interpretation of the
Peace Treaty. I do hope you all have read his book 'The Economic
Consequences of the Peace Treaty'. We thought it very, very good. He
told us a lot that he did not print about the personalities on whom the
fate of the world depended during those awful months, when they
were behaving in such a fatally stupid way.

To Bernard Berenson   17 July 1920   [London?]
I went to JD [Duveen] who was full of fervour and loving-kindness.
He said that the *only reason* those items weren't in the X list was
because he never put anything into the account *till it was paid for*.
Dionysus [Carl Hamilton], by the way, hasn't paid up, he owes over
£400,000 to the firm. *Per contra* he sold for a million pounds to the
Rockefellers, who are now beginning with Italian pictures! He showed
me various things, and I tremblingly gave the best opinions I could
muster. I turned down a 'Fra Filippo'. He has bought a *glorious* St
Paul dated 1326. He vows it is a Giotto. It is fine enough to be, but it
is more expressive. I did not say so, but I thought of the impressive-
ness of that marvellous fresco in Santa Croce. It might be Orcagna I
think. Thee will easily tell. . . . Lastly Lord Taunton's Bust of Lorenzo
the Magnificent*. That puzzled me. It is *too* powerful, too modern. . . .
'If it's right' he said, 'it's a GREAT thing.' I think it isn't terracotta, as
he believes, but only painted plaster—but on that point, as Bode's
letter said, only a craftsman can decide. JD was hacking it with his
knife, but I *made* him stop, as even when he got a piece off, he didn't
know what it was!!

To Bernard Berenson   23 September 1920   [No place given]
I dare say it may be quite as thee says, that during the last 25 years I
have had every conceivable reason to feel jealous and shut out and *less
now*! when age tempers both passions and poetry and dreams; but the
assurance is not one to make me happy. However there is very little
that is nice in human relations, anyhow ... the icy aloofness and

* This was the well-known and often reproduced terracotta bust of Lorenzo
now in the Kress collection at the Washington National Gallery of Art. Most
experts agree that it is by Verrocchio, although some think it is by a
contemporary imitator.

eccentricity in which we all live. I cannot understand why one goes on living once that becomes clear.

To Nicky Mariano   16 November 1920   Paris
I had such a nice letter from Geoffrey. I will send it to you, though I prize it very much and beg you to send it back to me. It was just that, that we had seemed to come into real touch with each other that made it so ghastly for him to do a thing I couldn't (and can't) in the least sympathize with, which shocks and horrifies me. Apparently he feels it has not altered him essentially, and perhaps it is true. At least he feels it leaves our friendship untouched, and of course I am very fond of him and sometimes I manage to think of him as if he weren't the husband of that appalling woman.... I cannot see very well how life will go on in any congenial or happy way, in outward matters. But it is a great deal to have the inner relations affectionate.

CHAPTER FIFTEEN

Guardian Angel

December 1920–July 1923

When the Berensons had settled in again at I Tatti, after their various
wartime activities, they decided that it was desirable, once again, to
pursue and consolidate their business contacts in America. This trip
was to be their last—neither B.B. nor Mary crossed the Atlantic
again.

On their arrival in New York they found themselves involved in a
complicated intrigue involving Duveen and Carl Hamilton. Hamilton
had been encouraged by Duveen to accumulate and house a large
number of valuable paintings, and by the time of the Berensons' visit
it was becoming increasingly clear that he would not be able to raise
the money to pay for them. Hamilton pounced on the Berensons when
they arrived and insisted on their occupying his apartment, where the
pictures were displayed, thus involving them—unwillingly—in his
affairs and obtaining their involuntary support.

B.B. and Mary soon began to realise that both Hamilton and
Duveen were using them as bait in their tortuous dealings with one
another, but there was little they could do about it. In the end
Hamilton lost his money and dropped from view, though Mary
retained a soft spot for him, while Duveen disposed advantageously of
the pictures he had so satisfactorily advertised.

To Nicky Mariano   5 December 1920   New York
It *is* an utterly unimaginable world, as you say. But we do not belong
to it, and we are dreadfully homesick. B.B. betrays his sense of misfit
by fiendish brilliancy which leaves people gasping and uncomfortable
—and hostile—and I betray mine by extreme and heavy amiability.
... You can't think what a difference it makes to us having you,
and also having your sister and her family in the villino. It has come
to me as heavenly healing after the crushing disappointment of

Geoffrey's marriage and the break-up of the architects' partnership which used to interest me so much.

To Alys Russell   7 December 1920   New York
I do not think we shall ever come again. It isn't our life. It happens, however, that it was *the* time for us to come from a business point of view, with many new buyers entering the field, and also with the Germans making a desperate push to get B.B. out and some of their own people in. *Les absents ont toujours tort*, so fortunately we are on hand at the crystallizing moment.

To Ray Strachey   17 December 1920   New York
We are trying to get Carl [Hamilton] married to a very nice girl ($15,000,000, incidentally) [Alice de Lamar]. He is very much in love, for the first time in his life, and hardly knows what to make of it. The match is eminently suitable, as she comes from the same stratum as he, her father having risen from (but not above) the gutter ... he is also, I am rather surprised to find out, what Sir Joseph Duveen calls 'deep', which in Italian we call *'furbo'*. He is getting from us as much as he gives, and he knows it. He says he will give us a fine automobile. I should not hesitate to accept it, for we have already saved him two hundred thousand dollars!

To Alys Russell   21 December 1920   New York
Our daily fare is Squillionaires ... and we find them *very* hard to digest. Yesterday (typical) we spent the morning with Miss Frick ($30,000,000), and we had Mrs Otto Kahn (endless millions) to lunch to meet Tagore, and the Rockefellers to tea, and we dined with Archer Huntington ($180,000,000). Let us hope it is good business. 'May some droppings fall on me!'

To her Family   24 December 1920   Boston
We went out to see Mrs Gardner today. She will soon die, and she must know it, but she is unchanged in her egotism, her malice, her attachment to detail, to nonsensical things. All this, in the days of her vitality, when it seemed as if she couldn't grow old and die, were actually part of her charm. But now it is purely pathetic, and a little ugly. She is paralyzed, but can be carried downstairs and can pour tea and talk, and she is still determined to thwart everyone of seeing her treasures. The law requires her to open her Palace so many days a year, I think 8. She does so, selling the tickets in a very inconvenient

way, but since her illness she only lets the Palace be opened for *one hour* a day, and she is always there, being carried about, so that no one feels free to enjoy. But the worst of all is that her great Palace, in spite of the marvellous pictures in it, looks to our now enlightened eyes *like a junk shop*. There is something horrible in these American collections, in snatching this and that away from its real home and hanging it on a wall of priceless damask made for somewhere else, above furniture higgledipiggled from other places, strewn with *objets d'art* ravished from still other realms, Chinese, Japanese, Persian, Indian objects, that seem as if they were bleeding to death in those dreary super-museums.... But this is not a gospel I can even allude to here, under the circumstances!! Where should we be?

To Nicky Mariano   17 January 1921   New York
The table literally groaned under orchids, caviar, turtle soup and gold plate. Twenty-two gross old people sat about it guzzling champagne and all sorts of wine (in spite of 'prohibition'), the women all over 50, all fat and all (except myself) nearly naked and hung with ropes of pearls and diamonds. After dinner, opera singers came in and yelled horrible music. B.B. nearly fainted. We came away 'early' (i.e. at midnight), and he actually said he was glad I *didn't* 'look like other women'!!

To Alys Russell   19 January 1921   New York
To tell the truth we want him [Carl Hamilton] to marry very much, for we have found out that he hasn't paid for his pictures! This is a deep and deadly secret, which we share with Sir Jo Duveen, who has believed in Carl's lucky star to the extent of letting him have about 3 millions' worth of pictures! Carl is now using these to advertise himself, with us as decoy-ducks, in order to strengthen his credit, for the money crisis has caught him and he has to 'carry' several millions of debt over till July, if not further. If he makes this fabulously rich marriage* his credit will be established and the Duveens will certainly be paid. I do not think all this was plotted. I believe his offer [of his apartment for the Berensons to stay in] was spontaneous and affectionate; but he is very acute, and having us here, he has proceeded to use us to his own advantage. His collection has also

* Mary was over-optimistic. Alice de Lamar had no intention of marrying Hamilton.

boomed the Duveens tremendously, and I think he means to get substantial reductions from them on that ground.... Sometimes between those two astute business men—and I suspect Carl is a slyer serpent than Sir Jo himself!—B.B. and I feel VERY QUEER. Not that we care, really. What is New York to us? The only thing that would really matter is that the patent evidence of the (non-existent) plot might undermine our prestige, which is what we make part of our money by! But even that is a side show, the real thing is that B.B. knows his Italians, and nobody dares to buy without his authorization. Still the 'situation' is odd.

To Nicky Mariano   8 February 1921   New York
Every few days we get into a perfectly new set of people and some of these sets are interesting and delightful. There is the *New Republic* set, very congenial, the art set (horrible!), the doctor set (absolutely enchanting), the musical set (not at all intellectual), the business pirates, as we call them (fascinating and breath-taking), the collectors (rather dull), the old society hacks we've known for years (I don't care for them) and lots of others. One could live for years in New York and never come to the end of the really interesting people and movements here.

To Isabella Gardner   28 February 1921   Baltimore
President [Carey] Thomas asked me to give a lecture at Bryn Mawr, and I was lost for days preparing it. I hadn't 'lectured' once since 12 years, and did not feel at all sure I *could*, so I wasted lots of time preparing what, in the end, I could have done just as well extempore.

To Isabella Gardner   21 March 1921   New York
My dear, we saw a picture today that made our hearts ache for you. It is the greatest of early Bellini's*, a severe yet radiant Madonna—as beautiful as anything of his in our country—except of course the *Bacchanal*. You have no Bellini—no Giovanni, that is—and he was the Tree of Jesse of the whole Venetian School, perhaps the very greatest artist of all the Renaissance. We have always mourned his absence from your collection, as I am sure you can understand. Well this picture is here and for sale ... the price was $100,000 but is now $75,000 and this is cheap for prices now!

* Mrs Gardner did buy this Bellini, for $50,000.

238

To Isabella Gardner   16 July 1921   I Tatti
We are all playing a losing game—you play it better than anyone in the world, and the splendid example you give heartens up all the rest of us. Whenever I don't speak of my rheumatic knees and my sleeplessness, I feel I am following in your glorious footsteps.

To Bernard Berenson   7 September 1921   Chilling
Bertie [Russell] has sent word that the Decree (due at Xmas) must be made absolute *'at once'* which we think means that Miss Black* is going to have a baby. There is machinery provided for it and it has been set in motion. Alys is very glad to be far away in a new set of interests.†

To Bernard Berenson   9 September 1921   Chilling
Of course I realize that I am outside their life, the dimmest background, though useful for presents and reading (I am definitely too old to play). But that is really about as close as one gets anyhow to anyone. It is impossible to express the ice that I feel imprisoned in, thinking of thee touring round Italy with a woman who lives as thy wife.‡

After the war Karin and Adrian had both decided to train as Freudian psycho-analysts, a profession Mary found fascinating, though Bernard thought it to be discreditable nonsense.

To Bernard Berenson   11 September 1921   Chilling
Karin is really most interesting about her Psycho-analysis. She feels on the brink of very important 'discoveries'—an exciting sensation, and expects to work out a new method.... It is certainly a wonderful moment in her life, how well I understand it! I don't believe it will come to much, to tell the truth.... There is an *appalling* amount of nonsense in it. I wish I didn't see it so clearly.

To Nicky Mariano   11 September 1921   Chilling
Karin is here, very full of their Psycho-analysis and of their yacht, which she and her husband have lived in all summer. He cares

* Dora Black, whom Russell married as soon as the divorce came through.
† Alys had been invited to spend a year at Bryn Mawr as a house-mother, by her cousin Carey Thomas.
‡ Mme La Caze.

absolutely nothing about his two sweet little daughters, it bores him to see them, and Karin is much influenced by him in this respect. Ray has had them since May, and they often call her 'Mother'! Yet Karin knows, or at least believes, from her psycho-analysis, that in the child before 6 is formed the character of an individual throughout life, and she is aware that her little Ann is timid, and unhappy and almost pathologically meek: but she does nothing about it except discuss it as a 'case'. Next summer she is planning a *six*-months' cruise with her husband, for their first real holiday since they took up medicine. Fortunately the nurse she has is quite good.

To Mrs Berenson   2 October 1921   Salsomaggiore
We were rather anxious about money, but Duveen made it all right for the moment. He owes us a *lot*, but we thought he might put off payment, as times are so desperately hard, and no one is buying pictures. However he has filled the gap, and we now see our way to going to Egypt as we long to do.

To Isabella Gardner   5 November 1921   I Tatti
The 'Ramus seems to have lost all his interest in his fashionable friends. It is curious, for he used to enjoy the pageant. But now he only wants to see people who share our interests, people whose minds stimulate his, and people he loves. Our present guests, the Walter Lippmanns*, fulfil all these categories. They really are the dearest people imaginable; and we hope to decoy them into coming over whenever he wants leisure for writing a book. His book called 'Public Opinion' will soon appear, and it ought to be extremely interesting. The dear little pair, with shining happy young faces, went off to San Gimignano or Siena in our motor yesterday. It is delicious to see people so happy.

In 1921 the Berensons visited Egypt, sending for Nicky to help them in their study of what was to them a new and fascinating art. Thereafter all three of them frequently travelled together, and Mary was able to pass on some of the burden of cherishing B.B. to Nicky, who considered it a privilege. By this time she had been welcomed by both the Berensons as a friend as well as an employee, and it was not long before she was truly loved by both of them. And even though the

* Walter Lippmann, American editor, political theorist and author. This was his first wife, Faye Albertson.

240

affection between B.B. and Nicky soon developed into a love affair, Mary's love, trust and sympathy remained constant.

To Alys Russell and Logan Pearsall Smith   27 November 1921   Cairo
We have sent for Nicky to come out in December as B.B. has (of course) become so keen on the things here that he means to 'annex it all as his province', and he wants Nicky, who is very keen and very intelligent, to be in it all. She is a perfect treasure to us, and grows more helpful every month. So, although it is expensive, B.B. thinks it wise to have her come, and it will be delightful to give the dear creature such pleasure. She will add to the happiness of us all.

Diary   16 January 1922   Cairo
Packing!! Eliza got back from the hospital only at 3. Nicky has been an angel of helpfulness. 'Things love her' and they seemed to fly into their places. B.B's only contribution was 'I don't like to see you using my sponge to wet the labels.'

To Ray Strachey and Karin Stephen   17 March 1922   Cairo
On the whole it has been the greatest experience B.B. and I have ever had. I haven't begun to digest it, I shall probably forget most of it, before I even begin to assimilate it. Anno Domini begins to tell in regard to our memories. Even B.B's. He has struggled terribly to become an Expert in this fresh field, but it is not as it was. Nicky, who has taken hold of it with great zest, will return a fair Egyptologist, while B.B. and I stagger home dazed and mazed and overwhelmed and undone, having forgotten nearly everything except our amazement. We call Nicky our 'External Memory' in imitation of the ancient Egyptians who used to hide their souls in trees or wells for safe-keeping. However, some things are clear, especially that Egyptian religion is the loudest bray the human donkey ever brayed in the presence of the mysteries of life and death.... Here there is no humility, no resignation, no abnegation of self, no annihilation; on the contrary, it is a tremendous assertion of the power and glory and domination of the individual.... Nor does their self-assertion stop with death. They are represented trampling on through the next world exactly as in this, with the same retinue of slaves, and the same tables laden with food. So little did any conception of spiritual life enter into their scheme, that *the chief preoccupation* was to provide themselves with lots and lots of FOOD in those dark sealed-up caverns in the rocks where their jewelled mummified bodies were to be laid. Incredible!!!

To Alys Russell   Easter Sunday [16 April] 1922   Venice
Blaydes is attending me, he is the English doctor here ... he is bald
and fat and clumsy, but we cannot say much to that. But we can
criticize him for being very dull and stick-in-the-mud, not even
keeping up with his own profession. His mind has gone to sleep. I AM
glad not to be married to him. *I should prefer Obrist*—!!! But praise the
Lord Barebones!

Diary   24 April 1922   I Tatti
I was overcome by a horrible feeling that these people we have come
back to are only flies, with their feet stuck to fly-paper, buzzing—
buzzing—I buzz too. What else is there? ? But my interest is no longer
there. I'm still looking at Egyptian reproductions and reading. So
simple to feel sure that the next life is only Eternal Eating.

Diary   28 April 1922   I Tatti
Geoffrey came over, very pale and thin, trembling as he used to when
he was 20, and most miserably unhappy. He said if there had ever
been any harmony between him and Sybil, to make a *fund* of happy
relations, and he had then got her on his nerves as he now has done,
he would say he had to go clear away and be left to himself for two
years. But she has been so considerate within her limitations that he
feels he cannot ask for it.

Diary   24 May 1922   I Tatti
We decided to settle £5000 on Nicky, invested in good Brazilian stock
that pays 7%, so that she will be provided for if we should die suddenly. I
am very glad about it. And someday I want to do the same for my
grandchildren, whose future I care *awfully* about, and wish to preserve, if
possible, from money sordidness. If this could be done, I should be
almost more than ready to die, as my *élan vital* is nearly exhausted. Egypt,
however, was proof that it wasn't quite at an end. I *could* die without
really upsetting anyone, for the children and grandchildren have
glorious full lives, and B.B. would be extremely happy married to Nicky,
who would make him a more satisfactory wife than I have ever been.

Diary   2 July 1922   I Tatti
B.B. said, *à propos* of a Castle half-ruined and ivy-clad, that when he
was young such a sight filled him with ecstasy. I asked him if it didn't
now. 'O I like it now' he said, 'but it gives me no longer that *tu-whit tu-
who feeling* it had when I was young!' What a good expression!

Diary   17 August 1922   I Tatti
Nicky writes full of happiness in her trip, the dear thing. She was nervous at being alone with B.B. but that has all passed away.

To Bernard Berenson   25 August 1922   Chilling
Well, so I'm to tackle the redoubtable Jo!! Thee must tell me exactly the points I am to make.... I'm to deal with him about payments, telling him how we could exact much more, but are easy-going and *let him draw the interest* on money that really belongs to us. In return he really should pay up when we ask. As to policy, we must have a free hand and he must trust our judgment.... Thee must be free to offer things they don't want to others, so as to keep the dealers faithful to thee and the market busy. Any other points?

To Bernard Berenson   9 September 1922   Paris
Well, Ray and I FLEW over yesterday, and it was so easy and quick and untiring that I am determined THEE shall never cross to England any other way. And you can take all the luggage you want. At 3 we got into a nice motor at the Victoria Hotel in Northumberland Avenue and motored to Croydon and there got on to an aeroplane. Ray forgot to bring her passport, but apparently it didn't matter!!! Nor over here either. With a great buzzing we trundled out and gradually rose to about 150 ft and began to fly at 75–80 miles an hour. This height and this pace we kept till we reached Paris in 1 hour 50 minutes. The car was large with comfortable seats and even a WC. You can walk about, though with a high wind.

Diary   12 September 1922   Paris
I called at the Duveens and Jo promised me we should now hear of all sales as they are concluded—'hour by hour' he said, since the 10% tax has now been reduced to 5%, which he intends to pay in an open and aboveboard way. I lunched with the Duveens at the Ritz, most uncomfortable, as he and she are on each other's nerves and show it every second. He bought her some gorgeous pearls afterwards, which she didn't want, as she found them too white.

To her Family   17 September 1922   Berlin
This life of pleasure is so exacting that I have no time to write, from the moment when I hurriedly dress to rush off to a Museum to the hour when, after a long opera with 5 hours of *Sitzfleisch*, I sink exhausted but melodious into a German feather bed! Everything is

243

going on oiled wheels, only it seems so odd to come back to a person whom the slightest hitch throws into an agony of nerves, after a month with easy-going people! Poor old B.B., I see him searching round to blame me, before he recollects that it is only exhaustion, and eats a biscuit and finds the world again harmonious. I believe I really *like* his capricious and changeable skies, at any rate when my own are serene. It is a constant melodrama!

Diary   22 September 1922   Berlin
How one's characteristics go *through everything*. B.B. finds mine do, and he adds to ferocity, cynicism and mechanism; *worrying*. That I swear I don't do! But he says I'm totally unconscious so perhaps I don't know. His awful remarks have given me a great distaste for life. Such a person as he describes had better not exist, and whatever may be the truth, that is apparently the impression I make on the person who knows me best. And I swear I am absolutely an *angel* about Nicky, not ferocious but gentle, not cynical but sympathetic, not mechanistic but understanding. It is really hard that he gives me no credit for this, but as it is so much to his advantage he takes it for granted, for a right which it would be monstrous to make objections to.

To her Family   29 September 1922   Berlin
Punctually at 12.30 Hermann Keyserling and his Bismarck-grand-daughter wife appeared. He had made us order a diet for him, but like most people who diet, he ate that and everything else too, drinking also wine and coffee. The wife is a sweet-looking girl, at least 20 years younger than he, speaking English perfectly. She evidently adores him for she never took her pretty eyes off his queer Mongol face, while he talked and talked and TALKED. I could not help thinking of Gram's 'Thirteen Christs in the suburbs of London'*. B.B. was quite unhappy, but I enjoyed myself like a goat, and the more monstrous he was the more fun I had. He thinks he is the Western equivalent of a Bhodissatva, an incarnate Buddha, and there are two other celestial Beings now alive, one Tagore, the other a Rabbi, whom he has just discovered. These three are to save the world, but (here his shrewdness came in) not at once, perhaps it will take 50 to 100 years. ... The odd thing is that I liked him, which I never did before. Behind his pose I discovered a witty, worldly, keen man, and in past time I

* Hannah had claimed to know thirteen people in the suburbs of London who believed themselves to be Christ.

really could see nothing but a conceited clown. But B.B., who had always appreciated him as a friend, was sunk in gloom.

To Alys Russell   1 October 1922   Lucerne
Thy letter somewhat reassures me, hearing that thee and Logan laughed at the idea of my being 'ferocious and worrying'. B.B. says I inspire terror wherever I go, while no one is afraid of him, unless I make them so by representing him as a monster. When can I live down those years of illness—Never I suspect. But B.B. certainly— exaggerates! However, when all is said and done, I am what I am, and I can't change fundamentally, I fear, so I'm not going to bother.

To Alys Russell   16 October 1922   I Tatti
Oh, what a difference it makes to feel well! For the last 5 or 6 years it has been a sort of agony to shop, and I never did half of what I had on my list. This time I did all and more than all the things I set out to do, and could have done still more.

To Alys Russell   23 October 1922   I Tatti
Living in a Götterdämmerung of languages, as we do here, brings some disadvantages in its train. We can't help having our Italian and French and German friends here, and then Zangwill cannot hold the stage. He is very good-natured and nice, I must say, but one feels it a weight.... I do all I can to make them happy, let them have the motor, take them to villas, etc. But there it is, a slight un-mixable element I cannot eliminate. However, they will not, I am sure, talk of us with spite and hatred when they leave, as Vanessa Bell did. They are really nice people, and I think in spite of all drawbacks they are enjoying their visit. I took them to see Mrs Ross yesterday, and then to Villa Medici, where Lady Sybil fainted at our approach, so that we had a pleasant time with Geoffrey.

To Alys Russell   26 October 1922   I Tatti
I really think he has forgotten how violent he was. That remains hard for me to remember, even after all these years—how little his violence means. As I haven't any instinctive clue, I often go wrong either by thinking it means something when it doesn't, or by saying it's only words when by an unlucky accident he actually means it. I am in fact rather stupid about it, but we are so different that my lack of instinctive sympathy causes me to be tactless.

245

Diary   28 November 1922   I Tatti

Poor Geoffrey has written that his heart has been 'truly broken' by my having Nicky here. The 'happiness' Sybil attributes to him comes from a despair which ends the fearful agitation that (more than anything else) made everyday life impossible. Of course he would have fallen in love with someone anyhow, probably with Nicky living at San Domenico even if she had not come here. But I understand that *her being here* has ruined his old home for him. She would never have returned his love. That he doesn't quite realize.

To Senda Berenson Abbott   7 January 1923   I Tatti

It is curious that I do not mind the big things that can be carried off without sordid squabbles and hateful words. He is always in love and I put up with it all right, except when his mistress is an out-and-out vulgarian like Belle Greene. Indeed, I sympathize in a way, for it is not the worst thing a human being can do, to find another human being supremely attractive. But what does me in are nasty little injustices and the betrayal of a suspicious, self-seeking, exacting egoism, and 'scenes'. B.B. rather likes scenes, they clear the air for him. Me they poison, more and more since my breakdown. However, it's no use repining. Such is my fate, and I am aware that if I went home to live among people whose lives are, at any rate outwardly, harmonious, I should miss his stimulating mind and his amusing talk. It is quite silly of me to break out about it, for he will never change but only grow worse, but every six months or so I feel as if I couldn't bear it, as if I must live with 'nice' people, who don't fly into unholy rages at little things and tell me that no man ever had a wife that did so little for him as I do, such a silly doddering incompetent imbecile, whose malice and stupidity have ruined his life etc. The next day he may say affectionate things, then he wonders I am not moved by them, but I cannot forget what has gone the day before. It is all so undignified and sordid. He is very like his father. Well, Well!!

To Mrs Berenson   28 January 1923   I Tatti

I am now finishing my sixth day of a milk cure that has been recommended to me for the kidney and bladder weakness I have. It consists in drinking about 3 quarts a day of warm milk, eating at the same time a few dates, apples and oranges and sucking a lemon. It was rather hard at first, but I am getting to like it, and am already better in every way.

246

Diary   *8 February 1923*   *I Tatti*
Heartbreaking talk with B.B. when Nicky went down to meet her
sister at 11. He expects far more than anyone should expect, really the
utter immolation of other people to himself—and lives in a state of
resentment at not getting it. Yet in a way, Nicky *does* give it, but it is
not enough. It is something so monstrous one can't grasp it. Suppose *I*
put up such a claim—!!

To Mrs Berenson   *14 March 1923*   *I Tatti*
Bernard has finished his long article, and his translator is very
enthusiastic about it, thus undoing all the good effects of my attempt
to put the fear of the Lord into him over it. It *is* very interesting and
opens a new field in our studies, so that in its way it is a considerable
effort of originality as well as a monument of patient scholarship. But
it was certainly very carelessly written, and it took two weeks of very
hard work on my part and on the part of Bobby Trevelyan, the poet,
who is staying here, to put it into possible English. Bernard fought at
every point almost, so it became very thorny, and when at last we sent
it off to be translated, I said it was really a miracle that divorce
proceedings were not to follow immediately!

In the spring of 1923 the Berensons, their friends Arthur Kingsley
Porter, Professor of Art at Harvard, and his wife Lucy, Nicky and
Logan, with Mary's maid, Elizabeth, and the chauffeur, Parry, went
on a long tour of Greece. B.B., as usual, was indefatigable in
sightseeing, but Mary was beginning to flag, and was grateful that the
young and agile Nicky could take over.

Diary   *21 April 1923*   *Athens*
Logan and I went to the gallery. The others arrived for lunch. The
Porters' motor was standing on the quay at Colchis and some children
got playing with the brakes and the car rushed down into the sea. It
wasn't very deep and they got it hauled up, but I fear quite ruined.
What bad luck!

Diary   *15 May 1923*   *Greece*
One of the most awful days of my life. 6 hours on a donkey, on a
frightful path of rocks, going and coming from Bassae. My knees were
agonizing but it was too hot to walk up, and too steep, and although I
walked halfway down my knees made it nearly impossible. Nicky and
Elizabeth [her maid] washed me and put me to bed. I could only

247

drink some tea. Two *bugs* roused me, and the breaking down first of Lucy's and then of Elizabeth's bed. The privy was so *awful* I could not enter it. Besides the door did not close and it was in face of the porch where all the town took hours sitting from 6 am till midnight.

Diary   28 May 1923   Delphi
Logan says he never talked with anyone so monstrously unjust to people and things he doesn't like, nor so calm and full of insight towards art and literature. It makes it hard for me who have so much to do with him on the life side. . . . he [Bernard] has the opportunity of continual contrast with dear Nicky, who is young and active and most most lovely as a character and absolutely devoted to him in the most slavish ways. He lets her do far too much for him. I am so old that all I can do is to take care of my own health. . . . It is a very difficult situation for me, this continual contrast between my age and infirmities of body *and* character with a young woman who is such an angel. Fortunately I love her very much, and if B.B. would only behave politely to me I could manage. As it is I lie awake hour after hour with almost desperate thoughts and plans.

To Alys Russell   10 June 1923   Venice
Logan got off yesterday morning, very quietly, with no fuss, as is his way. . . . By the way a funny tale went about Venice that Logan and B.B. had had an awful quarrel in Greece. It came from B.B.'s writing that he was intensely enjoying his trip, in spite of the outrageous behaviour of 'Brother Ass' (the Franciscan name for the body).

To Bernard Berenson   5 July 1923   London
I induced Aunt Janet [Ross] to fly, on the ground that we did not rise higher than 250 feet in the air, as Dr Giglioli had forbidden her to go for fear of heart failure in the heights. He thought they rose to 6000 ft. As a matter of fact they run between 2000 and 2500 feet high, and if I had known this I should not have dared to take her. However it all went off very well and she thoroughly enjoyed it.

To Bernard Berenson   19 July 1923   Chilling
Jo [Duveen] left a pleasant impression on me, from the point of view of encouraging business and of friendliness. But my, how he boasted. . . . But I can bear it, once in a way, for Jo triumphant is necessary to us—and besides it is a vital spectacle. But what tremendous gaffes he must make in English society. . . . Jo was *most cordial* . . . and we got so

confidential that I told him we had settled £5000 on Nicky, and he got up and shook my hand and said 'It's the best investment you ever made. She's a wonderful person.' And he beamed all over when I said that it was because of him we could do it. I think it really attached him to us humanly, if such a cockatoucan *can* become attached.

CHAPTER SIXTEEN

The Grandmother

December 1923–April 1927

More and more friction developed between Bernard and Mary during the years that followed. Mary felt that she was entitled to some proportion of Bernard's earnings in return for her work for him, but he disapproved of the way in which she handled money and above all of her incessant and often devious efforts to shower it on her children and grandchildren, and to persuade him to make them—and not Harvard University, as he intended—his heirs.

Mary tried to enlist Nicky in her support, but Nicky did not have Mary's feminist background, and remained a staunch—though tactful—supporter of Bernard's point of view. In spite of fierce quarrels B.B. nevertheless was and remained invariably generous. He was not fond of children, however, and when Mary filled the villa with her relatives he tended to rage fiercely or to absent himself in dudgeon.

Mary's peace of mind was disturbed by another factor: she was beginning to discover yet again, with another generation, that there were snags as well as delights in the physical presence of the young.

To Alys Russell   28 December 1923   I Tatti
Barbara is so desperately absorbed in reading that she leaves poor Leslie* far too much alone. She is a difficult child. Dermod† could manage her, but Leslie is too meek.

To Alys Russell   30 December 1923   I Tatti
Leslie is a very good follower, but Barbara is a bad leader, for she is so subject to moods and whims and sudden lazinesses. I do wonder if we couldn't get Dermod just for a month or five weeks, from the time I

* Leslie Scott, Geoffrey's niece, a schoolfriend of Barbara's. Barbara was eleven at this time.
† Dermod MacCarthy, son of Desmond MacCarthy.

leave England till we go to Constantinople.... As they are now, they are really almost as much trouble as pleasure, and last Christmas they were so delightful.

To Alys Russell   7 January 1924   I Tatti
I'm in a sad hope for B.B. *absolutely refuses* to let me have Karin's children unless for short holiday visits. The sting is that he has got it into his head that Karin despises him intellectually, because she said, half laughing, that when people were hot against PA [psycho-analysis] it was a sign they needed it! My way is thorny, he is so unreasonable, so selfish. He objects to *my* being concerned with the children, even if *he* never sees them and is not disturbed by them. But he has it firmly in his mind that he has a Right to all my time and attention and energy. I must break it to Karin about this spring (he won't change so soon) as she wants to send Ann, and indeed it would be very good for her. I feel very bitter to have my house so closed against my grandchildren, but there it is. I have no hope of a peaceful life, till I can get where I DON'T CARE, and not caring is so awfully close to dislike.

To Alys Russell   9 January 1924   I Tatti
I daresay, Alys, my letters sound gloomier than my life is. I write sometimes from gloomy moments, and it has been a relief to express what I really do keep to myself here. The bottom truth is that B.B. and I grow more and more uncongenial every year. No doubt *my* faults multiply or deepen, as I see his do. And he has taken on the attitude that his will is law (a reversion to type) and he will not discuss it, but says 'I will have it so'. The way we live horrifies me since the war, and the bothers with this big house of servants are great. But of course it is the difficulty about the children and grandchildren that makes the worst, the things he says.... I'm not living the life I should enjoy, nor the life I can approve of, but there is no way out while I remain with him, for he is dreadfully suspicious about every kind thing I do for others, and will not hear of a more reasonable *train de vie*.... When I'm well, I can get along somehow. But B.B. always falls into a rage with me for small illnesses, and the fact of being below par makes me take it hard.

To Alys Russell   10 January 1924   I Tatti
Dear dear! How I wish B were living nearby. It is a joy to watch her from a certain distance. She's rather overwhelming for a sick old lady.

251

To Senda Berenson Abbott   3 March 1924   I Tatti

The only difference is having little Christopher here—a great joy to me, but rather mixed pickles for him [B.B.], I should have thought, though they get on better than I could have dared to hope. Christopher admires 'Uncle Bergen' enormously, and stands rather in awe of him. I am hoping he will let me have Karin's elder little girl, for it is evident that Karin doesn't care for her, partly because she looks very much like Adrian,* and has his rather slow hesitating ways, and partly because the younger child is such a witch, so fascinating and gay and winning that you can't notice little Ann when she is about. It is evident to everyone, even to Karin, that Ann is tragically unhappy. So I want to get her out here and give her a good petting, if only B.B. will allow it. He practically needn't know she is in the house.

To Bernard Berenson   Undated [probably 1924]   I Tatti

Bernard dear, Thee often accuses me of dribbling away £1400 on my children. I went into my accounts with Alys in Paris and I find that this is a *very great* exaggeration. Please I do beg of thee—for these discussions are so painful to us both—look carefully at the enclosed list. Thee will see on P1 my practically fixed expenses, which come to £811. Only three of these relate to the children and grandchildren, the Xmas and birthday presents which come to £50, the holiday board of which about £50 is for them at Alys's and the Education Insurance of £105, which will automatically end as each child becomes 14.

From this, and from the next list†, thee will see that it is not true that I am grasping and avaricious and never do anything but for my children.

On P2 are the things that always come up, £360, of which extra illnesses and educational things amounting to £80 go towards the grandchildren.

The total of these two lists is £1171, and of course there are lots of little things that cannot be reckoned, like cabs and teas and so on which make it easily £1200.

Sometimes I spend £10 more on the bulbs, sometimes an extra present to the Nowerses or helping some friends through dentists' or doctors' bills.

From Grandpa Smith's estate I receive an *average* of £1300, and

* Karin and Adrian had decided to separate in November 1923, but came together again after barely a year.

† The lists also included clothes, her maid's wages, bulbs for the garden, books and private charities.

from Life Insurance £160 = £1460, and this leaves about £260 that I 'waste' as thee calls it. But that is really not very much, and I cannot bear to think that such a small sum, spent, after all in no wicked way, but one which gives me ten times its value in pleasure, should cause such bitterness between us....

I want to have it out once and for all, because we cannot go on into old age so sordidly. I hate concealing and cheating, but I like it better than fierce reproaches that do not correspond to the facts. Yet it is an annoying method, and God knows I should love to be open and aboveboard. Yet where a person has power, the underdog cannot come out into the open unless the power is used justly and with fairness. And certainly, dear, the facts are there to prove that I do not dribble away $7000 solely upon my children, that I am not avaricious, thinking of no one but them—many of the other charges thee hurls at me when thee is angry.... Now Bernard dear, is it worth our while to get so bitter over so little? In view of what we spend for our own comfort and convenience and pleasure, of all we do for Nicky (amounting to about as much as I 'waste' on my 6) it does not seem to me very monstrous.

B.B., on his side, was concerned to spend every penny he could spare on creating his superb library and in building up an endowment for the Institute he passionately wished Harvard to found at the Villa after his death.

To Senda Berenson Abbott   9 June 1924   I Tatti
We are, from my point of view, living in a foolish way. He is spending oceans in making his library complete, and then what? I do not see that we shall ever have the money to properly endow the place as an Institution for Humane Studies (which is his ambition), for it would take more than a million dollars (I worked it out in some detail with a lawyer) so why buy all sorts of books that we shall never open which might be of *possible* use to some hypothetical students. Nicky is a good deal worried about it too, and often she actually does not order the books he marks in catalogues, and then he forgets about them. But that is not the worst, the worst is the dreadful expensiveness of running this big house up to his standards, and entertaining so continuously. I cannot bear to know what it all costs and yet as I pay all the accounts I *do* know. And it is more than we can really afford. However, when I put it before B.B. he says he doesn't see how to change, and there it is. A Muddle, like so many things in life....

Bertie Russell does seem to do a lot of inferior work as potboilers, and I regret it very much. But on the other hand he is one of the few utterly disinterested people in Europe who stand up for world peace, and I admire him for that and think he is doing his best, much more than the rest of us who grumble in our caves!

In one respect Mary retained B.B.'s full trust, and that was in their difficult relations with the firm of Duveen Brothers. B.B. avoided meeting Sir Joseph as much as he could, and often deputed Mary to take his place. Duveen's now worked with a lawyer, Louis Levy, who had become a great friend of the Berensons, and who endeavoured to dispel B.B.'s suspicions of the firm.

To Bernard Berenson   19 July 1924   London
Bernard, he [Duveen] said so much to me about his entire trust in thee and spoke with such real appreciation of thy work and thy general culture (thy answers in the Leonardo case did a lot of good: Levy said he never had anyone to equal thee to examine!) and seemed so solidly established on the Facts as we see them—indeed as they are—that I cannot think of any disaster but his death that can break the association. He says he is *afraid* to take the opinion of anyone else, though he has to use people who can run at his bidding. He added that having *me* there gave him increased confidence, for he felt he could say things to me he would be afraid to say to thee! I think he really has a feeling of friendship for us. There was no chance to speak of money—but I told Edward [Fowles] we would go into it on Tuesday in Paris and perhaps Levy will advise Jo to make regular payments. If Levy does, it is a pretty sure thing, for Edward says Levy holds Jo in his hand.

To Sir Joseph Duveen   25 July 1924   I Tatti [Draft, with proof of receipt]
I still keep the feeling of exhilaration with which every contact with you fills me—fills everyone, really!—and I wish I had matters to write of which were *à la hauteur.* ... And now I must turn to two subjects which are really more difficult for me to write about, because I could wish our association to be free from all questions of money between us and to depend on all the other interest there is in it. You pay us half yearly remittances on account and they are most useful to us, only we never see the accounts! We are in a sense partners in your great Italian adventure but still in spite of many remonstrances, we only know casually and accidentally, as it were, what is going on. I repeat

254

what I have often said that B.B.'s advice would be more valuable to you if he knew what you sold, and how much you got for each picture, and who your clients were. . . . We are in the dark to a degree that really is unnecessary and actually hampering. We are not in the position of people drawing a salary from you, but are your associates. B.B. hasn't your genius for selling, you haven't his knowledge for authenticating, here we need each other. It is true you could get other connoisseurs, but you would run the risk of being badly let down from time to time; and B.B. could advise other firms, but they would not be the great J.D. with whom it is a pleasure and an honour to work. No, we are better together than apart, but we should like to be kept better informed about the sales, and also we *should* like to be able to count on your remittances on account at definite dates, that is to say in January and July. You do not understand, I am sure, the importance to people like ourselves of a certain regularity, for you swim in ever widening and deepening golden floods, and have endless credit for times of drought. We sail our little bark on a shallow stream, and go aground if there is an unusually delayed season of dryness. Not only ourselves, but many people who are dependent on us, who sail lighter barks on still shallower seas.

As Mary's relations with B.B. worsened, those with Nicky became more and more trusting and loving.

To Nicky Mariano   31 July 1924   I Tatti
B.B. has given me the best news I have had for an age—namely that you like housekeeping so far as it relates to eating!! I loathe it like poison, and if you could take it over for me I should bless you forever. I'm bad at it, to start with, I hate interviewing servants, I've never properly learned the names of foods or utensils, and altogether it is a tiresome muddle. If only you will take it on your, I fear, already overburdened shoulders how glad I shall be!

To Nicky Mariano   5 August 1924   I Tatti
We know each other too well, all our past mistakes are latent in each other's minds, and we see too clearly the follies and horribilities of each other's characters. That perhaps makes it unwise for us to be too much thrown on each other's exclusive society! Yesterday, which we had all to ourselves, was verily a black serpent day, in which all my worst mistakes and failures were trotted out and all B.B.'s secretly pondered on by me without a word said—which is perhaps worse!

255

To Nicky Mariano   8 August 1924   Poggio allo Spino
Yours is the only friendship we have whose harmony hasn't been
jangled and put out of tune again and again, so that if Death comes
one is full both of remorse and indignation. If you died (which God
forbid) there would be nothing but a clear track of sunlight left behind
you. But great gloom *ahead*, so don't go and do it!

To Nicky Mariano   4 September 1924   I Tatti
They [the Duveens] arrived at midnight, Jo bubbling over with spirits
and energy.... I have a difficult task ahead of me, to screw money out
of him and arrange somehow we are kept *au courant* of the Accounts.
B.B. wants to be kept like a god on an altar, free from human
wrangling. I daresay he is right.

To Alys Russell   11 October 1924   Rome
How funny Oliver is never to dine at home. It is an unsatisfactory life.
I almost wonder Ray doesn't do as Karin has done. However Oliver is
not so depressing, only unsatisfactory. I cannot say either of them
made good marriages. What a pity. Still we should be grateful for the
children, and indeed I am, and have no unkind feelings towards the
'biological factors' who produced them.

To Mrs Berenson   12 October 1924   Rome
I am preparing some 'surprises' for Bernard. Three of our modest
pictures that had modern imitation-old frames have been put back
into really antique frames and ought to look ever so much better.
Then I am having an open fire put in his bedroom, for he is reading
several hours every morning. Besides this, I am installing a water-
softener, and changing all the hot-water pipes and putting the wine-
cellar and the servants' hall in different places, and building two small
houses for some tenants. Also I am putting a clock-tower on our roof,
but I don't quite like the design Cecil Pinsent has made me, and have
asked him to prepare another. He has ceased being our architect, but
I get designs from him, as he has taste and ingenuity. I have an
Italian architect, who is inexpensive, punctual and careful—quite the
opposite of Cecil.
    You will probably be shocked that I say always 'I am doing so and
so', but the truth is that Bernard, though he loves to walk about the
garden and see how things are growing, will not take any practical
interest in anything except his profession. I build and plant and
change and plan, and he generally approves the result.

To Mrs Berenson   26 October 1924   Rome
Bertie Russell's wife is a candidate for Chelsea, where Alys lives,
and it would make it awkward for Alys to work there*—the more
so as Bertie permits his wife to speak against Alys in public. She
said 'that horrible woman' (Alys) tried to delay the divorce so
that her child should be illegitimate when Bertie knows that Alys
began divorce proceedings the very day she had word that he wished
it! I do not think his present wife does any good to her candi-
dature by such statements. What can have come over Bertie to
permit it?

To Mrs Berenson   22 February 1925   I Tatti
Bernard really dislikes children, and although he does not see Ann
and Christopher more than once or twice in ten days, he hates the
idea of their being here, and makes it so difficult for me, that I think in
future I must always arrange to see them elsewhere. I suppose, deep
down, and perhaps unconsciously to himself, he is jealous.

To Nicky Mariano   15 August 1925   Vallombrosa
As we walked along, we talked of what an angel you were! Only, you
do spoil him!! I began that way, and gave him the impression that
only *his* pleasures and wishes were to be taken into account, and it was
a mistake which I have repented for years. In any association there
should be equality of consideration, or *tôt ou tard* it goes on the rocks.
However, perhaps you are made that way, so I won't bother you. He
says you like it, when I remonstrate with him.

To Mrs Berenson   3 October 1925   Munich
I was in bed with my throat raw from ear to ear, in the sort of way it
always takes 2 or 3 weeks for me to get rid of (and even then it leaves a
bad cough, if it doesn't turn to influenza), and this extraordinary man
came and laid his rather dirty hands on me, and in two hours I was
well! He has also cured me of an inflammation of the eyes which I
have had for 11 months, and which no oculist could get at, and of an
earache which had been slowly creeping on me for six weeks. So how
can I help believing that he really is a healer? He is now at work on
Bernard, of whom he says that there is nothing the matter but his gall-
bladder, and this he proposes to set right by a few layings-on of hands.
We shall see!

* For the Labour Party.

257

B.B. had begun to nurse the hope of finding some cultured young man who could be trained to become, to some extent, his intellectual and professional heir. The first promising discovery in this field was Kenneth Clark. He met the Berensons when he was visiting Janet Ross, and made such a good impression that B.B. promptly asked him to work with him on the revision of the lists for the new edition of the 'Florentine Painters', and the even more crucial 'Florentine Drawings'.

To Alys Russell   5 January 1926   I Tatti
Kenneth [Clark] turns out to be a very remarkable youth, so learned and with such good taste. He is a splendid worker, too, puts his mind into all he does. And he has no side, no pretentiousness. I like him more and more.

B.B.'s fancy, meanwhile, had turned for a while to a girl called Pellegrina del Turco, who was working at the villa as a secretary. Nicky was much cast down, but Mary did her best to comfort her.

Diary   6 January 1926   I Tatti
Poor old Nicky is in real trouble over B.B.'s having taken a slightly amorous fancy for Pellegrina. She suffers, but quite needlessly.

To Alys Russell and Ray Strachey   12 January 1926   I Tatti
Kenneth Clark develops well. Logan likes him immensely and he fits in wonderfully well. He is apparently full of enthusiasm about settling in Florence and devoting his life to working with B.B. and carrying on his work, but of course when a youngster speaks about 'devoting his life' it means 'two years and then see'. We have all advised him not to break it rudely to his parents, who simply hate the idea, as art has no prestige whatsoever for them and they would feel that he was throwing himself away, but to tell them that he wanted to associate himself with B.B. in the revision of the 'Florentine Drawings' and would learn languages in the meantime, Italian here and German when working in Berlin etc, so that if later he wanted to go into Diplomacy (their ideal for him) he would not be unprepared. He objects 'But it's a lie: I don't mean to take up a diplomatic career.' But it will be time to tell them that two years hence, and anyhow one never knows what life may prepare for young people. But as it seems to be turning out, from *our* point of view, it is about as nearly perfect as it could be. I will not say another Nicky, but another very congenial and reliable and satisfactory prop for our declining years.

The rise of Fascism in Italy involved the Berensons in considerable worry. Although they were not politically active, they were violently opposed to the regime, and many of their Italian friends were exiled or imprisoned. They themselves were threatened with expulsion, and were forced to advise their more political acquaintances to keep away, lest their presence should prove compromising.

To Walter Lippmann   18 February 1926   I Tatti
Your letter has been a great unhappiness to us. At first we could not believe there was any need for such precaution, and as you know, one of our greatest pleasures is to have a visit from you both.

But considering that B.B. has been warned not long ago by our Consul, a very kind and sensible man, that he was not regarded favourably by the Government, and considering that there actually was some talk of using the opportunity of his leaving Italy to ask him not to return, the best thing seemed to be to lay the case before him. And his advice is against your visit until things have quieted down. It is known that the most hated of them all, Salvemini*, has found a home with my brother and sister in London, and that does not increase their love for me.

So, heartbroken as we are about it, we have to say that your decision not to come is probably wise. Comments unnecessary!

Diary   23 February 1926   I Tatti
The derrière of the Princess† is a most mysterious thing. She goes out like a shelf and then there is a mass that gyrates, but whether it is herself or something she wears, we cannot determine.

Diary   19 March 1926   I Tatti
A fiendish day . . . B.B. has been like a crazy man, shaking his fists at me, shouting, beating his head against the wall, damning Nicky and saying he never wanted to see her again, saying he hated my children and that I had utterly ruined his life, that none of us, not even Nicky, were 'in his world', that he was going away and I should never see him again. I rang for Elizabeth to pack his things. This brought him around a bit.

* Professor Gaetano Salvemini, Italian historian who fought Fascism and was imprisoned. He fled first to France and then to England, where he stayed with Logan and Alys. Later he taught at Harvard and Yale and became an American citizen.
† Princess Mary of Thurn and Taxis was a highly cultured member of the Italo-Austrian aristocracy, and a long-term friend of the Berensons.

Diary   28 March 1926   I Tatti
I love having Ray here, she is so calm and reasonable and competent. Would that Karin had her good sense! She has written me a quite horrid letter asking me never to thrust my advice upon her again. And we all think her so utterly incapable of acting sensibly on her own! I replied mildly and sent her £25, which Ray thought a remarkable answer to such a silly and unkind letter. But what can one do? She is my child. I must, however, put her career and life off my mind. After all she's not as idiotic as Geoffrey.

Diary   5 April 1926   I Tatti
I saw Judith* and her nurse Daisy off at 3.30. Funny little mite. She is perhaps less attaching than any of the others, partly because of her obstinate nature—which she inherits from her mulish father, no doubt.

To Walter Lippmann   19 April 1926   I Tatti
We call him [Mussolini] 'Teddy' now, and that makes things safer, and also a bit ridiculous. We are apparently threatened with exile, at least all our friends tell us so, and we are officially informed that warnings against us have come through from Teddy's headquarters. Our minds refuse to take it in, but anyhow, now that we are going off for two months [to Naples], we have lent the villa to the American Vice Consul, Henry Coster†, so that should secure it from attack. Meanwhile I hope the agitation will die down as we have stopped being in opposition. Really we feel that things are the way people want them to be, and how can one strive against that? It may even be that there will be internal reforms that will produce a fairly decent state of affairs in the end. There is still a lot of violence that does not appear in the papers, of course, but it is growing less, I think, to judge by this small corner at least.

  B.B. remains a convinced, dyed-in-the-wool Liberal, which he says is the same thing as an Aristocrat in sympathy. But in a general way we are trying to stick to our own interests, which is the best thing anyhow, for people politically impotent.

To Mrs Berenson   8 June 1926   Naples
Then we motored up to Caserta Vecchia, a deserted town with a

* Judith, Karin's younger daughter, had insisted on having a pet pig, and on calling it Celestino, after the butler—not a popular move.
† A good friend, who married Nicky's friend Byba Giuliani.

260

glorious castle and a most fascinating Arabo-Byzantine Cathedral. There we stayed for hours, watching the light change over the plain and shine on the sea beyond, and seeing the ever-fascinating spectacle of Vesuvius throwing out columns of smoke, sometimes red with flame. The air was mountain-like, we needed our warmest coats. Up there we pulled out the invaluable tea-basket and had our tea, and then as evening was closing in we came back, well content with the day. I describe this, as it is typical. We often say to each other that Bernard's 'profession' is the most agreeable one in the world. Who knows the beauties of this enchanting land as we do? And yet everything we see and enjoy adds to his capital, so to speak, deepening his understanding of beauty, of art, of Italy, of history, so that we don't feel like mere idle or self-indulgent tourists.

To Mrs Berenson and Senda Berenson Abbott   *3 July 1926   I Tatti*
Carl Hamilton now writes that he is again prosperous. He has paid off nearly $2,000,000 of his liabilities, and hopes to have soon another three million. But we have ceased to believe him.

To Nicky Mariano   7 August 1926   Consuma
He had a letter from Belle Greene which upset him a lot. It was evidently one of her sex-boasting letters, when she gets her silly head turned by people who make up to her thinking she is Morgan's mistress and can do great things for them. She has the worst taste in letter writing of any female I have ever known. Still it seems the trip is on. I do not know whether I said the right thing, but I told him I thought you would as lieve not go on that trip, although you were prepared to receive her if she came to I Tatti. But maybe I am mistaken. You had better tell him quite frankly what you prefer. He is prepared for either event, though of course he loves to have you always and everywhere.

To Nicky Mariano   11 August 1926   Consuma
I am hurrying along with the typing of B.B.'s Friedsam Catalogue, and hope to have it done this week, so as to return to the Index of his Oxford book; and one is fortunately so made that one gets absorbed in even the meanest of tasks—among which I do not really count this typing. B.B. has taken a turn in his way of writing and there have been no more of those dreadful snags, and he is even modifying the two that cast me into such gloom. In fact he is doing a really

admirable piece of work, and it is a pleasure to be associated with it in however humble a capacity.

To Alys Russell   13 August 1926   Consuma
I have promised Mr Sulley to go round to his place and sit with him a while before that glorious new picture we have been able to get him. B.B. would not believe till the last moment that the thing had gone through, and even brought me the letter to see, because he was 'sure' it had bad news, that the picture had slipped through our hands. I was equally 'sure' that it was all right, and as it happened I was correct; but what a difference in general outlook on life between us such a little incident betrays. He always expects misfortune. I generally expect good luck. It must mean a very different set of nerves to live on.

To Bernard Berenson   8 September 1926   London
Dear Bernard, it was horrible being with the D [Duveen] family, and dependent on their caprices. They are brutally selfish in all the things that matter, and to be their guest is humiliating in the extreme. I hope I need never go through such an experience again.... I tried to pretend to like it—it was the only thing to do. Jo will give me (I think) the extra 5, so I daresay it was worth it. And my friendship with him and Levy was, as far as I can see, very much strengthened—and I got on well with all the women, I think. Still—— It will be joyful to see you again, thee and beloved Nicky.

To her Family   10 November 1926   Verona
It is quite moving to see how Kenneth admires B.B. Nothing is lost on that boy, he is so marvellously cultivated that he can follow intelligently almost every intellectual path that B.B. opens. He says he has never before been with a person who, in three weeks, never repeated himself, or with any older man whose mind did not seem poured into moulds.

To Alys Russell   18 November 1926   Padua
He [Kenneth] has got very fond of him [B.B.] and B.B.'s rages and unfairness do not put him off, though he sees them with the sharp eyes of youth. They aren't directed against him, that is one thing, and they are in any event less fearful than similar traits in his own father. Kenneth really understands him, and Nicky too, sympathetically, affectionately. This is a great blessing. I fear I don't altogether, I

suffer too much from all the animus that is directed against me, my ways, the people I love, my desires.

To Ray Strachey and Alys Russell   8 January 1927   I Tatti
Barbara came up today full to bursting of the glorious time they are having. The della Stufas [the family of their agent, with whom Barbara was staying for the holidays] are members of a band of about 20 who are up to the maddest pranks, with midnight suppers and dancing and flirting and dressing up in each other's clothes. B is enraptured and of course they make a lot of her. Nando della Stufa tries to kiss her!! I fear it isn't just what she needs, but we all thought them such a quiet stodgy family. At least her Italian is coming on and she is enjoying it. But oh my! They go ahead of their English contemporaries. Dear me, what a responsibility, I couldn't have imagined such a thing.

To Bernard Berenson   27 January [1927]   Berne
She [Alys] says she likes Kenneth's 'Jane'* who is neither dressy nor smart, but seems very sensible and keen on work. But of course it's a leap in the dark. I think our policy is to make the best of it, while it lasts, and not speak against either of them. What we say will inevitably come round to them. And we must start Kenneth on his job. He evidently needs directing. . . . I hope we can be good friends to him, even if we don't get what we too hastily imagined we should get. Besides he is young, and may improve with guidance. I've had all this very much on my mind. Alys says he is *perfectly devoted* to all three of us.

Diary   3 February 1927   Berne
Being alone is a *fearful* ordeal. There is nothing to hide one's self from one's eyes and I've got to face myself for ten days to come. I hate it really, deep down. The being alone appeals to the laziness and selfishness and wilfulness in me, and these old records†—I can hardly bear them without taking refuge in a shallow fatalism. *Basta!*

* Jane Martin, whom Kenneth Clark had recently married. There was considerable disapproval at first, because B.B. and Mary felt that Clark would not be the devoted pupil they had hoped for, and also because Jane had broken off her previous engagement to Janet Ross's great-nephew, of whom they were fond.
† Mary was re-reading her own and Bernard's old letters, in the course of working on a biography of him. The nine chapters she completed went no further than 1891.

To Bernard Berenson   4 February 1927   Berne
Mixed up with them (though a bit later) are love letters from me, which have moved me strongly. They sound very genuine, and were, I know. I like to come on something convincingly and spontaneously real in my past. So much has been imitation and conformity and parrotism. Although, apparently, it was because thee found me *real* in a world of shadows that thee cared so much. Well, well! Life took its course. But thank the gods it left us still together, still loving, still pursuing many of the same ends.

To Mrs Berenson   6 February 1927   Berne
Alys could not come to visit us in Italy, as we had planned, for she had shown kindness and hospitality to Prof Salvemini, a political exile and a great friend of ours, and the Consul thought her coming to visit us would compromise us and perhaps lead to our all being asked to leave Italy. We are living under a tyranny *at least* as bad as Russia in the old days. So, as Alys had to come to Switzerland anyhow, to see a sick friend, I decided to meet her here, and, since I was here, to take advantage of the famous Dr Kocher and his Cure. I couldn't scrape up any symptoms, except perhaps a bit of old-age laziness, and he rather laughed at me. However he said that fat old ladies did tend to lose their grip, and that he could help them by his system of feeding the glands by means of injections of (as I understand) gland extract. So I am trying it. It takes three weeks and I hope to get home by the middle of February.

To Bernard Berenson   7 February 1927   Berne
What a quick and thorough revulsion thee had from Catholicism! It is almost frightening. The psychology of that period is very strange, for thee saw the beauty and felt the glow of Catholicism in scores of ways unconnected with being in love. And yet in 2 years thee can write 'It has not been a very merry Xmas. But better so. Why should I be merry on the day that the institution I most hate in the world has chosen for its birthday!'

Diary   20 February 1927   I Tatti
B.B.'s rage was awful. He fell on his knees and made shocking faces at me. He beat his head on the wall and shook his fists at me and called me a tactless brute who never considered his feelings, selfish, inconsiderate and always working against him. Two separate outbursts.... Of course it is pathological, and I try to estimate it that

way. But the nerve shock of those faces and gestures and that high voice—yes and the things he says—put me off, hurt something deeper than reason. At Berne I read of just such a scene 35 years ago, because I was slow in bringing a lamp from my dressing-room, where, as a matter of fact, I was doing my hair. And then I said 'What will it be like if such scenes go on and on into our old age? How hideous it will make life.' And they *have*! But so much else to balance against this unpleasantness. Never could there be a more *interesting* companion, and to the Will with which he has planned our lives and brought them out on the whole successfully I owe nearly everything.... And no doubt I am more provoking than I realize. That is my blind spot.

To Alys Russell   11 April 1927   I Tatti
There was a lady (American of course) here the other day, who remarked in the Library 'What I say is "Where there are books there is peace"', a remark which caused bursts of laughter from Logan and Nicky and Bertie von Anrep [Nicky's brother-in-law] and myself, as only a few hours before B.B. had been making a dreadful scene and had gone out of the door shaking his fists! Today, in spite of the books, he has been much worse, declaring that I was killing him by inches, that Cecil [Pinsent] had done almost nothing he liked, that he couldn't stand any longer the life I made him lead etc etc. I felt so *desperately* sorry for him, just as if I had seen a person groaning in an agony of physical pain. The cause is at present the garden walk and the clock tower, but when I freely confess having made a mistake he glares at me and says 'You never learn anything! You simply don't care how I feel. Your one idea is to give that insolent unbearable Cecil something to do.' Nicky thinks he has been here too long without a break. He is certainly very ill. And what a pity. Life could be so pleasant, and sometimes it is next door to hell! *Pazienza*. How nice Logan is by contrast! Even when he is ill. Perhaps I am horrible, really, and make B.B. wretched. If only someone would tell me!

Diary   14 April 1927   I Tatti
Another of those devastating rages ... B.B. said I had always kept him in misery and disgust because I was keen on my home letters (if I hadn't them and were shut up with him I should die), that I had no self-control but pounced on them with revolting eagerness neglecting all his interests, that it was as bad now with grandchildren as it had been with children (a complete and demonstrable lie, this), that he humiliated himself having to do with dealers to keep up this

establishment *all for me*, that I let it go in horrid piggery, every day he saw disgusting signs of neglect on my part (can I give much attention to the house when he keeps me writing his business letters, sometimes all my working time). ... Fortunately I did not lose my temper even inside, but felt desperately sorry for him, it made him look so ill and tired and old and miserable. At the end I opened my arms and he came trembling and laid his silly furious unkind ungoverned throbbing head on my shoulder.

CHAPTER SEVENTEEN

Withdrawal

April 1927–February 1932

When the grandchildren stopped being babies, they began to develop characters of their own, of which Mary could not always approve, and she found that she was beginning to grow apart from her family, though she still spent her summers in England. Without this preoccupation with her descendants she became more and more aware that much of what constituted her life with B.B. was uncongenial to her, though she still found interest in her work with him, and there were many times when their old affection was renewed.

The social life at I Tatti had now begun to take on the pattern it retained until B.B.'s death. Except during the hot weather, when they went up to Vallombrosa or Consuma, or when they were on their travels, the timetable was very rarely varied. House guests were given breakfast in their rooms and were expected to look after themselves all morning, which was devoted to work, though transport into and out of Florence would be provided if required. There were usually some four or five important guests to luncheon, which was followed by a siesta. Then came one of B.B.'s much-loved walks, accompanied by selected guests. The car would drop the walkers at one end of the chosen walk and pick them up at the other. Tea was the occasion for less important visitors, or those with mere letters of introduction, while yet more guests (now in evening dress) would arrive for dinner.

Mary found this constant hospitality, and its complicated organizational requirements, increasingly boring, just as she had once found Frank's politics and philanthropy boring. During these years she tended more and more to absent herself, retiring to her bedroom and leaving Nicky to act as hostess.

Their travels, too, were beginning to exhaust her, though these she still found entrancing. Encouraged by the success of the Egyptian trip, they were now visiting the more remote (and uncomfortable) areas of artistic interest beyond the Mediterranean, in Turkey, Palestine, Syria and North Africa.

Up in her room Mary took to writing about these trips, and completed three books—*A Modern Pilgrimage* about Palestine and Syria, *Across the Mediterranean* about Libya and Algeria, and *A Vicarious Trip to the Barbary Coast* about Tunisia. The last of these trips she had been too ill to take herself, but she travelled in imagination and based her descriptions on the daily letters she received from B.B. and Nicky.

It gave her a great deal of pleasure to write the books, but they had none of the flowing ease and humour of her letters, and enjoyed only a limited success.

To Mrs Berenson   17 April 1927   I Tatti
Of course my life consists in doing a thousand snippets of things, what with the house and garden, the whole estate, the correspondence, the visitors, the charities and so on. There is no *one line* to it, and if I do half an hour of cataloguing pictures then have to write three or four business letters, then am called into the garden, or to see a workman or caller, then look up some photographs, then answer the telephone, then arrange plans for the household, and so on all morning, I do not retain any very clear idea of what I have done and what I only thought of doing. Dear Nicky attends to the food question, and this is an immense weight off my mind, but there are so many things that I alone can do, particularly in regard to B.B.'s business affairs and his correspondence about pictures. I do not think he could delegate this to anyone else, for by now I have a knowledge not only of the whole subject but of his attitude.

Diary   6 June 1927   Vienna
Fowles telegraphed he was coming on important business and B.B. was quite ill with anxiety. I simply couldn't feel anxious—and it turned out when he arrived ... that it was only that JD wants to pay twice as much for the Benson collection of pictures [as] they are worth. But the great Sir Joseph cares far more '*far figura*' than to make money.

To her Family   7 August 1927   Oslo
I went with him to see a very remarkable private collection of modern pictures.... I saw one of the most wonderful pictures I have ever seen—a huge Gauguin, with Samoan natives in the woods. For *Stimmung* I can compare it to Bellini's *Feast of the Gods* which Hamilton

used to own, or to Signorelli's great *Pan* at Berlin. I could not tear myself away from it, though Cézannes and Degases and Corots etc called for attention on every hand. The picture was one I ought to have hated, great lumps of arms and legs, heavy faces, wild indecipherable background, but it was a great 'Creation' all the same, and held me spellbound.

To Alys Russell   19 August 1927   Hamburg
B.B. is as nervous as a cat (*are* they nervous, by the way) over this business meeting with the lawyer tonight. I cannot quiver a nerve! I am *sure* Levy is friendly to us and will not propose anything against our interests. Once when I said I thought we got a very great deal of money from Duveen, he said 'You can't get too much. B.B. has made the whole reputation and prestige of Jo Duveen!' That was not the remark of a man secretly working against us in the Duveen interest.

Diary   20 August 1927   Cologne
Spent the morning talking with Levy.... A very great happiness came to me in the course of the talk, when it veered around to our disposition of property by Will. I said I should be glad to give up all my share of I Tatti to B.B.'s beloved 'Institute' if I could first ensure each of my grandchildren having a couple of hundred pounds a year—as a protection against entire destitution. B.B. up to now would never hear of this, and I confess I have worried a *lot* about it, and felt it to be very unfair, considering how much I have worked for and with him. Everyone says I have helped him *enormously*, and my own conscience says the same. But up to now he has been adamant on the matter. Suddenly he gave way and said yes, he would charge the estate with $2000 a year to each of my beloved 4. No words can say what a weight this takes off my mind!... I have always been so grateful to my grandfather who left all his grandchildren a share in his estate, saying 'I do not want any of my grandchildren to have to stand behind a counter.' It made my life with B.B. possible.

Karin was still suffering from a deafness which fluctuated and raised hopes of improvement. In 1927 she had yet another operation which did improve her hearing to some extent, but left her with a bruised facial nerve and permanent slight facial paralysis.

To Mrs Berenson   27 September 1927   Munich
I have better news, in a way, of Karin. While the side of her face

remains paralyzed, the probability is that it is only nerve shock from her slight operation, and not what we dreaded more than anything in the world, the cutting of the facial nerve. She has been quite splendid about it, faced up to the worst like a hero, and made up her mind to work out a successful life in spite of it. Indeed in one way, it might not be a misfortune, for it would put an end to her dreams of social gaiety, which, for some strange reason—perhaps for having been kept from all social life by her deafness and by Adrian's peculiar man-hating nature—she seems to have desired more than any intellectual eminence or achievement, for which she is so exceptionally gifted.

However, the really serious thing is that her husband has been so devoted and helpful during this crisis, that I am dreadfully afraid she will be persuaded into taking him back, and then the whole miserable history of incompatibility and uncongeniality will begin all over again. Well, we can only do so much for our children, and then just hope that they will be, as the old Quakers used to put it, 'rightly guided'. [In fact Karin and Adrian were on good terms at this time.]

Diary   11 November 1927   Paris
In the afternoon Fischer of Lucerne came to see B.B. and offered him money for having given certain attributions, but B.B. would not take it. He won't be classed with Gronau, van Hadeln and Venturi and the rest who exchange 'attestations' for banknotes.

To Alys Russell   13 November 1927   Paris
Nicky is enjoying herself too. People love her. Someone asked at tea the other day what her real name was, and was instantly told that her name was 'Nicky Darling'.

To Senda Berenson Abbott   8 December 1927   Hyères
I cannot face the approach of Christmas. It nearly overwhelms me to have Barbara come out, B.B. hates it so, although I have carefully arranged it so she will be at I Tatti only a couple of nights when he is there. It is so very difficult, he does so resent my caring for my descendants. Really, if I could stop loving them, I would, in the interest of a quiet life! I hoped Nicky's devotion would give me a free hand, but of course at Christmas she is entirely wrapped up in her nephew.

To Bernard Berenson   28 February 1928   Berne
I shall have to tell thee why I am so short, which I didn't in the least

want to do! But it's only fair, since I am asking to be helped out. It's on account of very old debts, which, to my surprise, my Bank insists on my paying up as quickly as I can.... The first was to help Mother out when, shortly before she died, she got into difficulties. She really did not like to come on thee again, so I borrowed £400 for her, which made her completely comfortable. The next was £250 for my share of putting Chilling in order, a thing I and mine have much profited from. Then again at Christopher's birth I borrowed another £100 and another £100 at another time, but I forget for what, and there have been one or two small overdrafts which they have considered as loans, making close on £900 altogether. They asked me at the end of last year to begin paying it back, and now I've got it down to £650 and shall be able, I hope, to pay it all back in the course of the year. But meantime it keeps me very short. Ray is so distressed that she will scarcely let me buy a flower and thinks of cinemas as most extravagant!!! ... Well, it is all out now, and I hope thee will excuse my keeping it secret from thee.

Diary   17 March 1928   I Tatti
All art is in a certain sense a lie, and the value of the art depends on the beauty of the lie, not on the veracity of the fact.

But some people pretend that *facts* are beautiful *per se*, and that the nearer you get to them the more beautiful your art must be.

Diary   13 April 1928   I Tatti
Someone asked me what my morning 'toilet' consisted of. I put it down for curiosity.

1. Rise at 7
2. Clean my teeth
3. Drink (Fiuggi)
4. Curl my hair
5. Exercises ½ hr

6. Bathe legs
7. Warm bath
8. Brush face
9. Frinz Branntwein (face and neck)

10. Brush arms
11. Cold sponge
12. Brush legs
13. Cold sponge legs
14. Frinz Branntwein (legs etc)

Then massage 8–8.30. Then tea and toast. Then read.

To Mrs Berenson   30 April 1928   I Tatti
At the moment it is the 'season' and the sins of our past life are upon us with all the fashionable people from America. Bernard used to think he liked them, and he still likes individuals who are his friends, but as a class he has come to loathe them. They seem to think wrong in all public questions and their ideals are chiefly dress, jewels, silly

271

gregariousness, and flirtation, and it takes on a most unpleasant aspect now that they are old.

To her Family   2 May 1928   I Tatti
It seems that it is the gout that is the cause of all my coughs, colds and rheumatism. It is a bore to have lost faith in Drs Freeman and Kocher! But I mean to have a few more trials before I settle down to the life of an old invalid.

Bernard was still deeply suspicious of the good faith and business methods of Duveen and his lieutenant Edward Fowles, while Mary as usual tried to act as a peacemaker.

To Bernard Berenson   11 June 1928   Bagnoles
How dreadfully suspicious thee gets! I do think it is an utter mistake to suspect Edward [Fowles]. He is immensely on thy side, as a dozen things showed me in Paris, then, as so often before. Those suspicions of thine grow up in absence and are always dissipated by a talk with him. As to his wanting to persuade thee that their geese are swans, there's not a word of truth in it. Jo yes, but Edward quite the contrary.... He *wanted* to see thee, said he had a hundred things to talk over with thee, proposed the £3000 extra for the new Bellini and two other pictures. Levy, by the way, said Jo must be urged to pay off what is still owing.

To Edward Fowles   27 June 1928   I Tatti [copy]
B.B. asks me to beg the firm NEVER to send up any Italian dealers or picture owners direct to him. A Conte Roberti of Venice has just been here, sent, he said, by Mr Edward Duveen, but without any letter. B.B. could not receive an Italian coming in that way—he might be any scoundrel.... But even with a letter, B.B. *does not want to see Italians*. He wants all communications to pass through the Firm, and no photos or pictures to be jumped upon him here. Italians run to blackmail and threats as readily as ducks to water, and if B.B. doesn't at once 'authenticate' their rubbish (for such it generally is) they became nasty and eternal enemies ready to do him all sorts of bad turns.

More and more, Mary and B.B. drifted apart on the question of money. Mary felt that by her own work for him she had earned the right to a set proportion of his actual earnings, while B.B.—as Nicky obediently explained—felt that keeping his wife in luxury fulfilled all his obligations. Furthermore he was convinced that she obtained much of the money she spent on her family by disingenuous means, and that left to herself she would have ruined them both. On her side Mary felt that in view of his obduracy she was entirely justified in getting hold of money in any way she could. This remained a bitter battleground for years.

To Nicky Mariano   20 August 1928   [No place]
I sent off a long letter to Levy about our Wills. I do not *einstimmen*, but do not see my way to change anything, as B.B. does not recognize that I have had any share in building up his career—though without me, in the beginning, he would have drifted and never written a line. I wish he would make one or two concessions which I have very much at heart, but he gets *furious* when I even approach them.

To Mrs Berenson   8 September 1928   Consuma
He [Duveen] left us all a bit breathless from the pace he set and the enormous vistas of success and affluence he dangled before our eyes. We persuaded him to found Chairs of Art at Oxford and Cambridge, and attach to them Fellowships for students at the Berenson Institute in Florence. We have 6 Fellowships already promised (all by Jews!), and can ourselves I think endow several more.

In the autumn of 1928 the Berensons took a trip to Constantinople and Asia Minor.

To Mrs Berenson   16 October 1928   Constantinople
I shall always see Bernard [in Konya], his hands clasped tight, stealing round from one pillar to another, gazing up in rapture at the cupola'd ceilings of these mosques, quivering with joy at finding so complete a realization of what he felt to be implied in the best Italian architecture. You *can't think* how he enjoys it all! It is a real pleasure to watch him.

Diary   3 November 1928   I Tatti
I saw Geoffrey Scott twice before he went to America to edit the Talbot de Malahide Boswell papers. The visits were eminently unsatisfactory and marked the end of our friendship. It is better to leave it embalmed in the past, for what it was. It meant a lot to us then, but means nothing now.

Geoffrey's marriage to Lady Sybil ended in divorce in 1926. His books, *The Architecture of Humanism* (published in 1914) and *The Portrait of Zelide*, a biography of Mme de Charrière (whose relations with Benjamin Constant, he admitted, resembled his own with Mary too closely for comfort), were highly regarded, and in 1928 he was asked to go to the United States to edit the recently surfaced Talbot de Malahide Boswell papers. The following year he fell ill, and died in a New York hotel, of pneumonia. Lady Sybil soon married again; her new husband was her old friend Percy Lubbock. She died in 1943.

To Bernard Berenson   29 December 1928   Vienna
Barbara has a nice social manner. I am encouraged about her. After all youth is an illness one recovers from, being thenceforward immune.

To Mrs Berenson   26 January 1929   I Tatti
She [Ray] does not quite know what to do with Barbara after she is finished in Vienna*, which will be at the end of April; she says she and her husband live in a way most unsuitable for the young and that their talk, friends and habits are so sophisticated that it would do Barbara no good to live in the midst of it. Of course Ray's husband is a Strachey, and any normal home life with a Strachey is impossible. Jane Harrison said that there were four classes in the world: men, women, children, and Stracheys! Ray's husband has ten brothers and sisters, the two eldest are normal ordinary people, but the others are all as queer as are made.

To Mrs Berenson   2 February 1929   I Tatti
I am getting on awfully well this winter as regards my health. I am very careful to rest my two days in ten, and look forward to these times with real pleasure ... these days of rest have given me a feeling that I never expected to have; all the weight of the things I ought to do and have not done has fallen off my shoulders.... Bernard is horrified with me, but says little as he is pleased to have me so good-humoured and so easy-going. Nicky has taken on the responsibility of the work, and I sometimes feel that it is too much for her. Bernard is so very exact in his work that he does not allow the least frailty on the part of his helpers; he cannot convict me any more, though; I have worked up

* Barbara spent two winters in Vienna, to study music and German.

274

to the limit of my ability for forty years, and now I feel no pang if I lose a photo or copy a date wrong!

To Alys Russell   8 February 1929   I Tatti
The Clarks arrived on Monday to stay till Monday next. He is certainly an unusual creature, but a bit stiff. We all find that she has absolutely *nothing to say* although she is very sweet, and always *looks* interested.

B.B. had become disillusioned with Kenneth Clark, who was too independent to fulfil the docile and laborious role he required of an ideal pupil.

To Alys Russell   9 February 1929   I Tatti
Nicky is very troubled about the business of Kenneth's collaboration with B.B. over the [revision of] the *Florentine Drawings*. Houghton says that K would like to get out of it and B.B. would like him to, but none of us ... dare to put in our oars. B.B. feels sure that K cannot help him, as he needs careful scholarship and not pretty writing *à la* Leonardo in *Life and Letters*. K has said to me that he loathed the pettifogging business of correcting notes and numbers and there will be a lot of that to do if he means to help B.B. But all he wants out of it is, I fear, whatever kudos he will get from the association. He has an ungenerous self-centred nature, and B.B. needs devotion. Will he ever get it from a man? He would repay it richly, opening ungrudgingly *all* his knowledge to his assistant, but the *assistant* must also be ungrudging. I do not interfere.... I *expect* it to end in a deplorable quarrel.

In the spring of 1929 the Berensons took an ambitious sightseeing tour of Syria and Palestine, and on their return Mary started writing about the trip in her first book, *A Modern Pilgrimage*, published in 1933.

To Mrs Berenson   13 July 1929   I Tatti
I am extremely well. I spend my mornings in bed dictating my book to my awfully nice young secretary. I am about three quarters of the way through the book and am already cackling about it like a hen who has triumphantly laid an egg.... In a sense I have never enjoyed myself so much as I have done in writing this book! It is wonderful what pleasures life stores up for one's old age.

275

To Bernard Berenson   20 August 1929   Chilling
Dearest B.B. Nicky is just waking up at Havre. We *hated* to let her go last night. But I rejoice that thee will have her soon—almost before this letter reaches thee. Everyone here adores her.

To Mrs Berenson   3 September 1929   Thorpe-le-Soken [Karin's house]
She [Karin] is revising her book.* I find her husband *incredibly* improved—so genial and cordial (he used to hate and despise us all), and so keen about his work. He already has 8 Psycho-analysis patients—about all he can deal with.

To Bernard Berenson   4 September 1929   Thorpe-le-Soken
J.D. is *wallowing* in money, and can perfectly well settle our past account. He must be pressed. The trial reinforced his (and your) position with the rich, convincing every collector in America that it is unsafe to buy without expert advice and, incidentally, that the safest advice is that of Berenson. Even Langton Douglas admitted that you were the first of living experts! . . . Levy said the money he is handling for us is now over $600,000 and he means to make it a million in another year.

Duveen had been sued by a Mrs Hahn for damages resulting from his declaring that a picture she owned, called *La Belle Ferronière*, was a copy of the Leonardo da Vinci painting in the Louvre. In spite of strong professional support, including testimony given by Berenson in Paris six years earlier, the jury in the 1929 trial could not agree, and Duveen, to avoid a retrial, made an out-of-court settlement of $60,000. Whether the case in fact reinforced Duveen's position, or Berenson's, is perhaps a matter of opinion.

To her Family   1 November 1929   Seville
It is the eve of All Souls, *Ogni Morti*, and so I thought of all the people I once knew who have died. I could recall nearly 200—and how few I could sincerely wish alive again, even if they weren't too old! These thoughts are dreadful.

To Alys Russell   3 December 1929   Barcelona
I am awfully sorry for her [Lina Waterfield]† for it is just the period of

* *Psycho-analysis and Medicine: A Study of the Wish to Fall Ill.*
† Lina Waterfield, Janet Ross's niece, correspondent in Italy for the *Observer* 1922–36. She was left Poggio Gherardo for her life in trust for her younger son, and ran it as a finishing school.

her life when she ought to be spared all worry, and no one spares her ... everything falls on her. It is a hard hard time for her. If I were in B.B.'s shoes, instead of storing up money and money for an 'Institute', I should use enough of it to make things easy for dear Lina. But I can do nothing. If I get the money out of him for R & K (and it's not always easy, even now) it is as much as I can do. And there's nearly a million dollars goes piling up compound interest in America for something *we* shall never get any benefit from, and which if it has any vitality will live on its own.

To Alys Russell   25 December 1929   I Tatti
Barbara and Christopher were *awful* yesterday. I could have cried at their hatefulness. Of course they were both dead tired: they are better today, though still a bit difficult.... The Ball at Poggio [Gherardo] was a tremendous affair ... Barbara danced only with Cecil [Anrep, Nicky's nephew] and English boys. She says she had too much of the other at the della Stufas. Perhaps this is true—one never knows with young people.

To Bernard Berenson   29 December 1929   I Tatti
Children are adorable, but they aren't orderly.... I remember old Walt Whitman who used to go and sit in the hall outside the dining-room when he had finished the little he ate. He always came for our school and college holidays. Once when I went out to him and asked him to come in again, he said 'No, Mary, I love to hear you laugh, but I don't care about your conversation.'

To Mrs Berenson   21 February 1930   I Tatti
Last night Bernard suggested to me the theme for another book—namely the attitude of the early Egyptians towards death. It was an extremely simple attitude, they refused to recognize it—a wonderful instance of the power of the human race to shut its eyes to facts. When I was there, I called it the very loudest bray the human ass has ever uttered in the face of the mystery of death, but Bernard says I must speak of it much more respectfully than this. I am already beginning to chew over the idea.

The truth is that I can't really be of the assistance to him I used to be in his special work. With age I have got to be inaccurate, and this does not do in preparing lists. Nicky, on the contrary, is extremely accurate and painstaking, so that I feel I am doing no wrong to Bernard in making her my substitute and shuffling off what had

277

become a real burden to me. Nicky is even better than I ever was, but of course she had hardly been born when Bernard and I started out on our great adventure.

To Alys Russell   28 April 1930   I Tatti
I can't seem to come to an end with my book. Logan's suggestion that I should embroider on the few words I said about stone-worship has taken me more than a week's reading (all very interesting), and now I must fit it into the text without dislocating things too much. I wish HE were writing this book with all the fascinating material I have gathered. I wish I had devoted my life to writing instead—Oh well, we do what we must. But writing and re-writing are fascinating and tormenting. I vaguely see what might be made of what I have in hand—and Logan could do it so wonderfully! What a blessing for me to have this work to retire into when things go wrong.

To Ray Strachey   7 May 1930   I Tatti
Our chief sorrow is that Nicky is away.... Alda [Nicky's sister] is *almost* a substitute, the dear creature; but yet there is but one *Nicky darling!*... Logan said I was to amplify the phrase 'stone-worship, to which mankind has ever been prone' and I got buried deep under megaliths and mud-towers and menhirs and cromlechs and all the rest. It led straight to Phallic Worship and then on to Baal, then to the worship of trees and fountains, and I know not what else. Salomon Reinach once apologized to me *on a postcard* for his delay in answering a letter by saying 'I have been entirely occupied with Incest this week'. So I apologized the other day *in a letter* for leaving a note of his unanswered 'I have been too much occupied by Phallic worship to reply sooner'. These be the mildly indecent jokes of archaeologists.

To Alys Russell   15 May 1930   I Tatti
I did another futile thing during the day and that was to go to Mrs Loeser's to lunch 'to meet the Sitwells'. I went really because she seemed so grieved at our not going to her large musical party last week, and I am rather fond of her. But when I entered the room, where they were drinking preliminary cocktails and saw one of the people I most abhor, Arthur Acton*, heave up his bulk to shake hands with me, and when I saw also the rather squalid though amusing

---

* English owner of Villa La Pietra, father of Sir Harold Acton.

Reggie Turner.... I regretted having accepted the invitation—that is the worst of Florence, you can go nowhere without meeting people you detest. Presently the Sitwells came in; Lady Ida and her son Sacheverel's wife, and a dubious young musician* who frequently stays with them, and a German girl from Darmstatt, also their guest. Last time I saw Lady Ida she was an extremely handsome woman, but drink and the devil have done for her, and she looked sodden and half paralytic, an old hag not really fit to appear in society. Osbert Sitwell I have not seen for several years and he has not changed for the better in looks, he has got thick and coarse. He asked at once about Logan but did not listen to what I said, interrupting my account with an indifferent 'ah'—in quite the most tiresome London manner. We had lunch, a very delicious lunch, in a pergola overlooking the most heavenly view, and I thought what an enviable scene it would be to someone from London or the States—a real 'Florentine Symposium'.

To Alys Russell   26 May 1930   I Tatti
Today B.B. handed me over his manuscript for correction. Correcting his writing is one of the things I least enjoy doing.... It is an absolute mystery to me how he cannot at least say things in a straightforward manner and how he, who I know is so extremely sensitive to bad style in what he reads, crowds his pages with confused and ungrammatical sentences, and occasionally offends seriously against good taste by some occult jibe, dripping with jocose bitterness. The worst of it is that when I attempt to eliminate these jeers and sneers he gets into a perfect fury. He has developed the theory that I have ruined his style, that if I encouraged him to let loose all the fury and rage that he feels against his fellow-connoisseurs he would have been a second Carlyle in invective (the thirty-fourth way in which I have 'ruined his life'!!!). The worst, or perhaps the best of it is that in the midst of all this dull writing, every now and then he strikes out extraordinarily original and suggestive ideas, any one of which would be enough for a historian or critic to seize upon and use as the basis for a whole treatise. He really does say things that nobody else says or thinks, and it seems a pity that they should be buried away like this under masses of detail and frightfully wearisome connoisseurship, and presented, when they are presented, in an insignificant and some-

* Presumably William Walton, a lifelong friend of the Sitwells.

279

times almost repulsive fashion. The correction of the manuscript took me all the morning and is not half finished yet.

To Alys Russell   2 June 1930   Assisi
Here they have stuck a lot of chimney-stacks just in the middle of the plain, but even worse, a quite new huge convent has sprung up below the town, out of all relation to the buildings and to the site. Curious how completely architects have lost what the most modest builders used to have—the sense of relation between a building and its site. Perhaps it is because they make their designs in offices, and it may be that the earlier builders planned out their edifices on the spot.

Following the American Stock Market crash of 1929 the question of money became an even more burning one between Bernard and Mary. Bernard was more determined than ever to build up funds for the endowment of the Institute, while Mary was still determined not to reduce the gifts she showered on her family—often to their embarrassment.

To Alys Russell   26 June 1930   I Tatti
It is B.B.'s birthday, and by a piece of good luck the garden seats were delivered this morning so they will do for a present for him—the only hitch in the affair is that he has to pay for them, and has never wanted garden seats—in which he is entirely wrong, as he has been in everything to do with the garden from the very beginning....
    Yesterday he came in in a very friendly nice mood and said he was not going to accept the proposal of Ray and Karin that he should diminish their allowance by a hundred pounds each; he said he would give them what they have always had in the hope that they would invest the hundred either for themselves or for the benefit of their children. He was really awfully nice about it and was speaking from the reasonable and considerate side of his nature. He said he did hate to see me concerned so much for their material welfare, but I told him that most mothers were like that and he would have to put up with it the way I put up with his getting agitated over what seemed to me to be unimportant things. But of course we shall go down to our graves fighting, but fighting, I hope, in a more and more friendly and understanding way.

To Nicky Mariano   1 August 1930   Rheinfelden
I do want a little freedom with money all for my own. *He* can give

280

motors to Naima, *he* can do this and that, but I never can. If I had more money it would by no means all go to R & K. They have *nearly* enough to enable them to lead the lives they like—and this is of course thanks to him. He doesn't give to his people a regular income equal to what he gives Ray and Karin, but he is always making them presents for special things, illnesses, holidays etc, so that it comes to quite as much. I am willing to help him all I can about his Institute but that is *sure* to attract money once it gets going, and I want him to feel free, and feel freer myself, to do certain things *now*, while we are alive and can enjoy them.

To Nicky Mariano   20 August 1930   Thorpe-le-Soken
Just as B.B. likes to have money to do as he wants with ... so I think I ought to have some of the same money to use in the same way. If he had never made any money *of course* I would have shared all I had with him. But he has made a lot, and for years I helped him, more than you or anyone can realize who knows me now old and tired. For all this help—*of all kinds*, I think I have deserved a share of the fortune that came to us. I will not say half, for his genius was of course the greater part of it, but *I should have shared the fortune*, not only had my board and living, but have had a definite share that was my own, as he considers the whole of it now is his.

To Bernard Berenson   26 August 1930   Fernhurst
The last sentence of your letter of the 23rd made me weep. Perhaps you did not mean it to be icily cold and breathing suspicion: 'When may we expect to have the pleasure of your society in these parts?' I must leave it at that. I am coming back *before I can*, so to speak. I think I am a great burden here. No doubt I shall be the same there, but perhaps the mountain air will help me. Scarcely in the worst moments of my breakdown have I felt so unhappy as here, such brain anaemia, such bodily fatigue, such depression.... In all my life I have never been so depressed as here this summer. I see all the defects of the people I love, and sometimes at night the vital spark of love itself falls very low. My only comfort is objective—they are all well and happy and intelligent, and I am glad, for in a way I am responsible. But they feel as remote as the polar stars, and within me is a black void.

To Bernard Berenson   30 August 1930   Fernhurst
Ray and Karin seem happy. Thanks to thee they live lives that give them all they want. In fact I think they are unusually happy, and this

is a great satisfaction to me, for sometimes the thought of being responsible for human beings coming into this ghastly world is almost more than I can bear. We know so little about each other—I daresay thee has never known how often I have bitterly regretted being a mother. Life would have been so much simpler and happier for us both if I had had no children, but not only that, *dentro di me* things would have been so very much easier. I often think I have had more anguish than delight from my affection for them.

To Nicky Mariano   30 August 1930   Haslemere
I feel the force of everything you say in your letter. At the same time, you must admit that where a man and a woman have both worked up to the limit of their abilities, the rewards of their labour should be divided between them, and not come as a largesse (subject to bitter criticism) from the one to whom the payments are made. In our case I should never have thought of the matter if B.B. had not made things so difficult about R and K—for it is much easier to slide along without insisting on abstract 'rights'. But he has for years humiliated me so cruelly every time he gave the allowance to them, and whenever the matter of my own money came up, that very serious bitterness has arisen between us—which is madness, considering that it is about a few hundred pounds. It has made me think things out a bit.

What would be fair would have been to put *all* our money together in the beginning and apportion it in three parts, 1) common expenses, 2) B.B.'s share, 3) my share. I do not pretend that my share should be as great as his. But ¼ would have been fair, considering all that I did.... I do not regard my sharing B.B.'s life and pleasures as a set-off against my sharing (in however small a degree) the cash profits of our labours. It would be humanly impossible for him to travel in luxury with me living in penury and travelling 3rd class. Nor do I owe him what I claim to have *earned* because he hasn't turned out a bounder. If that sort of reckoning were turned into cash, then he would have to pay me for whatever virtues I may possess. Those things cannot be put on a cash basis.

If he hadn't torn the very skin off my heart, I am sure I should never have raised this question, even though I do think that husband and wife *should* share, on a fair basis, the actual cash accruing from their joint labours. But one doesn't stand out for rights, when there is harmony. This attitude has led me, I confess, to take unoffered advantages, in giving a few presents to the children. This has been far from delicate but has he been delicate in the things he has said to me?

It is a disgusting muddle. I feel sorry you are drawn into it.

But if it ended by his putting 10,000 lire a month to my account—which would raise my income to something over two thousand pounds, I, for my part, would cease making any fuss, and *you* would not be bothered any more. I should pay everything outside connected with the children, even, if B.B. wished it, their food for the two weeks in the year in which they visit me (when he stays over Xmas at Edith's) and he and I need never mention money again, unless he brings up old grudges and repeats old sneers. I should pay everything that might be counted mine apart from our common life—that is to say, my charities, my dress, my presents to people, hairdresser, my summers, my 'Cures' etc...

Dearest Nicky, I *am* sorry you are involved in our hateful matrimonial disputes! Your loving Mary

To Mrs Berenson   29 October 1930   I Tatti
My brother has been here—but leaves today, and Mr and Mrs Kenneth Clark also are here, with whom we have just shared a quarrel—and I do hate quarrels, especially with anyone we have taken up so enthusiastically as we did young Clark. As time went on we came to perceive that he wasn't the person we hoped, and his marriage completed the disillusion. Bernard felt very bitter about him, but when he met them ten days ago at Cortona ... he himself took pity on little Mrs Clark, who was really ill, and invited them here for a rest. Nicky and I were very glad it came out this way.

To Alys Russell   9 November 1930   I Tatti
We have made a vow never again to rush anyone, as we did Kenneth. B.B. is too little to be depended on, too suspicious and quick to take offence for any such close relation to work well.... I am rather distressed—in fact *very* distressed—about the Eugénie Strong situation. She has begun writing me most affectionate letters, and she wants to come and stay. B.B. vows he will never see her again, and I think he means it. She is not a very loyal friend, but I do think it is a mistake to quarrel with her. Oh dear, I do wish B.B. didn't make things so difficult! It is dreadfully thorny, and I have to be rude again and again.

To Mrs Berenson   4 January 1931   I Tatti
B.B. could not have endured his home during the last fortnight! One

283

day the three younger children took it into their heads to flood the upper bathroom and 'swim' in it. Presently the water came sneaking through the walls and ceilings, and finally ran off in a cataract down the stairs!! Now they are marching round the house counting the old 'Madonnas' hanging on the walls. They have found 50 on this floor alone. They hope to get up to 100. The number of them is more interesting to these youthful minds than the beauty of them!

To Bernard Berenson   4 January 1931   I Tatti
Sometimes I wish I could disentangle my heart from them—they are really *so* far away—I mean the grandchildren. Their problems are too difficult for me, their faults too distressing. But it is a craze, like drink, to meet them sometimes. With Ray and Karin it is different; they are real friends and I am interested in their work, and on the whole approve of them. Well, there it is, I utter cries like a cat on a roof at pairing time.

To Bernard Berenson   7 January [1931]   I Tatti
We shall enjoy it very much [going off alone with Alys] especially having *no children* bothering around!! A sad confession I have spared myself in every possible way, but just *seeing* their muddles is distressing, late, careless, untidy and full of awful faults which time will no doubt cure, yet one is afraid it won't. I see now that old people cannot deal with children; they know too much the pitfalls of existence and it's agony to see the young stumble into them.

During 1931 the financial situation really began to affect them: unpleasant cuts had to be made in their lavish expenditure, and capital had to be broached.

To Mrs Berenson   30 September 1931   I Tatti
I take it as certain that Bernard's 'retaining fee', as adviser to Duveen's on their purchases of Italian Art will cease, as they have made no purchases for a year, and are not contemplating any. This was the chief source of our income! It looks as if we should have just one third of what we have been spending.

We are cutting down in all sorts of ways—first of all, I'm sorry to say, in the allowances we made to my daughters, who will have to earn their own livings now, and utterly change their manner of life.

Bernard has stopped buying books (his greatest pleasure), we are dismissing the butler and one of the gardeners, we shall entertain

284

much less—in fact we are tightening our belts, and waiting to see what will happen. We could always go and live in one of the smaller houses.

To Alys Russell   1 October 1931   I Tatti
What shall we do if the lira cracks? For us it will perhaps be an advantage, but it is awful to live in a country where people are suffering.... I can imagine getting really interested in saving!! I should positively adore it, if it meant I could give what I saved to R and K.

To Alys Russell   5 October 1931   I Tatti
I was again stricken down in the night by my enemy [cystitis] and I am keeping in bed today with a hot-water bottle. It is very disappointing, for I was feeling very well, and had been on 5 nice walks with B.B. As soon as Giglioli recovers from his motor accident I will arrange to be examined by a specialist to see if I need to repeat the sewing-up operation which Dr Aldrich Blake so successfully performed.

During 1931 Mary's health had deteriorated sharply. Never gifted with physical fortitude, she was now determined to have the operation for vaginal repair, in the hope of putting a stop to her continual nagging cystitis. Following the operation she developed a fever which nearly killed her.

To Mrs Berenson   27 October 1931   I Tatti
I love to be taken care of by these kind 'Blue Sisters' who add to the usual care and sympathy of nurses the enthusiasm of service that comes from a higher motive, namely to please the God they adore. They grumble at no trouble and make an offering of everything to the Heart of Jesus or Seven Rules of Mary or whatever other nonsense they have gotten into their dear heads. They have the intelligence of birds and twitter with little jokes and chatter like a flock of birds.

To Alys Russell   13 November 1931   I Tatti
I was better this morning, but they used a big glass something to wash me out and it bruised me and my *worst pains* are back. These 'dark fountains of pain' are pouring their dreadful floods through my veins, but not water—fire, writhing snakes with fiery heads. In other ways I am better, and I daresay I shall get over this attack. The analysis is

285

always showing improvement. But *is* it worthwhile to make such a fight for a few more years of an old woman's existence?

To Mrs Berenson   9 January 1932   I Tatti
During the time that my sister has been with me she has read to me extracts from my mother's letters beginning in 1848 and ending at her death in 1911. They are the history of a deeply religious soul shaking itself free without any aid from others, and in fact in such deadly opposition to the circle she lived in that even her parents said they would rather she were dead than holding the beliefs that had forced themselves upon her.... Those old disputes over justification by works, sanctification by faith, the out-pouring of the Holy Spirit, the personal guidance of the same 'Honourable Pigeon' as the Japanese called the third member of the Trinity when an attempt was made to set Christian Truth before them, are to us like 'Old unhappy far-off things and battles long ago'. But the spectacle of an eager indomitable soul striving to find Truth in all this maze of superstitition and convention is a very exhilarating one. Therefore, in spite of my illness I have been profoundly interested in my mother's history and have even been able to think a great deal about the problems such as the story presents, and, if one's mind keeps even a little spark of activity, things are not hopeless.

To Mrs Berenson   25 February 1932   I Tatti
I was recovering quite nicely when suddenly a fiery sheet of irysipalas [erysipelas] was wound around my waist and began to eat into my very bones. I went right down and for two days they thought I could not survive. Then on the evening of the 2nd day I began to slide away—a most delicious sensation. I heard one doctor say to another 'She is going'—and I felt happy to go. Then I heard, from what seemed to me a hundred miles away, Bernhard's voice crying out: 'Don't desert me, Mary'. He was really kneeling by the bed, but it seemed very far away. There was so much love and despair in his voice that I had to respond to it and I said in my mind 'I won't desert you', and held myself back from dying. One of the doctors said 'What has happened?' and the other said 'She will live' and I am very glad that I am alive.... One thing that this illness has taught me has been very surprising to me and that is that I am loved by the people whom I myself love. I never thought much about it, but always had the idea at the back of my mind that I was nothing in myself and only shone of a light of the reflected merit of my gifted husband. But now I know

286

that I am loved and even when I was in most pain I have had a feeling of being like a small boat floating on a lake of affection. It is a very beautiful thing. But I cannot tell you all that this illness seems to have done for me. It has taken away every bitterness and grudge or resentfulness that experience seems to have scarred on my soul and especially with regard to Bernhard, for we have had in our lives a good deal of dissension and even unhappiness, although of course not enough to overbalance the real love that has always existed; but at any rate, now that is all gone and the dear man has responded so warmly to the change in me that we both feel a new period of happiness is opening before us. The first symptom on his part is that all the jealousy he has felt for my children and grandchildren has dropped away from him, but *completely*, and as this has been the chief element of discord between us, his change of attitude fills me with bliss and happiness. I myself feel as if I am just beginning to understand what love and affection mean.

CHAPTER EIGHTEEN

The Invalid

March 1932–May 1944

Mary never really recovered after the operation, despite an exhausting summer spent in the Vienna Cottage Sanatorium in 1935. She became almost a complete invalid, though she still managed to recover sufficiently each year to undertake the journey to England to stay with her daughters.

Money troubles continued, but Mary was becoming less urgent in her demands. As she dropped out of active life she took a more resigned and reflective view of Bernard's character, and a greater peace descended on the villa.

To Mrs Berenson   24 March 1932   I Tatti
Up to now during the period of more than 40 years when I have always gone over his articles and always discussed them with him, our discussions have always ended in what I might inelegantly describe as bloody rows! And Nicky and my daughter were extremely anxious about this article when I told them I was ready to go over it with B.B., for they did not realize what a change had come over us both since my illness. Instead of looking for defects and sneering at B.B. for careless writing, I looked out for the good things first and praised them while he, on his side, fully recognized that I was actuated by nothing but a desire to have work as good as possible and that I was putting my best pains into smoothing out the angles and knots that his hasty writing had left in his article. We therefore discussed the thing with complete harmony and satisfaction to ourselves.

To Carey Thomas   6 April 1932   I Tatti
I expect to take up again in about a week the revision of our list of Beautiful Italian Pictures*, this ought not to take very long and we

* The work was finished and sent to Yale University Press, but it was never published.

have our prefaces already written. Then I shall have to look for a publisher. The *we* consists of myself and the most talented and delightful pupil we have ever had, the young man from Pittsburgh—of all places! named John Walker. When he was sent to us a year and a half ago from Harvard, B.B. was too busy to direct his work, so I took him into this scheme thinking it would be good training for his taste. To my surprise and delight his taste needed very little training. We united independently upon almost every picture. What he needs training in is writing, and I am putting him to a severe course of sprouts, as we used to call it, in that respect.

To Alys Russell   *17 July 1932*   *Consuma*
It looks as if we were up a tree, but we shan't *know* till we've seen Levy in September. We fear the worst, why should he alone have been able to keep his investments, for us and for himself, profitable? Meantime we LOST the £10,000 a year we got from Duveen, and £50,000 of Duveen's investments are *absolutely gone*. He cannot allow me the £1200 a year he gave me, and I shall have to do everything on the Cemetery money*—which itself is dwindling. We shall probably shut up I Tatti, dismiss the servants, suppress the motor, and live perhaps in Rome very economically—at any rate for a few years. Alas, they are the years when the children need money for their educations. I have to cut off all my charities, and this is very painful to me. Otherwise, I mean apart from thee and the children, I shall be *glad* to live more economically.

To Bernard Berenson   *15 August 1932*   *Fernhurst*
Logan is very remote and illish and Alys seems cased in a metal armour that is very hard to pierce. The first shock of 'Mud House' [Ray's cottage in Fernhurst] is upsetting, but it was nice yesterday. . . . They are all, of course, very reduced as to money, but not depressed.

Mary's pessimism was excessive. Louis Levy, the Duveen lawyer who was in charge of their investments, was able to salvage a good part of their capital, and they were able to remain at I Tatti and live in much the same way as before. B.B. continued to work with Duveen, on a reduced scale, until late in 1937, when their agreement came to an end.

* Mary's grandfather, John Jay Smith, had left his grandchildren shares in the family cemetery, Laurel Hill, in Philadelphia.

To Alys Russell   4 October 1932   I Tatti
He [B.B.] was unable to come to any agreement with Duveen, and is full of gloomy anticipations. Nicky said things would have gone better, she thought, if I could have gone to Vienna in his place—as I have so often done when I was well.

To Bernard Berenson   17 October 1932   London
The first splash of the rising tide came up to the arid rock where this human seaweed has been stranded, dry and withered. Curious, the way life creeps back, little by little—just like the tide, imperceptible, almost, but quietly insistent.

To Senda Berenson Abbott   18 October 1932   London
The doctors, with their examinations and endless 'remedies', seemed to make me worse, so at last I threw away all their horrid brews and betook myself to the Milk Diet that cured me last spring. They were sceptical and even disapproving, but *in a week I got well.* I mean the bladder trouble has gone; but I am so weak that I can hardly take a step alone, and I am very weary.

To Mrs Berenson   5 February 1933   I Tatti
The day before he [John Walker] left Italy he was received into the Catholic Church. I feel very sorry, but somehow I knew that the world or the devil or God would get him. As Emerson says 'So many promising youths, and never a finished man'; or as Logan wrote, 'How full is the world of Fallen Angels.'

To Edith Wharton   10 February 1933   I Tatti
Except for pain and discomfort, and for the distress it gives B.B.—I have enjoyed this time in bed. As I felt too wretched to read a good deal of the time, I let my mind wallow, so to speak, and then found I had an unexpected visual memory for our motor trips. I have been all over Tunis and Algiers, and saw everything again, even to the wild flowers that grew along our roads. It has been a joy beyond all telling, and I am gradually writing the chief things I remember* only—*I can't write.* Everyone writes better, though few have as much to say.

To Bernard Berenson   28 February 1933   I Tatti
Dearest Bernard. It is awfully selfish of me, but I *can't bear* to have

---

* This book was published in 1937 under the title *Across the Mediterranean.*

thee go away! I nearly weep every time I pass the closed doors of thy empty rooms. It is most desolate, and I miss thee *dreadfully*, just thy presence that informs the house with life and interest. And when Nicky is gone *too*, it is really too much for this sick old lady to endure.

To Mrs Berenson   11 April 1933   I Tatti
Germany—! We are heartbroken at this terrible streak of brutality that has appeared in them. So many of our friends, too, are rendered destitute—because they belong to the cleverest race in Europe!

To John Walker   11 March 1933   I Tatti
I have just sent off the corrected proofs and index of my first book—*A Modern Pilgrimage*—and I feel like Sarah when in extreme old age she gave birth to Isaac! You would think, from the fierce way I fall upon the writings of others, that I was satisfied with my own effort. On the contrary, I could have wept over the horrid style of my book. I am trying to do better in a book on North Africa that I'm doing now, but I fear I am a hopeless case. The reasons are deeper than the pen can probe.

To Mrs Berenson   10 June 1933   I Tatti
Even if his nerves get the upper hand and fierce words rise to his lips, I don't let myself get upset any more, I only feel sorry for him, as if he had a fever, and try to find a cure for it. Nicky has *always* been like that, having been severely disciplined by a fierce and undisciplined and very selfish father, to whom Bernard, at his worst, is a lamb! But I grew up in a family where no one ever lost their temper, so it was hard for me not to take it too seriously.... The chief good of life for us is to *be together*, and we appreciate it as a fresh benediction every day. How strange it is that a choice made under the influence of the blindest of gods, at the silliest time of youth, should turn out to be the real essential thing we need in old age!

To Mrs Berenson   10 July 1933   Gazzada
I was much amused the other day to receive a review of my book which began 'The very kernel of Christianity is to be found in Mrs Berenson's *Modern Pilgrimage*'. *That* I could never have anticipated.

To Alys Russell   21 July 1933   I Tatti
I had to take an opium suppository to quiet my pain, which was rather bad, so I feel better now, but of course I shan't move or eat till I'm well again. What luck I like being in bed.

To Walter Lippmann   20 August 1933   Consuma
B.B. is just leaving for Vienna to meet his lawyer and find out where he *really* stands. This lawyer, Louis Levy, has charge of all our American investments. He guarantees us against any loss of capital, but of course cannot create the old income.... Now Harvard hasn't yet accepted the future legacy. Naturally they hesitate, unless the endowment is adequate, and we sympathize with them. If things had gone normally, we could have left it properly endowed (and we still may be able to), as the money Levy was taking care of was mounting up in a very satisfactory way. But now, we may have to use it for ourselves.

What B.B. would like would be the assurance that Harvard will accept the legacy provided B.B. leaves a sufficient endowment, or subscription from the outside, sufficient to run it properly, can be found.

To Nicky Mariano   [7 September? 1933]   Consuma
Barbara arrives soon. I dread it, though I suppose I do love her. Christopher gets more and more delightful as his shyness wears off. Barbara hasn't *enough* shyness.

To Alys Russell   11 September 1933   Consuma
Barbara is remote and strange. She will have to unscramble her own problems. She is awfully vehement and at the same time silly and ill-judged. I have a grandmotherly sympathy for her, but not much personal sympathy at present. The young people's way of taking love is very foreign to all my ideas and feelings.

To Alys Russell   13 September 1933   Consuma
She [Karin] does seem to me so wonderfully improved. Her mind worked so well, she seemed gay, carefree, detached, yet friendly and benevolent, poised, mature, sure of herself (but not obstinate), happy, serene, in short what the Buddhists call 'enlightened'. Her eyes had a new expression, very lovely. She did not say one foolish or ill-judged or unkind thing. I simply cannot say how beautiful the character she revealed seemed to me. I remarked on the change in her, and she smiled and said she was just finishing (she hoped) her analysis, at last with a perfectly satisfactory analyst, which Dr Glover was not. It is very striking. As to Christopher, Alys, he is an *Angel*! Poor, scrawny, self-absorbed, turbulent Barbara was another tale, but even she melted to Karen and became nicer and nicer.

Barbara, after leaving Oxford, embarked on a trip to Australia on a sailing ship.

To Barbara Strachey   14 September 1933   Consuma
I want once more to tell thee how grateful I am for thy visit! Thee gave up a lot to give me this pleasure, and I appreciate it. Now thee is about to set sail on unknown seas, real and spiritual. Both will probably be stormy. The first command of the Wise of all nations is 'Know Thyself!' and this, I think, is what thee means to try to do. But the aim of knowledge is, in a sense, to be *freed from self,* and not to be self-absorbed. I mean, when one *knows,* one has command of all one's powers and can pursue the path one's nature provides without hesitation and further introspection. I do not think it is easy to know one's self. It took the mature Buddha seven years of solitude. I believe the best way for us Westerners to get our feet set on this path is not solitary introspection but introspection under a trained physician— a P.A. in fact! Karin is a remarkable example of the benefit to be derived from analysis. Thee must have noticed how gay and serene and kind and *free* she seems. But thee cannot know the unhappy, struggling, resentful creature she was. The change is very remarkable, and I think it is due to her being (at last!) near the end of her analysis, this time with a skilful and wise physician. Still, people have different ways of attaining self-knowledge and self-control and freedom from self, and maybe thy extraordinary voyage may be *thy* way. Whatever it is, *bon voyage* on thy adventurous trip. My loving if not always comprehending thoughts will follow thee.

To Bernard Berenson   23 September 1933   I Tatti
I've taken up work on ... the Berensonian Anthology. I find the writing sometimes *very good.* My *œil dénigrant* did not give thee enough credit.

To Mrs Berenson   31 December 1933   I Tatti
Bernard is going on the 8th to spend two weeks with Edith Wharton, while I have Alys with me here for part of the time. The rest of the time I shall be alone, and this I enjoy greatly, long spaces of time for working without interruption. I shall get on with his 'Life'. He thinks Alys will be here *all the time* but she can stay only a week out of the three he will be away. But I haven't told him! He hates being alone, himself, and cannot believe I like it! One must deceive people sometimes for their good.... As the heroine of a story I once read

293

said—'The Lord has given us the faculty for deceiving: He must have meant us to use it sometimes!'

Diary   17 February 1934   I Tatti
Trevy left for Austria and Nicky went to Florence, so B.B. and I were left to ourselves—which I greatly enjoy! We began to read Rhys Carpenter's *The Humanistic Value of Archaeology*—a *delightful* little book.

To Mrs Berenson   28 May 1934   London
My dear Mother—Another week has slipped by most agreeably— full of interest to me. For I heard Karin give a really first-class lecture to the Medical Students of the British Medical Association —the President said it was the best lecture they had ever had!—I heard Ray give an excellent talk over the Radio, on Unemployment, and Adrian Stephen (Karin's husband) another Radio talk on 'Normal and Abnormal Personalities'. Alys also made a witty after-dinner speech at a meeting of College Alumnae; Logan read me a really fine paper he has written for the Carlyle Centenary; and finally I got my book all in order and took it to the Publishing agent.

To Bernard Berenson   6 June 1934   London
Dame Ethel Smyth was the only other 'convive', I may say the only person present, for she talked steadily in her loud emphatic voice. She dresses as much as possible like Vernon [Lee], but her head was covered with a large grey felt man's hat, especially made for her. Her clothing was a man's soft shirt and tie, and a reach-me-down of rough tweed. She is deaf, like Vernon, but uses a thing in her ear. Not quite so deaf, and infinitely more vigorous—a dynamo of energy, over 70, but determined to keep a hold on everything that ever interested her. She would wear me out in a day, but *completely*, though I should faint, gasping with admiration at that boundless energy.

Diary   22 June 1934   London
The Kenneth Clarks lunched here. He is a queer mixture of arrogance and sensitive humility. She looked most flourishing.

To Bernard Berenson and Nicky Mariano   August [1934]   Fiuggi
I have come to think of myself as already passed out of human life. Pain and exhaustion have killed all that. But I still love you, and I still

enjoy my memories. And I have made a little discipline, which is to neglect the deathly side but enjoy, yes enjoy, each little second of relief or interest that comes along, if it is only taking hold of the side of my chair, or sinking back on my pillows. There are hundreds of such tiny pleasures still to be had.

To Bernard Berenson   26 September 1934   Fiuggi
He [the doctor] is *sure* I will get over this attack. I do want to finish my 'Life' and (thee will be horrified!) I want to hold in my arms my first great-grandchild!! As to *us* we have had our day, and I am no longer a companion to thee, but a heavy burden, in spite of thy dear affection. This time I want to go for thy sake, as well as to escape from suffering. Love has nothing to do with death.

The great-grandchild was born in October. On arriving in Australia, Barbara had rashly married a Finnish fellow-passenger on the sailing ship; the marriage broke down almost immediately, leaving her with a baby. In March she brought the child out to I Tatti, and Mary was once again able to find in him the magic of childhood which had always so delighted her. The child, Roger, came to be almost the only thing which could bring her comfort, and he spent his first three winters in Florence with her. In 1937, however, his mother married again and wanted him at home.

Diary   23 March 1935   I Tatti
Barbara arrived 5.53 with ROGER!!! Barbara dined up in my room. Motherhood has improved her. The Baby is *perfectly heavenly*. Such blue eyes and long curling lashes.

To Bernard Berenson   1 April 1935   I Tatti
Each day with a baby, though it seems the same as all the other days, is really entirely different from the inside, as it were. To the child there is no monotony but drama and melodrama from moment to moment, since each little event is surprising and thrilling; and you share the feelings.... Its bath is as exciting to it as if *we* were to dive over the Niagara Falls, its being wheeled to the terrace as long and wonderful as our motor ride to Palmyra. Its sunbath is indescribable, its crawl on the floor more than Aurel Stein's exploration of the Gobi Desert. And my days pass amid these excitements. But alas they are not exciting to write about to travellers just landed on the Barbary Coast.

To Bernard Berenson   Easter Sunday [21 April] 1935   I Tatti
There is little to say, except gurgles of laughter from Roger, moans of pain from me, and nothing from Barbara, who stays in her room, finding even me too much of a strain.

All my energy was taken up by keeping the 'chronic' pain at bay. I had come to the conclusion—and Ray confirmed me in it—that it was a mixture of fright and 'nerves', rather than real bodily defect, and I grappled with it most successfully. That is *I had no pain*, but the effort to control my nervous fright from its usual time of coming till bed-time was all I could do.

Diary   8 June 1935   I Tatti
Roger began to cry at 4.20. I misread the clock and thought it was 5.20, so I went out to him [he slept on her loggia]. He was lying naked and I thought he was cold so I brought him into my bed. Then I saw it was 4.25, so I said 'You must sleep' and he did, snuggled up in my arm. And so did I, both of us till 5.30, but I was conscious all the time of having an Angel at my side.

To Alys Russell   12 June 1935   I Tatti
B.B. says he looks forward to seeing him in the morning, when I come in for my second visit about 9.15. Roger tramps on B.B.'s stomach and pulls his beard, and B.B. *loves* it!

To Ray Strachey and Alys Russell   30 June 1935   I Tatti
B.B., the former President of the Herod Club, today said that a Lending Library of Babies should be started by the League of Nations, to send those little joy-bringers into old people's houses, to relax them and bring them back to the innocent pleasures of childhood!!! This is really *true* though inconceivable.

To Bernard Berenson   25 July 1935   Vienna
I nearly telegraphed for thee to come, but it would be a *great mistake*. I am very close to thee, dear Bernard. I feel thy sympathy, and I really don't want thee to sit by, unable to help, and see me suffer. Better the little creature who confides his tiny self to my love and has no idea that I am anything but a laugh and a smile of encouragement. It might easily break thee down to be here.

To Bernard Berenson   2 August 1935   Vienna
I could not help laughing, though it was very painful, and I groaned

at the same time, when all the doctors, peering with mirrors into the confusion and wreckage at 'Clapham Junction'*, all exclaimed *'Sehr schön! Merkwürdig!'* Thee could not have been happier over a recently cleaned Titian!

To Ray Strachey   21 August 1935   Vienna
I am most awfully ill. The treatment has been too strenuous for my exhausted body. If I die (I should like to) I want thee to know that thee has always given me the greatest happiness. I have written to B.B. and Nicky to keep a friendly eye on Roger.... Dr Steinlechner, the consultant, and most famous doctor in Vienna, agrees with me (he came this morning) that the cure has been too severe. I am to have a complete rest for several days. Alas he says my heart is good for 20 years more. But if it is to beat on in a tortured body, I *hate* it. Yet I am better today, after 3 days in the lowest circle of the Inferno.

Diary   10 September 1935   Vienna
All this time it hasn't seemed worthwhile to keep any record of my ebbing life. But now the tide has turned. I am even sending off to Yale the corrected MS of 'List of Beautiful Italian Pictures'.

Diary   27 October 1935   I Tatti
Reached Florence at 3.45.... Sat and chatted till 10.30, most enchanting to get back to Bernard's delightful talk, like an oasis after 4 waterless months in the desert.

To Mrs Berenson   18 November 1935   I Tatti
I have been negligent about writing, because I felt so very slack. It will take a long time, I think, to get over my nervous breakdown, a very natural thing to have after all I've been through, but a very paralyzing thing. The mere thought of writing a letter makes me sleepless and anxious. Even the postcards that I try to send every day to my family are a very great burden.... Life in the household goes on very much as ever with people coming and going and Bernard so astonishingly able to talk with them all on endless subjects. I am ashamed to say that I often go to sleep while these talks are going on, as one of my symptoms is an inability to fix my attention upon anything.

* A railway junction of considerable complexity in South London.

Diary   5 February 1936   I Tatti
Being set aside from most things gives a splendid relish to the few
contacts I am able to make. I enjoy them almost impersonally, as it
were, the way I enjoy Roger, having nothing to gain from them any
more than if I were dead. It is a wonderful way to appreciate the it-
ness of each person.

Diary   10 March 1936   I Tatti
B.B. and Nicky arrived for dinner. Heavenly to see them again,
though the fatigue of talking to them gave me a bad night.

Diary   11 April 1936   I Tatti
Ray left for London. She is a Rock of Ages for me. But I was almost
too ill to talk to her.

To Bertrand Russell   28 July 1936   Fernhurst
My dear Bertie—Might I motor over and call upon you and your wife
on Thursday or Friday of this week, or sometime next week?
　I've been very ill, and one of the results of illness is to make me
understand what things have been precious in my life, and you were
one of the most precious. I do not want to die without seeing you
again and thanking you for so many things.

To Bernard Berenson   21 August 1936   Fernhurst
Well, I motored over to see Bertie Russell today—after—is it?—thirty
years. Christopher, full of desire to see the man he reverences as a
Mathematician and laughs at as a *donnaiuolo* [lady-killer], was my
chauffeur, and little Roger came, who weeps if he is left behind when
the car starts.... Bertie came out to meet me, looking scarcely older,
but for his white hair. He was *émotionné* and rather embarrassed, but
sincerely glad I had come (so was I). Then his wife*—40 years
younger than he, and a beautiful red-haired creature—came and we
went in and sat around a table loaded with sandwiches and cake and
honey and jam, of all of which Christopher and Bertie's two children,
Kate, about 10, and John, perhaps 8—partook plentifully. Talk
stagnated a bit, because his wife did not understand how not to
interrupt, but it was helped out by cats and kittens and a wonderful
story Bertie told of his charlady at the time of the *Titanic* disaster.
They spoke of it and Bertie said 'You know it was supposed to be a

* Russell's third wife, Patricia (Peter) Spence.

298

ship that could not sink'. To which the charwoman replied 'Oh Sir, they forgot that there is One Above as could sink *any* ship.' ... He seemed very keen to hear about the people he used to know—even Alys, of whom he spoke almost tenderly, but with biting comprehension*, of Logan, of Algar, and then particularly of B.B. He said nothing in his life quite compensated him for losing your conversation. It was in many ways the most stimulating he had ever known, and particularly in regard to books and history. He begged me to give you all the nice messages I could think of. 'Nothing would be too nice to be true' ... We parted affectionately: I cannot help being very fond of him and it was somehow as if the long separation went for nothing in our friendship. He said that though he agreed with you that Religion is man's greatest art-creation, he also agreed with me in hating to have his friends turn religious—and they often do. My dear, how quickly he understands everything one means! Such a pleasure, never any 'explaining' necessary.

To Bernard Berenson   15 October 1936   Fernhurst
Our visit to Lady Jekyll was very interesting though it tired me to death.... We were met at the door by the butler, House, who is as famous in his way as Lady Horner's Graham. He took a more active part in the conversation at table than Graham usually takes, laughing inordinately at Logan's jokes, and when Logan accused Lady Jekyll of being such a vamp that her tenant's wife would not even let her husband call upon her, House intervened: 'Now Mr Pearsall Smith, you are really exceeding yourself today.' ... We were taken upstairs to see a 'certified' Giotto ... I got out of the hole into which the sight of it plunged me, by saying 'How noble!' Logan disappeared behind a Japanese screen to conceal his laughter.†

To Bernard Berenson   23 October 1936   Fernhurst
Yesterday Bertie lunched here and we spoke much about the philosophy of Berkeley, from which I have never been able to shake myself free. Nor he—but he carries it further, as indeed I have done, carries it to include internal scepticism as well as external scepticism.

* Alys lived on until 1951, and the last months of her life she and Bertie met again, in amity, for the first time in nearly forty years.
† Logan had now become subject to the crippling swings of mood of a true manic-depressive, and though he continued to write, his output was less and achieved with more difficulty. He lived through the Second World War and died in 1946.

Our thoughts, our feelings, are quite as much artefacts as our impressions of the world outside us. We talked a lot about Santayana. Bertie does not regard him as a thinker, but as one who has blended and expressed in modern language Plato and Medieval Scholasticism. ... He asked me to tell you, B.B., that meeting you again was one of the greatest pleasures he had ever had, and I could see, too, that he liked being with me, for he stayed late and said again and again that he was grateful to me for holding out the olive branch.

To Nicky Mariano   8 November 1936   I Tatti
I am still full of gratitude for the way you took care of me in Paris. Ray did the same in London, and I feel as if I had two beloved and kind daughters.

To Mrs Berenson   25 November 1936   I Tatti
I am thinking out the sort of invalid's life I want to lead, that will be the least troublesome to the people who have to live with me. It is the greatest good fortune in the world that darling Nicky is here and so well able to fill my place in most respects, and in some respects improve on anything I ever did. If I don't get tired, especially if I don't get bored, I can manage pretty well, because I have a dope against pain, if it becomes very bad, that suits me admirably, and makes it possible for me to go out sometimes in the motor and to enjoy seeing a few people. Even at my worst, I had great delight in little Roger, whose photograph I enclose for you to see what a jolly little being he is.

Diary   27 January 1937   I Tatti
I had a chance to read some of the Michael Field letters to B.B.... I read those Field wrote when she knew she had only a few months (of agony) to live. Very beautiful and touching. B.B. and I both wept.

To Bernard Berenson   14 May 1937   Viareggio
Nothing new to tell you, only an intensification of my wonderful mystical experience. At any moment the clouds may show a rift and a Golden City is revealed, while the waves begin to say Something I cannot understand but only apprehend. It makes my solitude a time of Bliss and ... I can hardly be brought back to earth by ordinary things. Roger's exquisite poses, his sweet voice, the look of his eyes are all part of an unearthly dream.

To Bernard Berenson   4 July 1937   Fernhurst
My pain seems to have paralysed my brain and my energy. But it has set free my soul in a way I cannot describe, and I feel very wonderful 'intimations of immortality'; and along with this my affections still persist, which are perhaps what we carry with us across the border.

To Bernard Berenson   5 September 1937   Fernhurst
Bertie Russell came over for tea today. It has tired me *fearfully* but I did want to see him before he moved away to Oxford, which he is just on the point of doing. But I was in trouble all day. It went off very well, however, and he was at ease and charming. He says Cambridge is no use any more for philosophy: it has hardened into a set of lifeless formulae. There is much more life at Oxford.

To Bernard Berenson   4 September 1938   Fernhurst
I suffer a lot, *not* the bladder, for that is practically cured, but all sorts of aches and discomforts and mental ruin. But of course I mustn't get dependent on dopes; and I bear the discomfort with resignation.

In September 1939 the Second World War broke out, while Mary was in England staying with Ray. After a struggle it proved possible for her to return to Florence, as everyone urgently desired. The prospect of her having to spend the whole war with them was as alarming to her family as it was disagreeable to her.

Mary got home safely, but she was now too ill to face a further upheaval, and as it proved impossible to get a passport for Nicky, after much heart-searching the Berensons decided to go neither to America nor to Switzerland (both of which ideas had been canvassed) but to remain quietly at I Tatti.

To Bernard Berenson   7 September 1939   Fernhurst
I shall come and join you as soon as travelling is possible. This visit has done a great deal to detach me from everything except you. Although I still feel a more or less responsible interest in the doings of my descendants, they are so different from ourselves, their interests and amusements are so little the same that I feel I must leave them to lead their own lives without suggestions or criticism from me. We, on the contrary, are *Zeitgenossen,* and I want to come back to a more congenial atmosphere, although I hate to leave Roger's blue eyes and the sound of his merry laughter.

301

To Senda Abbott and Bessie Berenson   30 December 1939   I Tatti
We understand that Rezia* has become a frantic Jew-hater, and this naturally breaks off all intercourse with her. One by one our friends fall away, either through politics or death or mere absence, and very few new ones come to take their place.

To Bernard Berenson   20 May 1940   I Tatti
I have not been at all agitated since the first day, and as one only lives one day at a time anyhow, I feel that somehow we shall get on. I fully expect to carry out my program of cure and aftercure ...

God knows if any of us will have money enough to feed him [Roger] when he gets bigger. His step-father will probably be called up in August. Then I suppose Barbara will be on the loose and ready to make some other utterly foolish marriage. But I have entirely ceased worrying about my grandchildren.

To Senda Abbott and Bessie Berenson   30 May 1940   I Tatti
B.B. was assured that no American over 60, having a home in Italy, would be disturbed, *no matter what happens*. So B.B. is peaceably re-seeing the Roman antiquities with Prof Rhys Carpenter (a *great* friend of ours), and now is going to Naples for more museum work.... Meantime I have been getting marvellously better in the new Cure I have undergone—Youth and Music. I have had a most brilliant young Russian pianist and his sweet Hungarian wife (only 19 years old) staying here; also Elisabetta Picolellis [Placci's niece by marriage, a singer] and Nijinsky's daughter and little grandson of 3. Magalov (the pianist) plays to us by the hour and Elisabetta sings, Nijinsky's daughter dances, the baby is a fascinating imp, and I have been living in an enchanted world of Beauty and Youth. They are all kept here by defective passports or other difficulties, but as their world is Art, they are not unhappy, but enjoying everything. We do not listen to the Radio, and know only vaguely that the world is brutal and horrible and painful.

This new 'Cure', however, worried B.B. and Nicky, for rumours had been going round that the villa was full of foreign agents, and the police had called there to enquire about noisy late-night parties. More keenly aware of the dangers of life in an unfriendly country in wartime, they urged her to be more cautious.

* Principessa Lucrezia Corsini, a Florentine friend.

To Bernard Berenson   31 May 1940   I Tatti
I hope to get Kyra [Nijinsky] and the darling little boy established in
Casa Boccaccio in a day or two. I see that you think I am a case of
euphoria at present. It may be true, but I will try not to let it lead me
into rash commitments.... It is wonderful to feel tranquil and happy
(in myself) at such a time, and I am really better.

To Nicky Mariano   7 June 1940   I Tatti
Your letter, dearest Nicky, has just come. How could you imagine I
should try to go against your wishes? I respect your judgment
more than my own, and if I did not, I should desire with all my
heart to accede to your wishes. I am absolutely in your hands, and
gladly.

When Italy entered the war in June 1940 it became impossible to
write direct to England, but Mary was still able to give her news and
receive news of her family via the United States. In July her euphoria
was shattered when she heard—this time through the Red Cross—
that her daughter Ray had died in London.

To Lina Waterfield   29 July 1940   Fiametto
I need at the moment all the moral and spiritual strength the universe
can give me. For Ray is dead. Suddenly she died from heart failure
under an unexpected operation.... The strength and calmness and
good sense of my beloved daughter, and my memories of 53 years of
unclouded companionship, have made these ten days, since I knew,
very beautiful, very blessed. I live with her again all those years, and
sometimes I surprise myself in the quiet of the night laughing at
something amusing we shared together.... I do not want to make
anyone else grieve for me. B.B. and Nicky would have come, but it is
better to be alone with my memories.... I am joining B.B. and Nicky
in two days and we shall be at Casa al Dono, Vallombrosa, till the
middle of September—unless America joins the war.... But one
cannot foretell the course of future events, and I am really living in
another world, 'out of space, out of time' and Ray has 'outsoared the
darkness of our night'.

To Christopher Strachey   15 October 1940   I Tatti
We here are walking on a knife edge. We may be obliged to leave for
Switzerland, but Nicky cannot get a visa, and we hardly know how to
face life without her. We should be like the Children in the Wood,

with no kind robin to keep us warm by spreading leaves over us. In any case we shall not cross the ocean. I should rather die in Europe than live in America, or, closer to fact, suffer great discomfort here than live in luxury there. Most of our acquaintances have already deserted us, and even some whom we thought of as friends. But I like the quiet. I almost hate to see the people we do see, for the chief topics of conversation are how to get away and where to go, and then the War, about which we know so little. But people can't keep off it. I generally plead perhaps more illness than I feel (for I am better) and creep up to my room and my books.

To her Family   19 August 1941   Consuma
Today for the first time in years I woke up to a feeling of being a human being and not a sack of pain. . . . I have begun to walk a little, and I sit out of doors a great deal. The only thing I do not get any better of is my worse than indifference to most people and the boredom I feel in their conversation. B.B. and Nicky keep the house crawling with guests and in order to please B.B. I join them after lunch, coffee and tea. If I were well enough to walk without assistance my feet would carry me away very quickly from these gatherings, the way my mother's feet used to do when she was bored. The worst of it is that these people are often people I should normally have been interested in, but somehow I have got into a different world and their talk does not interest me any more than if it were the chirping of insects.

When America joined the Allies, things became more difficult for the Berensons, and when Germany took over Italy in 1943, B.B., as an enemy alien and a Jew, was really at risk.

He and Nicky were taken into the home of a friend in Florence who was a diplomat—Minister for the Republic of San Marino to the Court of the Vatican—and there they were able to find sanctuary. The pictures and some of the books were hidden, and Nicky's sister and brother-in-law moved into I Tatti to look after Mary, who was by then too ill to be moved, even though the Germans requisitioned the villa.

In the autumn of 1944 the Germans were ejected and B.B. and Nicky were able to return. The Anrep home, near the Ponte Vecchio, together with some of the treasures which had been hidden there, had been blown up, but the majority of the pictures were recovered.

To Nicky Marino and Bernard Berenson   21 September 1943   I Tatti
Dearest N and B. It is a great comfort to think of you in a safe
place. I know we should hear if anything happened to you, and I
feel at peace (for the present) about you both. I am fatalistic about
everything else—which is a kind of peace—'from hope and fear set
free'. So I enjoy my reading, though much missing not being able
to share a lot of it with you. But I am keeping notes of some of the
things I want to speak of to you WHEN we are together again. Cecil
[Nicky's nephew, Cecil Anrep] will give you all the 'news' about
this household. I must say that Alda has been *splendid*. She has a
strong and helpful character, no matter what fairy tales occupy her
imagination. They comfort her, and who, *now*, would take away
anybody's comfort.... One thing is certain, and the rest is lies. The
flower that has once bloomed forever dies. But while we live, if we
retain our minds, we have memories. My memories of both of you
dear ones grow in beauty and fill me with gratitude to you. Your
truly loving old Mary.

To Bernard Berenson   8 October 1943   I Tatti
Dearest Bernard—as I write these two words and see the date above
them, I can hardly believe that they belong together. I look back to 55
years ago when it was all so difficult that it seemed *impossible* that I
should ever be able to write so freely, and when a stretch of years as
great was unimaginable. I was glad indeed to get your letter. It helps
me to put substance to the vague Somewhere and Somehow that
wrapped your familiar presence.... I feel almost sorry you should
think of me, dear though it is of you, so faithful and loyal. But as my
memory grows and grows—there being practically no life to fill the
empty spaces of my brain—I see that I have been a humble person,
and I should like to fade out of the memory of everyone—my own,
first of all. It makes the possibility of *Annihilation* by death almost
attractive.

To Bernard Berenson   16 January 1944   I Tatti
I may not be able to hold out very long, for the pain I suffer passes
description. It terrifies me and I may quietly slip off one of these
days, although I hope I can hold out to see you again. The two or
three strands I have found woven into my character were first of all
You and Italy, and secondly the love of a family, which is more
primitive and deeper than I could have believed, but You come
first of all.

To her Family   5 February 1944   I Tatti
[Despite the war, letters reached England via America.]
My dearest Family—if any of you exist when the devil has worked his will upon the world. This is to say goodbye. I have been a selfish creature but still I think I have loved you. As for Roger I have felt for him an absolutely perfect unselfish love. It was one of the greatest experiences of my life. I knew he could not return my love in any way or even remember me.... I have said goodbye to everything in this world and only hope for death to come quickly and end my pain which is severe and continuous.... I think I shall not see B.B. and Nicky again, and who knows if any remembrances go with us beyond the grave?

To Nicky Mariano   5 February 1944   I Tatti
Dear Nicky, I am very sorry not to write this with my own hand but neither hand nor eyes are working well. The truth is I am dying only I cannot die. The doctors will not give me receipts for medicines that might kill me and I am too ill to go out of my room to look for anything or to die in the garden. I suffer so much that the gate is already open on the long road we have to travel alone, but I cannot start. However all this is not important. What I want to express I never could express even if I had the use of my hand and eyes. It is the love and admiration and affection of many years. There is no cloud in the thought of you as there is in almost everything else. The end of life, if you remain conscious, is a sort of purgatory in which all your sins and mistakes come crowding upon you, but between you and me there is nothing of the kind—all is perfectly serene and I think of you with the deepest love. If I die in time I hope you will marry B.B. You will have my deep sympathy, but all the worldly things are fading away....

I am almost glad that B.B. should not see me in my pain and weakness. I love to think how in spite of all our failings and so-called infidelities we have always stuck together and stuck to Italy and when I am able to think at all I think of him with tender affection.

To Bernard Berenson   19 February 1944   I Tatti
In spite of all the wise and loving things you said I did try to make away with myself two nights ago, but the medicine which was said to kill you with two doses, seemed to have no more effect upon me than grape-shot on the hide of a rhinoceros. The medicines are not what

they were. . . . I try to think of the pleasant things, but the others come crowding upon me like a swarm of hornets.

To Bernard Berenson   22 May 1944   I Tatti
I have a very good memory and thousands of things come back to my mind in their settings, and it is in a way so impersonal now—as if I were really dead and reading my own autobiography. I am at present like a fly on one of those gummy pieces of paper called 'Tanglefoot', for I cannot seem to get beyond the different so-called love affairs that took up a good deal of time and thought when I was younger; I can explain a good many of them and one or two I deeply regret, but they are falling off like dying leaves from a tree, and only what refers to you has any vitality left. The one I chiefly regret is Geoffrey, because it gave you so much annoyance and inconvenience, and was so full of absurdity in itself. I am for the moment tanglefooted in my first marriage, for I begin to see it from the point of view of Frank Costelloe. It was very hard for an ambitious man in the full tide of party politics to be tied to a green schoolgirl, and every day I seem to see more clearly the difficulties he had to contend with. . . . I have begun to read *David Copperfield*. I had utterly forgotten it, but as I read, it all became familiar again. The character of old Mrs Gummidge who 'felt things more than other people' gave me my family nickname of 'Gummy'.

Epilogue

Mary and B.B. did meet again, when he and Nicky returned to the villa in the autumn of 1944. The following spring Mary died.

B.B. lived on, entering a new, mellow and remarkably productive period, in which he published three volumes of his diaries, and books on aesthetics and art history, travel and autobiography, and even conducted a column in the Milan *Corriere della Sera*. Cherished and supported, as ever, by Nicky, he entertained the learned, the famous, the high-born and the wealthy. As he moved into his nineties, he himself, with his brilliant conversation and his beautiful setting, became an almost legendary figure.

He died in 1959, and Nicky in 1968. They did not marry. Nicky said that though he had asked her, she had declined, because she wished to avoid confusing, and perhaps embarrassing, people who had known her for so long, in the same setting, as Miss Mariano.

B.B. duly left the villa to Harvard University, and although his long life had forced him to make considerable inroads into his capital, and the endowment was not as large as Harvard would have wished, the bequest was accepted. The Harvard University Center for Italian Renaissance Studies now occupies an enlarged I Tatti and receives a contingent of fellows every year, while the library, B.B.'s particular pride, continues to grow.

Shortly before she died, Mary asked to be cremated, but as cremation was forbidden by the Catholic Church, Nicky persuaded her that it would give great offence to her staff and the *contadini*, and both she and B.B. now lie in their own little chapel, just inside the gate of the villa, where they were married.

308

Appendix One

Notes on characters not fully identified in the text

Barnett, Henrietta Octavia, later Dame Henrietta Barnett, 1851–1936. Wife of the English clergyman Samuel Barnett. Both husband and wife were well-known philanthropists.

Bode, Dr Wilhelm, 1845–1929. Leading German art historian. Longtime rival of B.B.

Bunting, (Sir) Percy, 1836–1911. Chairman of the National Vigilance Association, devoted to social and moral reform.

Carpenter, Dr Rhys, 1889–1980. American author and archaeologist. Professor at Bryn Mawr.

Clark, Kenneth (Lord Clark) b.1903. Art critic, writer and broadcaster. Director of the National Gallery of London 1933–45.

Colvin, Sidney, 1845–1927. Art critic and writer, Keeper of Prints and drawings, British Museum.

Connaught, Duke of. Younger son of Queen Victoria.

Cook, Herbert, 1868–1939. Wealthy English art collector and patron. Old friend of the Berensons. One of the founders of the *Burlington Magazine*.

Costa, Enrico. A wealthy connoisseur and collector, half Genoese and half Peruvian.

Cunard, Lady (Emerald), 1872–1945. Of American birth, she had married Sir Bache Cunard, and became a prominent London hostess.

Dawson, Emily. A cousin of Mary's.

Douglas, Robert Langton, 1864–1951. English historian, art expert and Director of the National Gallery of Ireland 1916–1923. Longtime rival of B.B.

Dowdeswell, Walter. A 'scout' for Duveen in Italy.

Elliott, Maxine, 1868–1940. Stage name of Jessie C. Dermot, American actress and beauty.

Emin Pasha (Eduard Schnitzer). German explorer in Equatorial Africa. Imprisoned and killed in 1892 by Arab slave traders.

Fry, Roger, 1866–1934. English painter, art critic and champion of Post-Impressionism.

Galton, Sir Francis, 1822–1911. Father of the science of Eugenics.

Gronau, Georg, 1868–1939. Eminent German art historian. Longtime friend of B.B.

Hapgood, Norman, 1868–1937. Writer. He was a contemporary of B.B. at Harvard.

Harrison, Jane, 1850–1928. Cambridge classicist and friend of Gilbert Murray.

Horne, Sir William Van, *see* Van Horne, Sir William.

Kelly, Frederic Septimus, 1881–1916. Australian-born pianist and composer.

Labouchere, Dora, who had married an Italian prince, was the daughter of Henry Labouchere (Labby), noted English Liberal politician, at that time retired and living in Florence.

Leslie, Mrs Leonie Jerome. Sister of Jennie Jerome, Winston Churchill's mother. She married Col. Leslie (later Sir John) in 1884.

Northcliffe, Lord (Alfred Charles Harmsworth), 1865–1922. English newspaper proprietor. In 1917 he was director of the British War Mission in the USA.

Okakura, Takuzo. Japanese art historian. Curator of Japanese and Chinese art at the Museum of Fine Arts, Boston.

Palmer, Mrs Potter (Bertha Honoré), 1849–1918. Prominent Chicago social leader.

Parnell, Charles Stewart, 1846–1891. He had been one of the ablest and most popular of the leaders of the Irish Home Rule movement. The discovery of his affair with Mrs Kitty O'Shea caused a disastrous scandal in 1890. He died a year later.

Peabody, Elizabeth Palmer, 1804–1894. American author, educator and philanthropist.

Phillips, Claude, 1846–1924. Art critic and writer. Keeper of the Wallace Collection, London.

Santayana, George, 1863–1952. American philosopher of Spanish descent, author and Harvard professor. He and B.B. had been class mates and co-editors of the *Harvard Monthly*.

Sassoon, Lady (Aline). Daughter of Baron Gustave de Rothschild and wife of Sir Edward Sassoon. She was an artist and collector and a member of international high society. It was probably she who introduced B.B. to Duveen. She died in 1909.

Siren, Osvald, 1879–1966. Swedish art historian.

Smyth, Dame Ethel, 1858–1944. English composer.

Tagore, Sir Rabindranath, 1861–1941. Indian philosopher and poet.

Thorold, Algar. Nephew and biographer of Labouchere.

Tovey, (Sir) Donald, 1873–1940. Composer and writer on music.

Van Horne, Sir William, 1843–1915. Wealthy Canadian collector. Chairman of the board of the Canadian Pacific Railway.

Wharton, Edith, 1862–1937. American novelist.

De Wolfe, Elsie. A pioneer interior decorator, with a wealthy and fashionable clientèle on both sides of the Atlantic. She married Sir Charles Mendl when she was sixty.

Williamson, George Charles, 1858–1942. Writer on art.

Appendix Two

Letters to the following people will be found on the pages listed

Letters to Hannah Whitall Smith, Alys Russell, Bernard Berenson and to her family jointly can be found throughout.

Letters to Mrs Berenson are to be found from 1900 on and to Nicky Mariano from 1920 on.

Index

313

315

318